LARGE PRINT
WEBSTER'S
DICTIONARY

**This book was not published by the original publishers of
the Webster's Dictionary, or by any of their successors.**

Rules Of Spelling

(1)   The most common way to form the plural of a noun is to add an s (Example: girl, girls; town, towns; hall, halls).

(2)   The plural of nouns which end in y following a consonant are formed by dropping the y and adding ies (Example: country, countries; baby, babies; family, families).

(3)   The plural of nouns which end in y following a vowel are formed by adding an s (Example: toy, toys; boy, boys; attorney, attorneys).

In this quick reference dictionary, a double dash (--) indicates a hyphenated word, and a single dash (-) indicates syllabication.

Each entry is in bold type followed by the part of speech in italics. Sub-entries are indicated in bold type after the main definition.

Abbreviations Used In This Dictionary

abbr.	abbreviation	*L.*	Latin
adj.	adjective	*Mech.*	Mechanics
adv.	adverb	*Med.*	Medicine
Aeron.	Aeronautics	*Meteor.*	Meteorology
Aeros.	Aerospace	*Milit.*	Military
archit.	architecture	*Mus.*	Music
Astron.	Astronomy	*Myth*	Mythology
Biochem.	Biochemist	*Naut.*	Nautical
Biol.	Biology	*N.*	noun
Bot.	Botany	*Opt.*	Optics
Brit.	British	*pathol.*	Pathology
Can.	Canada	*photog.*	Photography
Chem.	Chemistry	*physiol.*	Physiology
Elect.	Electricity	*pl.*	plural
Econ.	Economist	*poet.*	Poetry
Fr.	French	*pref.*	prefix
Geol.	Geology	*pron.*	pronoun
Govt.	Government	*psychol.*	Psychologist
Gram.	Grammar	*Rom.*	Roman
Gr.	Greek	*Scot.*	Scotch
Theol.	Theology	*suff.*	suffix
Interj.	Interjection	*surg.*	surgery

A

A, a The first letter of the English alphabet.

aard-vark *n.* A burrowing animal.

aard-wolf *n.* A hyena-like mammal.

a-back *adv.* Unexpectedly surprised.

ab-a-cus *n.* A frame with beads for counting.

a-baft *adv.* Toward the stern of a ship.

a-ban-don *v.* To desert; to forsake. **-ment** *n.*

a-base *v.* Lower in rank, or position. **-ment** *n.*

a-bash *v.* To embarrass.

a-bate *v.* To reduce in quantity, or value.

ab-bey *n.* A monastery.

ab-bre-vi-ate *v.* To make briefer; to shorten.

ab-bre-vi-a-tion *n.* A shortened form of a word.

ab-do-men *n.* The stomach.

ab-duct *v.* To carry away wrongfully by force.

a-beam *adv.* Right angles to the keel of a ship.

ab-er-rant *adj.* Straying from the right course.

a-bet *v.* To incite.

ab-hor *v.* To dislike intensely.

a-bide *v.* To tolerate.

a-bil-i-ty *n.* Being able. **-ties** *n., pl.*

ab-ject *adj.* Sunk to a low condition. **-tion** *n.*

ab-jure *v.* To renounce solemnly.

a-blaze *adv.* On fire.

a-ble *adj.* Having sufficient ability.

a-ble--bodied *adj.* Having a strong body.

ab-lu-tion *n.* A washing of the body as a part of religious rites.

ab-ne-gate *v.* To deny; to refuse or renounce.

ab-nor-mal *adj.* To be not normal. **-ity** *n.*

a-board *adv.* On board a ship.

a-bode *n.* A dwelling place.

a-bol-ish *v.* To put an end to.

a-bom-i-na-ble *adj.* Being detestable; loathsome.

a-bort *v.* To terminate.

a-bor-tion *n.* An induced termination of pregnancy.

a-bound *v.* To have plenty.

a-bout *adv.* To be approximately.

a-bove *adv.* To be higher or greater than.

ab-ra-ca-dab-ra *n.* A word believed to have magical powers.

a-brade *v.* To wear or rub off. **-ing** *v.*

a-breast *adv.* **or** *adj.* To be side by side.

a-bridge *v.* To make

smaller.

a-broad *adv.* Widely.

ab-ro-gate *v.* To put an end to.

ab-rupt *adj.* To be happening suddenly.

ab-scéss *n.* An infected sore containing pus.

ab-scind *v.* To sever; to separate.

ab-scond *v.* To flee from justice.

ab-sent *adj.* To be not present.

ab-sent--mind-ed *adj.* Always forgetting things; not paying attention.

ab-so-lute *adj.* To be unconditional.

ab-solve *v.* To set free from guilt.

ab-sorb *v.* To take in.

ab-stain *v.* To refrain from doing something.

ab-ste-mi-ous *adj.* To be showing moderation.

ab-stract *v.* To summarize something.

ab-struse *adj.* To be difficult to understand.

ab-surd *adj.* To be clearly unreasonable.
 -ness *n.*

a-bun-dance *n.* Ample supply; plenty.

a-buse *v.* To use in an improper or wrong way.

a-but *v.* To border.
 -ed, -ing *v.*

a-but-ment *n.* A bridge support.

a-bys-mal *adj.* Im-

measurably deep.
 -ly *adv.*

a-byss *n.* A deep crack or gap in the earth.

a-ca-cia *n.* A thorny tree or shrub.

a-cad-e-my *n.* A private school.

acap-pel-la *adj.* Singing without accompaniment.

ac-cede *v.* To consent.

ac-cel-er-ate *v.* To work faster; to increase.

ac-cent *n.* Emphasize.
 -less *adj.*

ac-cept *v.* To take what is given.

ac-cept-able *adj.* Satisfactory; proper.

ac-cep-tance *n.* Approval.

ac-cess *n.* The admission, entrance.

ac-ces-si-ble *adj.* Easy access or approach.

ac-ci-dent *n.* An unexpected happening.
 -al *adj.*

ac-claim *v.* To greet with strong approval.

ac-cli-mate *v.* To become accustomed.

ac-co-lade *n.* An award; praise.

ac-com-mo-date *v.* To give room or lodging; to adjust.

ac-com-pa-ni-ment *n.* Something that goes well with another.

ac-com-pa-nist *n.* Someone who plays a

musical accompaniment.

ac-com-pa-ny *v.* To go along with.

ac-com-plice *n.* A companion in crime.

ac-com-plish *v.* To do. -ment *n.*

ac-cord *n.* Harmony. -ance *n.*

ac-cord-ing-ly *adv.* In a proper way.

ac-cor-di-on *n.* Type of musical instrument.

ac-cost *v.* To approach in an unfriendly manner.

ac-count *n.* A description; record. -able *adj.*

ac-count-ing *n.* A system of keeping business records or accounts.

ac-cred-it *v.* To give official power.

ac-crete *v.* To grow together.

ac-crue *v.* To increase at certain times.

ac-cu-mu-late *v.* To collect or gather.

ac-cu-rate *adj.* Be without mistakes; careful and exact.

ac-curs-ed *adj.* To be unpleasant.

ac-cu-sa-tion *n.* A charge of guilty.

ac-cuse *v.* To find fault with; charge someone with breaking the law.

ac-custom *v.* To familiarize by habit. -ed *adj.*

ace *n.* A playing card marked with one spot; score in tennis.

ac-e-tate *n.* Salt.

a-ce-tic acid *n.* A main ingredient of vinegar.

a-cet-y-lene *n.* An inflammable gas.

ache *v.* To have a dull, steady pain.

achieve *v.* To succeed. -ment *n.*

ac-id *n.* A chemical compound. -ity *n.*

ac-id rock *n.* The song lyrics suggesting drug related experiences.

a-cid-u-late *v.* To become or make acid.

ack-ack *n.* The anti-aircraft fire.

ac-know-ledge *v.* To admit the truth. -ment *n.*

ac-me *n.* The highest point.

ac-ne *n.* A skin disease; pimples.

ac-o-lyte *n.* An altar boy.

ac-o-nite *n.* A poisonous plant.

a-corn *n.* The nut of the oak tree.

a-cous-tic *adj.* Having to do with sound.

a-cous-tics *n.* The study of sound.

ac-quaint *v.* To make familiar. -ance *n.*

ac-qui-esce *v.* To agree without arguing.

ac-quire v. To become the owner. **-ment** n.

ac-quired im-mun-ity n. An immunity against disease.

ac-qui-si-tion n. Something acquired.

ac-quit v. To rule not guilty. **-tal** n.

a-cre n. A measurement of land. **-age** n.

ac-rid adj. A sharp, bitter taste. **-ity** n.

ac-ri-mo-ni-ous adj. To be bitter in speech or manner.

ac-ro-bat n. The one skilled in gymnastic feats. **-ic** adj.

ac-ro-pho-bi-a n. An unusual fear of heights.

a-cross prep. To be side to side.

acryl-ic fi-ber n. A synthetic textile fiber.

act n. A thing done; a deed. **-ing** adj.

ac-tion n. The process of doing or acting.

ac-ti-vate v. To put into action. **-tion** n.

ac-tive adj. Full of action; busy. **-ly** adv.

ac-tiv-ism n. An action to affect changes in government.

act of God n. An uncontrollable happening caused by nature.

ac-tor n. A performer.

ac-tress n. A female actor.

ac-tu-al adj. To be existing in fact; real.

ac-tu-ate v. To put into motion. **-tion** n.

a-cute adj. To be sharp and quick. **-ly** adv.

ad-age n. A proverb.

ad-a-mant adj. To be standing firm.

a-dapt v. To adjust to new conditions. **-tion, -ness** n.

add v. To join together.

ad-der n. Type of poisonous snake.

ad-dict n. A person with a strong habit. **-tion** n.

ad-di-tion n. Adding of numbers to find the total. **-al** adj.

ad-dle v. To become or make confused.

ad-dress v. To speak to; place where mail or goods can be delivered.

ad-duce v. To offer as proof or give as a reason.

ad-e-noids n. A lymphoid tissue growths.

a-dept adj. Highly skilled. **-ly** adv., **-ness** n.

ad-e-quate adj. To be sufficient.

ad-here v. To stick and not come loose.

ad-her-ent n. The one who follows a leader.

ad-he-sive adj. To be having a sticky surface.

a-dieu n. Good-by.

ad-in-ter-im *adj.* In the meantime.

ad-ja-cent *adj.* To be close to or nearby.

ad-jec-tive *n.* A word used to describe a noun or pronoun.

ad-join *v.* Be next to.

ad-journ *v.* To close a meeting or session. **-ment** *n.*

ad-judge *v.* To decide by judicial procedure.

ad-jure *v.* To ask urgently. **-tion** *n.*

adjust *v.* To arrange or change. **-ability** *n.*

ad-just-er *n.* A person who estimates damages for settlement.

ad-lib *v.* To improvise.

ad-man *n.* A person working in the business of advertising.

ad-min-is-ter *v.* To direct or manage.

ad-min-is-tra-tion *n.* The people who manage a school, or company. **-tor** *n.*

ad-mi-ra-ble *adj.* To be worthy of being admired.

ad-mi-ral *n.* The highest ranking naval officer.

ad-mire *v.* To regard with wonder.

ad-mis-si-ble *adj.* Capable of being admitted.

ad-mit *v.* To confess; give the right to enter. **-tance** *n.*

ad-mix-ture *n.* A blend; mingling.

ad-mon-ish *v.* To give a person advice. **-ion** *n.*

a-do *n.* A fuss.

a-do-be *n.* A building material made from clay.

ad-o-les-cence *n.* Between childhood and adulthood.

a-dopt *v.* To legally take into one's family. **-tion** *n.*

a-dor-a-ble *adj.* Being very likable.

a-dore *v.* To love greatly; to worship.

a-dorn *v.* To add splendor or beauty. **-ment** *n.*

a-drift *adv.* To be floating freely; having no purpose.

a-droit *adj.* Being skillful and clever. **-ly** *adv.*

ad-u-late *v.* To give greater praise. **-tion** *n.*

a-dult *n.* A person who is fully grown. **-hood** *n.*

a-dul-ter-ate *v.* To make impure.

a-dul-tery *n.* The voluntary sexual intercourse with someone other than a spouse.

ad-vance *v.* To move ahead. **-ment** *n.*

ad-vanced *adj.* To be ahead in time.

ad-van-tage *n.* The better chance. **-eous** *adj.*

ad-vent *n.* The four Sundays before Christmas.

ad-ven-ture *n.* An exciting experience.

ad-verb *n.* A word used to describe. **-ial** *adj.*

ad-verse *adj.* Opposed; against someone or something.

ad-ver-si-ty *n.* A bad luck or misfortune.

ad-ver-tise *v.* To draw public attention to a product. **-er** *n.*

ad-vice *n.* An opinion on a course of action.

ad-vis-ed-ly *adv.* Done deliberately.

ad-vise-ment *n.* A careful thought.

ad-viser *n.* The person who gives an opinion.

ad-vo-cate *v.* To write or speak in favor of.

aer-ate *v.* To purify.

aer-i-al *n.* An antenna for television or radio.

aer-i-al-ist *n.* An aerial acrobat.

aer-o-bics *n.* A strenuous exercise for the heart.

aer-o-nau-tics *pl., n.* The science of designing aircraft.

aer-o-sol *n.* A liquid substance under pressure.

aes-thet-ic *adj.* Having a love for beauty.

a-far *adv.* Far away.

af-fa-ble *adj.* Good-natured; friendly.

af-fair *n.* An event or happening.

af-fect *v.* To move emotionally. **-ing,** *adj.*

af-fec-tion *n.* The fond feeling for another.

af-fec-tion-ate *adj.* Being loving and gentle. **-ly** *adv.*

af-fi-da-vit *n.* A sworn written statement.

af-fil-i-ate *v.* To join or associate with. **-tion** *n.*

af-fin-i-ty *n.* A natural attraction or liking.

af-firm *v.* To declare positively. **-ative** *n.*

af-flict *v.* To cause suffering or pain. **-tion** *n.*

af-flu-ence *n.* A wealth; abundance.

af-ford *v.* To be able to provide.

af-fray *n.* A noisy fight.

af-front *v.* To confront.

af-ghan *n.* A knitted or crocheted cover.

a-fire *adv.* To be burning.

a-float *adv.* Floating on water.

a-flut-ter *adj.* To be nervously excited.

a-foot *adj.* Walking.

a-fore-men-tioned *adj.* To be mentioned before.

a-foul *adv.* Tangled.

a-fraid *adj.* Filled with fear; reluctant.

a-fresh *adj.* To something again.

aft *adv.* Being toward the rear of a ship.

af-ter *adv. prep.* To be following.

af-ter-math *n.* A consequence.

af-ter-thought *n.* An idea occurring later.

a-gain *adv.* Once more.

a-gainst *prep.* In exchange for.

a-gape *adv.* To be open-mouthed.

ag-ate *n.* A type of quartz.

age *n.* A length of time a person has lived.

aged *adj.* To be grown or become old.

age-less *adj.* To be existing forever.

a-gen-cy *n.* The business that acts for others.

a-gen-da *n.* A list of things to be done.

a-gent *n.* One who acts as the representative of another.

ag-glom-er-ate *v.* To collect.

ag-gran-dize *n.* To extend. **-ment** *n.*

ag-gra-vate *v.* To annoy.

ag-gre-gate *adj.* To gather together.

ag-gres-sion *n.* A hostile action.

ag-gres-sive *adj.* Being pushy; offensive.

a-ghast *adj.* Appalled.

ag-ile *adj.* Ability to move easily.

ag-i-tate *v.* To stir or move with violence. **-tion, -tor** *n.*

a-gleam *adj.* Gleaming.

ag-nos-tic *n.* A disbeliever in God.

a-go *adj. & adv.* Being in the past.

a-gog *adj.* To be excited.

ag-o-nize *v.* To afflict with great anguish. **-ed, -ing** *adj.*

ag-o-ny *n., pl.* **-nies** A mental distress.

a-gree *v.* To give consent. **-able** *adj.,* **-ness** *n.*

ag-ri-cul-ture *n.* The raising of livestock and crops.

a-ground *adv. & adj.* Stranded; beached.

a-head *adv.* In advance.

a-hoy *interj.* A nautical greeting.

aid *v.* To give help.

AIDS *n.* Acquired Immune Deficiency Syndrome.

ail *v.* To feel sick.

aim *v.* To direct a weapon; to direct purpose.

air *n.* A nitrogen and oxygen mixture; a breeze.

air con-di-tion-er *n.* Equipment to control temperature indoors.

air-craft *n.* A machine that flies.

air-field *n.* The paved

runways at an airport.

Air Force *n.* The aviation branch of armed forces.

air-mail & air mail *n.* The mail sent via air.

air-port *n.* The airplane terminal.

air raid *n.* A bombing attack.

air-ship *n.* A dirigible; lighter-than-air aircraft.

aisle *n.* A passageway between rows of seats.

a-jar *adv. & adj.* To be partially opened.

a-kin *adj.* Related, as in a family.

al-a-bas-ter *n.* A white, fine-grained gypsum.

a-lac-ri-ty *n.* Readiness; eagerness.

a la mode *n.* A pie served with ice cream.

a-larm *n.* A warning of danger; bell or buzzer of a clock. **-ing** *adv.*

a-las *interj.* An expressive of anxiety.

a-late *or* **alated** *adj.* To be having wings.

alb *n.* A white robe worn by the clergy.

al-ba-core *n.* A large marine fish.

al-ba-tross *n.* A large sea bird.

al-bi-no *n.* A person with abnormal whiteness of the skin and hair.

al-bum *n.* A book for photographs, etc.

al-bu-men *n.* A white of an egg.

al-caz-ar *n.* A spanish fortress or palace.

al-co-hol *n.* An intoxicating liquor.

al-co-hol-ism *n.* A habit or addiction.

al-cove *n.* A partly enclosed extension of a room.

ale *n.* A beverage similar to beer.

a-lert *adj.* Vigilant; watchful. **-ly** *adv.*, **-ness** *n.*

al-fal-fa *n.* A plant grown for forage.

al-fres-co *adv. & adj.* Outside.

al-ge-bra *n.* A form of math.

a-li-as *n., pl.* **aliases** An assumed name.

al-i-bi *n.* Form of defense.

a-li-en *adj.* Owing allegiance to a country.

a-light *v.* To dismount; to come down.

a-lign *v.* To arrange in a line.

a-like *adj.* Similar; having close resemblance.

al-i-mo-ny *n.* A court ordered allowance for support.

a-live *adj.* Having life.

al-ka-loid *n.* A nitrogen containing organic bases obtained from plants.

all *adj.* Being a whole amount.

al-lay *v.* To calm; to pacify. **-er** *n.*

al-lege *v.* To assert; to be true.

al-le-giance *n.* A loyalty to one's nation.

al-le-lu-ia *interj.* An expressing praise to God.

al-ler-gist *n.* A doctor specializing in allergies.

al-ler-gy *n.* **-gies** An abnormal reaction to environmental substances.

al-le-vi-ate *v.* To make more bearable. **-tion** *n.*

al-ley *n.* A passageway behind buildings.

al-li-ga-tor *n.* A large amphibious reptile.

al-lo-cate *v.* To assign.

allot *v.* To distribute or set aside. **-tion** *n.*

al-low *v.* To make a provision for; to permit. **-able** *adj.*

al-low-ance *n.* A regular amount of money, food, etc.

all right *adj.* Meets satisfaction; dependable.

all-round *adj.* Versatile.

all-star *adj.* Composed entirely of star performers.

al-lude *n.* Refer to something indirectly.

al-lure *v.* To entice; to tempt. **-ment** *n.*

al-lu-sion *n.* A hint.

al-ly *v.* To unite in a close relationship or bond.

al-ma ma-ter *n.* A school or university attended.

al-ma-nac *n.* An annual calendar publication.

al-might-y *adj.* Having absolute power.

al-mond *n.* An oval nut.

al-most *adv.* Not quite.

alms *pl., n.* The money given to the poor.

a-loft *adv.* Toward the upper rigging of a ship.

a-lo-ha *interj.* Hawaiian greeting.

a-lone *adj.* Away from other people.

a-long *adv.* Following the length or path.

a-loof *adj.* Distant; indifferent. **-ness** *n.*

a-loud *adv.* Audibly.

alp *n.* A high mountain.

al-pac-a *n.* A mammal related to the llama.

al-pen-stock *n.* A long staff used by mountain climbers.

al-pha *n.* The first letter of the Greek alphabet.

al-pha-bet *n.* The letters arranged in order.

al-pha-bet-ize *v.* To arrange in alphabetical order.

al-read-y *adv.* By this or a specified time.

al-so *adv.* Likewise; in addition.

al-tar *n.* An elevated holy table.

al-ter *v.* To change or make different.

al-ter-ca-tion *n.* A noisy quarrel.

al-ter-na-tive *n.* A choice between two or more possibilities.

al-ter-na-tor *n.* An electric generator producing current.

al-though *conj.* Even though.

al-tim-e-ter *n.* An instrument for measuring altitude.

al-ti-tude *n.* The height above sea level.

al-to *n.* A low female singing voice.

al-to-geth-er *adv.* Entirely.

al-tru-ism *n.* The selfless concern for others.

a-lu-mi-num *n.* A silvery metallic element.

a-lum-na *n.* A female graduate of a school.

a-lum-nus *n.* A male graduate of a school.

al-ways *adv.* Forever; at all times.

am *n.* The first person, singular.

a-mal-ga-mate *v.* To mix; to blend. **-tion,** *n.*

a-man-dine *adj.* Garnished with almonds.

am-a-teur *n.* One who lacks expertise. **-ish** *adj.*

a-maze *v.* To astound. **-ment** *n.*

am-bass-a-dor *n.* An official representative.

am-ber *n.* A brownish-yellow resin.

am-bi-ance *n.* An environment.

am-bi-dex-trous *adj.* Using both hands with equal facility.

am-bi-ent *adj.* To be surrounding.

am-big-u-ous *adj.* To be uncertain; doubtful.

am-bi-tion *n.* A strong desire to succeed.

am-bi-tious *adj.* To be challenging.

am-ble *v.* To move at a leisurely pace. **-er** *n.*

am-bu-lance *n.* A vehicle to transport the injured or sick.

am-bush *n.* A surprise attack.

a-me-lio-rate *v.* To make better.

a-men *interj.* Ending of a prayer.

a-me-na-ble *adj.* To be responsive. **-bility** *n.*

a-mend *v.* To correct; to improve. **-ment** *n.*

a-mends *pl., n.* A compensation for injury.

a-men-i-ty *n.* Agreeableness.

a-merce *v.* To punish.

America *n.* United States of America.

A-mer-ica-n *n.* A native U.S. citizen.

am-e-thyst *n.* A purple gemstone.

a-mi-a-ble *adj.* Being

friendly and pleasant.

am-i-ca-ble *adj.* Being harmonious. **-bility** *n.*

a-mid *prep.* In the middle of something.

a-mi-go *n.* A friend.

a-miss *adj.* Out of order or place.

am-mo-nia *n.* A colorless, pungent gas.

am-mu-ni-tion *n.* Projectiles fired from guns.

am-ne-sia *n.* The loss of memory.

am-nes-ty *n.* A pardon for political offenders.

a-mor-al *adj.* Neither moral nor immoral.

a-mor-phous *adj.* Lacking definite form.

am-or-tize *v.* To liquidate a loan.

a-mount *n.* A sum or total quantity.

am-per-age *n.* A strength of an electric current.

am-pere *n.* The unit of electric current.

am-per-sand *n.* The sign that represents and (&).

am-phet-a-mine *n.* A drug.

am-phib-i-an *n.* Able to live on land and in water.

am-ple *adj.* Sufficient; abundant.

am-pul *n.* A small, sealed vial.

am-pu-tate *v.* To remove a limb from the body. **-tion** *n.*

a-muck *adv.* In an uncontrolled manner.

am-u-let *n.* A charm worn to protect against evil.

a-muse *v.* To entertain. **-ment** *n.*

an *adj.* One sort of.

a-nad-ro-mous *adj.* Migrating up river to breed in fresh water.

an-a-gram *n.* A new word formed from another.

a-nal *adj.* Being related to the anus.

an-al-ge-sia *n.* An inability to feel pain. **-ic** *adj.*

a-nal-y-sis *v.* To be examining parts.

an-a-lyze *v.* To make an analysis of.

an-ar-chy *n.* A state of political disorder.

a-nat-o-mize *v.* To examine in great detail.

a-nat-o-my *n.* Structure of an organ. **-ical** *adj.*

an-ces-try *n.* A line of descent.

an-chor *n.* Device to keep a ship from drifting.

an-chor-age *n.* A place for anchoring a ship.

an-cho-vy *n.* A small fish.

an-cient *adj.* Being very old. **-ness** *n.*

and *conj.* Along with; as well as; added to.

an-dan-te *adv.* Slow in tempo.

and-i-ron n. A heavy metal support for logs in a fireplace.

an-dro-gen n. A hormone that maintains masculine characteristics.

an-ec-dote n. A short account of a story.

a-ne-mi-a n. A condition in which blood does not have enough red corpuscles.

a-nent prep. Regarding; concerning.

an-es-thet-ic n. A drug used during an operation to take away pain.

a-new adv. Again.

an-gel n. An immortal being. **-ic** adj.

an-ger n. A feeling of extreme hostility.

an-gi-na n. A disease marked by painful choking spasms.

an-gle v. Shape that forms a corner.

An-glo n. A root word meaning "English".

an-go-ra n. The silky hair of the Angora rabbit.

an-gry adj. Feeling of anger. **-ily** adv.

an-guish n. A great suffering or grief.

an-gu-lar adj. To be gaunt; bony; lean.

an-hy-drous adj. Does not contain any water.

an-i-mal n. Any four-footed creature; beast.

an-i-mate v. To give life or spirit to. **-tion** n.

an-i-mos-i-ty n. Hostility.

an-ise n. A licorice-flavored herb.

an-kle n. A joint that connects the foot with the leg.

an-klet n. A short sock.

an-nals n. A descriptive record.

an-neal v. To make glass less brittle.

an-nex v. To join a smaller thing to a larger one. **-ation** n.

an-ni-hi-late v. To destroy completely.

an-ni-ver-sa-ry n., pl. **-ries** A date on which something happened at an earlier time.

an-nounce v. To give notice. **-ment** n.

an-nounc-er n. A performer on radio or television.

an-noy v. To bother. **-ance** n.

an-nu-al adj. Recurring the same time each year.

an-nu-i-ty n. An annual payment of an income.

an-nul v. To cancel a marriage or a law. **-ment** n.

an-nun-ci-ate v. To proclaim.

a-noint v. To apply oil in a religious ceremony.

a-non adv. In a short

period of time.

a-non-y-mous *adj.* An unknown or withheld name, agency.

an-oth-er *adj.* To be additional.

an-swer *n.* A written or spoken reply.

ant *n.* A small insect.

an-tag-o-nize *v.* To arouse hostility.

ant-eat-er *n.* An animal with a long snout.

an-te-ce-dent *adj.* Event that precedes another.

an-te-lope *n.* A swift-running mammal.

an-te me-rid-i-em *n.* The time before noon.

an-ten-na *n.* The feelers of an insect; aerial.

an-te-ri-or *adj.* To be toward or at the front.

an-te-room *n.* A waiting room.

an-them *n.* A hymn of praise.

an-ther *n.* A part of the flower.

an-thol-o-gy *n.* A collection of stories.

an-thra-cite *n.* A hard coal.

an-thrax *n.* An infectious disease found in cattle and sheep.

an-thro-poid *n.* Gorillas.

an-thro-pol-o-gy *n.* A study on the origin, and development of man.

an-ti *n.* One who opposes policy or proposal.

an-ti-bi-ot-ic *n.* A substance used as a germ killer.

an-ti-bod-y *n.* The proteins that counteract diseases.

an-tic *n.* A mischievous caper or act.

an-tic-i-pate *v.* To look forward. **-tion** *n.*

an-ti-cli-max *n.* A letdown or decline.

an-ti-dote *n.* A substance to counteract poison. **-al** *adj.*

an-ti-freeze *n.* A substance, mixed with water to lower the freezing point.

an-ti-his-ta-mine *n.* A drug to relieve symptoms of allergies.

an-ti-knock *n.* A substance to reduce engine knock.

an-ti-mo-ny *n.* A silver-white metallic element.

an-ti-pasto *n.* An appetizer.

an-ti-per-spi-rant *n.* A substance to reduce perspiration.

an-ti-pode *n.* A direct opposite.

an-tique *n.* An object over 100 years old.

an-tiquity *n., pl.* **-ties** The quality of being old.

an-ti--Sem-ite *n.* A person hostile toward Jews.

an-tith-e-sis *n.* A direct

opposition.

ant-ler *n.* The horns of a deer.

an-to-nym *n.* A word opposite in meaning.

a-nus *n.* A lower opening of the alimentary canal.

an-vil *n.* A block for forming metal.

anx-i-e-ty *n.* A state of uncertainty.

anx-ious *adj.* Worried.

any *adj.* No matter which.

any-body *pron.* Anyone; any person.

any-how *adv.* In any way; whatever.

any-thing *pron.* Any occurrence.

any-time *adv.* Being at any time.

any-way *adv.* In any manner.

any-where *adv.* To any place.

a-or-ta *n.* The main artery from the heart.

a-pace *adv.* Being rapid in pace.

a-part *adv.* Being separate or at a distance.

a-part-heid *n.* The nonwhite racial discrimination in South Africa.

a-part-ment *n.* A suite in a building.

ap-a-thy *n.* A lack of emotions or feelings.

ape *n.* A large mammal.

ap-er-ture *n.* An opening.

a-pex *n.* The highest point.

a-pha-sia *n.* The loss of the ability to express ideas.

aphid *n.* Small insects.

aph-o-rism *n.* A brief statement of truth.

aph-ro-dis-i-ac *adj.* To be arousing the sexual desire.

a-pi-ary *n.* A place where bees are kept.

a-piece *adv.* For or to each one.

a-plomb *n.* Poise.

ap-o-gee *n.* A point most distant from earth.

a-pol-o-get-ic *adj.* Expression of apology.

ap-o-plex-y *n.* The loss of muscular control.

a-pos-tle *n.* A person sent on a mission.

a-pos-tro-phe *n.* A mark (') of punctuation.

ap-pall *v.* To overcome by shock or dismay.

ap-pa-ra-tus *n.* An instrument for a specific operation.

ap-par-el *v.* To adorn.

ap-par-ent *adj.* Open to the mind; visible.

ap-pa-ri-tion *n.* An unusual appearance.

ap-peal *n.* An earnest plea. **-ingly** *adv.*

ap-pear *v.* To come into public view. **-ance** *n.*

ap-pease *v.* To pacify.

ap-pel-late *adj.* Review the decisions of the lower courts.

ap-pend *v.* To add an appendix.

ap-pen-dec-to-my *n.* The surgical removal of the appendix.

ap-petite *n.* A craving or desire for food.

ap-pe-tiz-er *n.* The food served before a meal.

ap-plaud *v.* To express approval by clapping.

ap-ple *n.* An edible fruit.

ap-ple-jack *n.* A brandy.

ap-pli-ance *n.* The equipment designed for a particular use.

ap-pli-ca-ble *adj.* Being appropriate; suitable.

ap-pli-cant *n.* A person applying for a job.

ap-pli-ca-tion *n.* A request or petition.

ap-ply *v.* To put into use.

ap-point *v.* To fix or set officially. **-ment** *n.*

ap-por-tion *v.* To divide and share. **-ment** *n.*

ap-po-site *adj.* To be pertinent.

ap-prais-al *n.* An evaluation of property.

ap-praise *v.* To estimate the value of. **-er** *n.*

ap-pre-ci-ate *v.* To recognize the worth.

ap-pre-hend *v.* To anticipate with anxiety.

ap-pre-hen-sive *adj.* View the future with anxiety.

ap-pren-tice *n.* A person learning a trade.

ap-prise *v.* To inform.

ap-proach *v.* To come near. **-able** *adj.*

ap-prove *v.* To express a favorable opinion.

ap-prox-i-mate *adj.* Almost exact. **-ly** *adv.*

apri-cot *n.* An oval, orange-colored fruit.

apron *n.* A garment used to protect clothing.

ap-ro-pos *adv.* By the way.

apse *n.* A polygonal projection of a church.

apt *adj.* Appropriate. **-ly** *adv.*

ap-ti-tude *n.* A natural talent or ability.

aqua *n.* Water.

aqua-naut *n.* A scuba diver.

aquar-i-um *n.* An artificial pond.

aq-ue-ous *adj.* To resembling water.

ar-a-ble *adj.* Land suitable for plowing.

ar-bi-tra-tor *n.* A person chosen to decide a dispute.

ar-bor *n.* A type of garden shelter.

ar-bor-vi-tae *n.* A type of evergreen tree.

arc *n.* Something that is curved or arched.

arch *n.* A structure that spans over an open area.

ar-chae-ol-o-gy *n.* The scientific study of ancient times. **-gist** *n.*

arch-bishop *n.* A bishop of the highest rank.

arch-di-o-cese *n.* A district of an archbishop.

ar-cher-y *n.* Art of shooting with a bow and arrow. **-er** *n.*

ar-chi-tect *n.* A person who designs and supervises construction.

arch-way *n.* An arch over a passage.

arc-tic *adj.* Being extremely cold or frigid.

ar-dor *n.* An extreme warmth or passion.

ar-e-a *n.* A flat piece of ground.

a-re-na *n.* an area for public entertainment.

ar-go-sy *n.* A fleet of ships.

ar-gue *v.* To dispute, quarrel. **-ment** *n.*

ar-id *adj.* Being dry.

a-right *adv.* Correctly.

a-rith-me-tic *adj.* Branch of math.

arm *n.* The upper limb of the human body. **-er** *n.*

ar-ma-da *n.* A fleet of warships.

ar-ma-dil-lo *n.* A burrowing nocturnal animal.

ar-ma-ment *n.* A military supplies and weapons.

ar-ma-ture *n.* The main moving part of an electric device.

arm-chair *n.* A type of chair with armrests.

arm-ful *n.* As much as the arm can hold.

arm-hole *n.* An opening in a garment for the arm.

ar-mi-stice *n.* A mutual agreement; truce.

arm-let *n.* A band worn on the upper arm.

ar-moire *n.* A large wardrobe.

ar-mor *n.* A covering to protect the body.

ar-mory *n.* A place where military equipment is stored.

arm-pit *n.* The hollow area under the arm.

arm-rest *n.* A support for the arm on a chair.

arm-twist-ing *n.* The direct pressure to achieve a desired effect.

ar-my *n.* The land forces of a country.

a-ro-ma *n.* A distinctive fragrance or odor. **-tic** *adj.*

a-round *adv.* To or on all sides.

a-round-the-clock *adj.* Lasting for a period of 24 hours.

arouse *v.* To wake up from a sleep.

ar-peg-gi-o *n.* A chord

produced in succession.

ar-rack *n.* An alcoholic beverage.

ar-raign *v.* To be called before a court. -ment *n.*

ar-range *v.* To put in correct order or sequence. -ment *n.*

ar-rant *adj.* Extreme; without moderation.

ar-ras *n.* A wall hanging of tapestry.

ar-ray *v.* To place or set in order. -er *n.*

ar-rears *n., pl.* A state of being behind, as an obligation, etc.

ar-rest *n.* To capture; to seize.

arrest-ee *n.* A person under arrest.

ar-rest-ing *adj.* Very impressive or striking.

ar-rhyth-mia *n.* An alteration in rhythm of the heartbeat.

ar-rhyth-mic *adj.* Lacking regularity or rhythm.

ar-ri-ve *v.* To reach or get to a destination.

ar-ro-gance *n.* An overbearing manner. -gant *adj.,* -gantly *adv.*

ar-row *n.* A weapon shot from a bow; sign to show direction.

ar-row-head *n.* A striking end of an arrow.

ar-row-root *n.* A starch-yielding plant.

ar-rowy *adj.* To move

swiftly.

ar-se-nal *n.* A collection of weapons; place where military equipment is stored.

ar-se-nic *n.* An element used to make insecticide or weed killer.

ar-son *n.* A fraudulent burning of property. -ist *n.*

art *n.* A human expression of objects by painting, etc.

ar-ter-y *n.* A blood vessel that carries blood from the heart.

ar-te-sian well *n.* A well that produces water without a pump.

art form *n.* A form of an artistic expression.

art glass *n.* A glass designed for decorative purposes.

ar-thral-gia *n.* A pain in one or more joints.

ar-thritic *n.* A person who has arthritis.

ar-thri-tis *n.* An inflammation of joints.

ar-thro-pod *n.* An animal with jointed limbs and segmented body, as a spider.

ar-ti-choke *n.* A plant with an edible thistle-like head.

ar-ti-cle *n.* A term or clause in a contract; a paragraph or section.

ar-tic-u-late *adj.* Able to

express oneself clearly.

ar-ti-fact *n.* Something made by man showing human modification.

ar-ti-fice *n.* An artful or clever skill.

ar-ti-fi-cial *adj.* Not genuine; made by man. **-ly** *adv.*

ar-til-lery *n.* Weapons, especially cannons.

ar-ti-san *n.* A craftsman.

art-ist *n.* A person who practices the fine arts of painting, etc.

ar-tiste *n.* An expert in the theatrical profession.

ar-tis-tic *adj.* Characteristic of an artist.

art-ist-ry *n.* An ability, or quality of workmanship.

art-less *adj.* Being crude; simple. **-ly** *adv.*

art-mobile *n.* A trailer that carries an art collection for exhibition on road tours.

art-work *n.* The artistic work of an artist.

as *adv.* In the manner like; similar to.

as-bes-tos *n.* A mineral form of magnesium silicate used in fireproofing.

as-cend *v.* To rise up from a lower level; to climb; to mount.

as-cen-dant *adj.* Rising; moving up.

as-cent *n.* A way up; a slope.

as-cer-tain *v.* To find out for certain; to make sure.

as-cet-i-cism *n.* A practice of strict self-denial.

as-cot *n.* A scarf or broad tie.

as-cribe *v.* To assign or attribute to something. **-able** *v.*

a-sex-u-al *adj.* Lacking sexual reproductive organs. **-ity** *n.*

ash *n.* A tree with a hard, elastic wood.

a-shamed *adj.* Feeling guilt, or shame; feeling unworthy. **-ly** *adv.*

a-shore *adv.* On or to the shore.

ash-tray *n.* A container or receptacle for discarding tobacco ashes.

aside *adv.* Out of the way; to one side.

ask *v.* To request; to seek information.

askance *adv.* With suspicion or distrust.

askew *adv. or adj.* Out of line, not straight.

a-slant *adv.* In a slanting direction.

a-sleep *adv.* In a state of sleep.

a-slope *adv.* In a slanting or sloping position or direction.

a-so-cial *adj.* Selfish, not social.

as-par-a-gus *n.* A vegetable with tender

shoots.

as-pect *n.* The situation, position, view, or appearance of something.

as-pen *n.* A tree known as the trembling poplar, having leaves that flutter.

as-peri-ty *n., pl.* **-ties** A roughness in manner.

as-per-sion *v.* To false charges or slander; defamation; maligning.

as-phalt *n.* A sticky, thick, blackish-brown mixture of petroleum tar.

as-phyx-i-ate *v.* To suffocate, to prevent from breathing. **-tion** *n.*

as-pic *n.* A savory jelly made from fish, meat.

as-pi-rate *v.* To give pronunciation with a full breathing sound.

as-pire *v.* To desire with ambition; to strive towards something that is higher. **-ingly** *adv.*

as-pi-rin *n.* A medication used for the relief of pain and fever.

ass *n.* A hoofed animal; a donkey.

as-sail *v.* To attack violently with words or blows. **-ant** *n.*

as-sas-sin *n.* A murderer especially one that murders a politically important person either for fanatical motives or for hire.

as-sas-si-nate *v.* To murder a prominent person by secret or sudden attack. **-ation, -ator** *n.*

as-sault *n.* A very violent physical or verbal attack on a person. **-er** *n.*

as-say *n.* To evaluate or to assess; to try; to attempt. **-er** *n.*

as-sem-blage *n.* A collection of things or people.

as-sem-ble *v.* To put together the parts of something; to come together as a group. **-ly** *n.*

as-sem-bly-man *n.* A member of an assembly line.

Assembly of God *n.* The congregation belonging to the Pentecostal Church.

as-sent *v.* To agree on something.

as-sert *v.* To declare or state positively, to maintain; to defend.

as-sess *v.* To fix or assign a value to something. **-sor** *n.*

as-sess-ment *n.* The official determination of value for tax purposes.

as-set *n.* A valuable quality or possession.

as-sev-er-ate *v.* To state positively, firmly, and seriously.

as-sign *v.* To designate

as to duty; to give or allot; to attribute. **-able** *adj.*

as-sign-ee *n.* The person appointed to act for another.

as-sign-ment *n.* A given amount of work or task to undertake; a post, position, or office to which one is assigned.

as-sim-i-late *v.* To take in, to understand; to make similar. **-tion** *n.*

as-sist *v.* To give support, to aid, to give help. **-ance, -ant** *n.*

as-size *n.* A fixed or customary standard.

as-so-ci-ate *v.* To connect or join together *n.* a partner, colleague, or companion.

as-so-ci-a-tion *n.* An organized body of people having a common interest; a society.

as-so-nance *n.* The repetition of sound in words or syllables.

as-sort *v.* To distribute into groups of a classification.

as-sort-ed *adj.* Made up of different or various kinds.

as-sort-ment *n.* The act or state of being assorted; a collection of different things.

as-suage *v.* To quiet, pacify; to put an end to

by satisfying. **-ment** *n.*

as-sua-sive *adj.* Having a smooth, pleasant effect or quality.

as-sume *v.* To take upon oneself to complete a job or duty; to take responsibility for. **-able** *adj.*, **-ably** *adv.*

as-sump-tion *n.* An idea or statement believed to be true without proof.

as-sur-ance *n.* A statement made to inspire confidence of mind or manner.

as-sure *v.* To give the feeling of confidence; to make sure.

as-sured *adj.* Satisfied as to the truth or certainty. **-ly** *adv.*

as-sur-er *n.* A person who gives assurance.

as-ter *n.* A plant having white, bluish, purple, or pink daisy-like flowers.

as-ter-isk *n.* The character (*) used to indicate letters omitted or as a reference to a footnote.

a-stern *adv. & adj.* Toward the rear or back of an aircraft or ship.

as-ter-oid *n.* One of thousands of small planets between Jupiter and Mars.

asth-ma *n.* A respiratory disease marked by labored breathing, accompanied by wheezing.

-tic *adj.*, **-tically** *adv.*

as though *conj.* As if.

as·tig·ma·tism *n.* A defect of the lens of an eye resulting in blurred or imperfect images.

a-stir *adj.* To be out of bed, awake; in motion.

as to *prep.* With reference to or regard to; concerning.

as·ton·ish *v.* To strike with sudden fear, wonder, or surprise.

as·ton·ish·ing *adj.* Causing surprise or astonishment. **-ly** *adv.*

as·ton·ish·ment *n.* The state of being amazed or astonished.

as·tound *v.* To fill with wonder and bewilderment. **-ingly** *adv.*

as·tra·khan *n.* The curly fur from a young lamb of the southeast U.S.S.R.

as·tral *adj.* Resembling, or related to the stars.

a·stray *adv.* Away from a desirable or proper path.

a·stride *prep.* One leg on either side of something; placed or lying on both sides of; extending across or over.

as·trin·gent *adj.* Able to draw together or to constricting tissue. **-ency** *n.*

as·tro·dome *n.* A large stadium covered by a dome.

as·tro·labe *n.* An instrument formerly used to determine the altitude of a celestial body.

as·trol·o·gy *n.* The study of the supposed influences of the planets and stars and their movements and positions on human affairs. **-ical** *adj.*, **-ger** *n.*

as·tro·naut *n.* A person who travels in a spacecraft beyond the earth's atmosphere.

as·tro·nau·tics *n.* The technology and science of the construction and operation of a spacecraft. **-cal** *adj.*

as·tro·nom·i·cal *adj.* Relating to astronomy; something very large. **-ly** *adv.*

as·tron·o·my *n.* The science of the celestial bodies and their motion, magnitudes, and constitution. **-er** *n.*

as·tro·phys·ics *n.* A branch of astronomy dealing with the chemical and physical constitution of the celestial bodies. **-ist** *n.*

as·tute *adj.* Sharp in discernment; very shrewd. **-ly** *adv.*, **-ness** *n.*

a·sun·der *adv.* Separate into parts or positions apart from each other.

asy-lum *n.* A refuge or institution for the care of the needy or sick.

at *prep.* To indicate presence, occurrence, or condition.

at-a-vism *n.* A hereditary characteristic that skips several generations. **-ic** *adj.*

at-el-ier *n.* An artist's workshop.

a-the-ism *n.* The disbelief that God exists.

athe-ist *n.* A person who does not believe in God.

a-thirst *adj.* Having a strong, eager desire for something.

ath-lete *n.* A person who participates in sports.

ath-lete's foot *n.* A contagious skin infection of the feet.

ath-let-ic *adj.* Relating to athletes.

a-thwart *adv.* Opposition to the expected or right.

a-tilt *adj. & adv.* Inclined upward or tilted in some way.

Atlantic Ocean *n.* The second largest ocean.

at-las *n.* A collection or book of maps.

at-mos-phere *n.* A gaseous mass that surrounds a celestial body.

at-oll *n.* An island of coral that encircles a lagoon.

at-om *n.* The smallest unit of an element.

a-tone *v.* To make amends.

a-tone-ment *n.* The amends for a wrongdoing.

atop *adj.* On the top of something.

atri-um *n.* One of the heart chambers.

a-tro-cious *adj.* Cruel or evil.

a-troc-i-ty *n., pl.* **-ties** The condition of being atrocious.

a-tro-phy *v.* To decrease in size or wasting away.

at-tach *v.* To fasten or become fastened. **-able** *adj.*

at-ta-che *n.* An expert on the diplomatic staff of an embassy.

at-ta-che case *n.* A briefcase or a small suitcase.

at-tach-ment *n.* The state of being attached; a tie of affection or loyalty.

at-tack *v.* To threaten with force, to assault.

at-tain *v.* To arrive at or reach a goal. **-ability** *n.*

at-tain-der *n.* The loss of civil rights that occurs following a criminal conviction.

at-taint *v.* To disgrace or stain; to achieve or obtain by effort.

at-tar *n.* The fragrant oil

from flowers.

at-tempt v. To make an effort to do something.

at-tend v. To be present; to take charge of or to look after.

at-ten-dance n. The number of times a person attends.

at-ten-dant n. One who provides a service for another.

at-ten-tion n. An observation, or mental concentration

at-ten-u-ate v. To lessen the force, amount or value; to become thin. **-tion** n.

at-test v. To give testimony, or sign one's name as a witness. **-ation** n.

at-tic n. The space directly below the roof of a building.

at-tire n. A person's dress or clothing.

at-ti-tude n. A mental position; the feeling one has for oneself.

at-tor-ney n., pl. **-neys** A person with legal training who is appointed by another to transact business for him.

at-tract v. To draw by appeal.

at-trib-ute v. To explain by showing a cause. **-uteable** adj.

at-tune v. To bring something into harmony.

atwit-ter adj. Excited; nervously concerned about something.

au-burn adj. A reddish brown color; moderately brown.

au cou-rant adj. Fully familiar or informed.

auc-tion n. A public sale of merchandise to the highest bidder. **-neer** n.

auc-to-ri-al adj. Having to do with an author.

au-da-cious adj. Bold, daring, or fearless; insolent. **-ly** adv.

au-di-ble adj. Capable of being heard.

au-di-ence n. A group of spectators or listeners.

au-di-o adj. Relating to sound or its high-fidelity reproduction.

au-dit n. A verification or examination of financial accounts.

au-di-tion n. A trial performance given by an entertainer as to demonstrate ability.

au-di-tor n. A person who listens or hears; one who audits accounts.

au-di-to-ri-um n. A large room in a public building or a school that holds many people.

au-di-to-ry adj. Related to the organs or sense of hearing.

aught n. Zero (0).

aug-ment *v.* To add to or increase; to enlarge.

au jus *adj.* Served in the juices obtained from roasting.

auk *n.* A sea bird living in the arctic regions.

aunt *n.* A sister of a person's father or mother.

au-ra *n., pl.* **-ras, -rae** An emanation said to come from a person's or an animal's body.

au-ral *adj.* Relating to the ear or the sense of hearing.

au-re-ate *adj.* Of a brilliant golden color.

au re-voir *interj.* Used in expressing farewell to someone.

au-ri-cle *n.* The two upper chambers of the heart.

au-ro-ra *n.* The brilliant display of moving and flashing lights in the night sky. **-al** *adj.*

aus-tere *adj.* Stern in manner and appearance.

aus-tral *adj.* Southern.

au-then-tic *adj.* Real; genuine; worthy of acceptance.

au-then-ti-cate *v.* To prove something is true or genuine. **-ity** *n.*

author *n.* A person who writes an original literary work.

au-thor-i-ty *n., pl.* **-ties** A group or person with power; an expert.

au-thor-ize *v.* To give authority; to approve; to justify. **-zation** *n.*

au-tism *n.* An absorption in a self-centered mental state, such as fantasies, daydreams or hallucinations. **-tic** *adj.*

au-to-bahn *n.* A highway in Germany.

au-to-bi-og-ra-phy *n., pl.* **-phies** The life story of a person, written by that person. **-er** *n.*

au-toch-tho-nous *adj.* Native to an area.

au-toc-ra-cy *n.* A government by one person who has unlimited power.

au-to-di-dact *n.* A person who has taught himself.

au-to-graph *n.* A handwritten signature.

au-to-mate *v.* To operate by automation.

au-to-mat-ic *adj.* Operating with very little control. **-ally** *adv.*

au-to-mat-ic pi-lot *n.* The device for automatically steering aircraft and ships.

au-to-ma-tion *n.* The equipment used to acquire automation.

au-to-mo-bile *n.* A four-wheeled passenger vehicle commonly propelled by an internal-combustion engine.

au-to-mo-tive *adj.* Relating to self-propelled vehicles.

au-top-sy *n., pl.* **-sies** The examination of a body after death to find the cause of death.

au-to-stra-da *n.* An expressway in Italy.

au-tumn *n.* The season between summer and winter. **-al** *adj.*

aux-il-ia-ry *adj.* Providing help or assistance to someone.

auxin *n.* A hormone in a plant that stimulates growth.

a-vail *v.* To be of advantage or use; to use.

a-vail-able *adj.* Ready for immediate use.

av-a-lanche *n.* A large amount of rock or snow that slides down a mountainside.

a-vant--garde *n.* People who invent new ideas and styles in a certain field.

a-venge *v.* To take revenge for something. **-er** *n.*

av-e-nue *n.* A street lined with trees.

a-ver *v.* To state positively.

av-er-age *n.* A typical or usual, not being exceptional.

a-verse *adj.* Having a feeling of repugnance.

a-ver-sion *n.* A feeling of strong dislike.

a-vert *v.* To prevent or keep from happening.

a-vi-ary *n.* A place where birds are kept.

a-vi-a-tion *n.* The operation of planes and other aircraft.

a-vi-a-tor *n.* A pilot of an aircraft.

av-id *adj.* Being greedy. **-ly** *adv.*

av-o-ca-do *n.* A pear-shaped edible fruit from the avocado tree.

av-o-ca-tion *n.* An activity in addition to the regular work; a hobby.

a-void *v.* To stay away from; to shun.

a-vouch *v.* To guarantee.

a-vow *v.* To state openly on a subject.

a-wake *v.* To be alert or watchful.

a-ward *v.* To confer as being deserved or merited.

a-ware *adj.* Being conscious of something.

a-wash *adj.* Flooded; to be washed by water.

a-way *adv.* At a distance; apart from.

awe *n.* A feeling of wonder.

a-wea-ry *adj.* Tired.

a-weigh *adj.* Hang just clear of a ship's anchor.

awe-some *adj.* Expressive of awe.

aw-ful *adj.* Very unpleasant. **-ly** *adv.*

a-while *adv.* For a short time.

a-whirl *adj.* To spin around.

awk-ward *adj.* Not graceful; clumsy. **-ly** *adv.*

awl *n.* A tool used to make holes in leather.

awn-ing *n.* A structure that serves as a shelter over a window.

a-wry *adv.* In a twisted or turned position.

ax *or* **axe** *n.* A tool used to split wood.

ax-i-om *n.* Something assumed to be true without proof.

ax-is *n.* The line around an object or body that rotates.

ax-le *n.* A shaft around which a wheel or pair of wheels revolve.

a-yah *n.* A nursemaid or maid in India.

a-zal-ea *n.* A shrub grown for their many colored flowers.

AZT *abbr.* Azidothymidine; a drug that improves the symptoms of AIDS.

Az-tec *n.* Indian people of Mexico.

az-ure *n.* The blue color of the sky.

B

B, b The second letter of the English alphabet.

baa *n.* The cry of sheep.

babble *v.* To chatter senselessly; talk with out meaning. **-bler** *n.*

babe *n.* A young child or infant.

ba-boon *n.* A species of the monkey family.

ba-by *n.* A young child; an infant. **-ish** *adj.*

ba-by-sit *v.* Taking care of young children. **-ter** *n.*

bac-ca-lau-re-ate *n.* A degree given by universities.

bac-ca-rat *n.* A card game that involves gambling.

bach-e-lor *n.* An unmarried male. **-hood** *n.*

back *n.* The rear part of the human body. **-er, -ing** *n.*

back-bite *v.* Slander.

back-bone *n.* The spinal column; the main support.

back-fire *n.* The premature explosion of a combustion engine; unexpected result. **-fired, firing** *v.*

back-gam-mon *n.* A game played by two people.

back-ground *n.* The area behind foreground.

back-hand *n.* A stroke in

the game of tennis.
-handed adj.

back-ing n. The support given to something or someone; an endorsement.

back-log n. The accumulation of unfinished work.

back-side n. The buttocks, the rump.

back-slap v. To express excessive goodwill.
-per n.

back-slide v. To lapse into a less desirable condition.

back-spin n. The reverse rotation of a ball.

back-stairs adj. Secret stairs.

back-stitch n. A stitch made in fabric by inserting the needle to the right and coming out in equal distance to the left.

back-stop n. Something that stops a ball, keeping it from leaving a field of play.

back-stretch n. The opposite side of the homestretch on a racecourse.

back-stroke n. A swimming stroke.

back-swept adj. To slant backward.

back-swing n. A movement with a racket that is the reverse of the forward swing.

back-sword n. A sword having a single-edge blade.

back-talk n. An insolent reply.

back-track v. To retrace previous steps.

back-up n. Something that serves as a substitute.

back-ward adv. Toward the back. -ness n.

back-wash n. A backward movement of something as water that is produced by a propelled force.

back-woods n., pl. A remote backward area.
-man n.

back-yard n. The ground located in the back of a house.

ba-con n. The side and back of a pig.

bac-te-ri-al adj. Caused or related to bacteria.

bad adj. Naughty.
-ness n., -ly adv.

badger n. A burrowing mammal.

bad-min-ton n. A court game.

bad-mouth v. To criticize persistently.

baf-fle v. To puzzle.

baf-fling wind n. A light wind that shifts frequently from side to side.

ba-gel n. A hard, round roll.

bag-gage n. The belongings of a traveler.

bag-pipe *n.* A wind instrument. **-er** *n.*

bail *n.* The money to guarantee appearance at a trial.

bail-iff *n.* An officer who guards prisoners.

bait *v.* To lure.

bake *v.* To cook in an oven.

bal-ance *n.* The amount remaining. **-anced** *v.*

bal-co-ny *n.* The platform projecting from the wall. **-nies** *n., pl.*

bald *adj.* Lacking nair on the head.

balk *v.* To refuse to go on.

bal-lad *n.* A narrative story.

bal-last *n.* A heavy material to give stability.

bal-le-ri-na *n.* A female ballet dancer.

bal-let *n.* An artistic dance.

bal-loon *n.* A bag inflated with air.

bal-lot *n.* A paper used in secret voting.

ball-point *n.* A pen with a self-inking writing point.

balm *n.* An ointment that heals.

bal-sa *n.* A light weight wood.

bal-us-ter *n.* A post that supports a handrail.

bam-boo *n.* A tall grass with hollow stems.

bam-boo-zle *v.* To trick or deceive.

ban *v.* To prohibit; forbid. **-ned** *v.*

ba-nal *adj.* Trite. **-ity** *n.*

ba-nan-a *n.* A yellow, edible fruit.

band *n.* A group of musicians.

band-age *n.* A strip of cloth used to protect an injury.

ban-dit *n.* A gangster.

ban-dy *adv.* To bent outward.

bane *n.* A cause of ruin.

ban-gle *n.* A bracelet.

ban-ish *v.* Force to leave. **-ment** *n.*

ban-jo *n.* An instrument similar to a guitar.

bank *n.* A slope of land adjoining water.

bank-er *n.* A bank manager.

bank-rupt *n.* A person who is insolvent. **-cy** *n.*

ban-quet *n.* An elaborate feast.

ban-yan *n.* A tree of the tropics.

barb *n.* A sharp projection.

bar-bar-i-an *n.* A person thought to be primitive.

bar-be-cue *n.* An outdoor fireplace. **-cued, -cuing** *v.*

bar-ber *n.* A person who cuts hair. **-shop** *n.*

bare *adj.* To expose to view.

bare-ly adv. By a little amount.

bar-gain n. Purchase of an item at a good price.

barge n. A flat-bottomed boat.

bark n. The outer surface of a tree.

bar-ley n. A grain. **-leys** n., pl.

barn n. A farm building.

bar-na-cle n. A fish with a hard shell.

ba-rom-et-er n. An instrument that records weather changes.

bar-rack n. Housing for soldiers.

bar-ra-cu-da n. A fish.

bar-rage n. The discharge of missiles.

bar-rel n. A wooden container with round, flat ends and sides that bulge.

bar-ren adj. Lacking vegetation. **-ness** n.

bar-rette n. A clasp to hold hair in place.

bar-ri-er n. A structure that bars entrance.

bar-room n. A place where drinks are sold.

bar-row n. A wheelbarrow.

bar-tend-er n. One who serves drinks at a bar.

bar-ter v. To trade something. **-er** n.

base n. The fundamental part.

base-ball n. A game played with a ball and bat.

base-board n. The molding where the wall meets the floor.

base-ment n. The foundation of a building or home.

bash v. To smash.

ba-sic adj. Forming the basis.

bas-il n. An herb of the mint family.

bas-o-lisk n. A tropical American lizard.

ba-sin n. A washbowl.

ba-sis n. The main part.

bask v. To relax in the sun.

bas-ket n. An object made of woven material. **-ry** n.

bass n. A fresh water fish.

bas-si-net n. A basket used as a infant's crib.

bas-soon n. An woodwind instrument.

bas-tard n. An illegitimate child. **-ize** v.

baste v. To sew a loose stitch.

bat n. A wooden stick. **-ted, -ting** v.

bath n. The act of washing the body.

bat-tal-ion n. A military unit.

bat-ten v. To make secure.

bat-ter v. To beat or strike continuously.

bat-tery *n.* A group of heavy guns.

bat-tle *n.* To struggle. **-tled, -tling** *v.*

bawd *n.* A prostitute.

bawl *v.* To cry.

bay *n.* An inlet of a body of water.

bay-berry *n.* An evergreen shrub.

bay-o-net *n.* A spear-like weapon.

ba-zaar *n.* A fair for charity.

be *v.* To exist.

beach *n.* A sandy shore.

bead *n.* A small round ball for threading. **-ed** *adj.*

beak-er *n.* A large cup.

beam *n.* A large, wooden plank.

bean *n.* An edible seed.

bear *n.* A carnivorous mammal. **-able** *adj.*

beard *n.* Hair growing on the chin and cheeks. **-less, -ed** *adj.*

beast *n.* A four-legged animal. **-liness** *n.*

beat *v.* To strike.

be-a-tif-ic *adj.* To show joy.

beau *n.* A sweetheart.

beau-ty *n.* Pleasing to the eye.

be-calm *v.* To make quiet or calm.

be-cause *conj.* For a reason.

beck *n.* To summon.

be-come *v.* To come, to be.

bed *n.* Furniture for sleeping.

be-dazzle *v.* To confuse with bright lights.

bed-fast *adj.* To be confined to a bed.

bed-lam *n.* A state of confusion.

be-drag-gled *adj.* Limp and wet.

bee *n.* An insect that makes honey.

beech *n.* A tree with edible nuts.

beef *n.* A cow, steer, or bull.

beer *n.* An alcoholic beverage.

beet *n.* A red root vegetable.

bee-tle *n.* An insect.

be-fore *adv.* Previously.

beg *v.* To ask for charity.

be-get *v.* To cause or produce.

be-gin *v.* To start.

be-grudge *v.* To envy someone.

be-guile *v.* To deceive.

be-half *n.* The support of another person.

be-have *v.* To function in a certain manner.

be-head *v.* To remove the head.

be-hind *adv.* At the back.

be-hold *v.* To look at.

be-hoove *v.* To benefit.

beige *n. or adj.* Light brown color.

being *n.* One's existence.

be-la-bor *v.* To discuss beyond the point where it is necessary.

be-lat-ed *adj.* Late.
 -ly *adv.*

belch *v.* To expel gas through the mouth.

be-lief *n.* Something that is trusted.

bell *n.* An instrument that rings.

bel-lows *n.* An instrument that produces air.

bel-ly *n.* The abdomen.

be-long *v., n.* To be a part of.
 -ings *n., pl.*

be-loved *adj.* To be dearly loved.

be-low *adv.* Lower level or place.

belt *n.* A band around the waist. **-ed** *adj.*

be-muse *v.* To bewilder.

bench *n.* A long seat.

bend *v.* To arch.

beneath *adv.* Below; underneath.

ben-e-dict *n.* A bachelor recently married.

ben-e-dic-tion *n.* A blessing.

ben-e-fit *n.* Aid.
 -ed, -ing *v.*

be-nev-o-lence *n.* An inclination to be charitable.

be-nign *adj.* Having a kind disposition.
 -ly *adv.*

ben-i-son *n.* A blessing.

bent *adj.* Curved.

be-numb *v.* To dull.

be-queath *v.* To give or leave to someone by will.

be-reave *v.* To suffer the loss of a loved one.

berg *n.* A large mass of ice.

ber-i-ber-i *n.* A nervous disorder.

berry *n.* An edible fruit.

berth *n.* A space for a ship to dock.

be-ryl-li-um *n.* A metallic element.

be-seech *v.* To ask earnestly.

be-side *prep.* Next to.

be-siege *v.* To surround with troops.

be-spat-ter *v.* To soil.

be-speak *v.* To foretell.

best *adj.* Exceeding all others.

be-stir *v.* To rouse into action.

be-stow *v.* To present.

be-stride *v.* To step over.

bet *n.* An amount risked on a wager.

be-take *v.* To move or to go.

be-think *v.* To remember.

be-to-ken *v.* To show by a sign.

be-tray *v.* To be disloyal.

be-troth *v.* To promise to marry.

bet-ter *adj.* To be more suited.

be-tween *prep.* In the middle.

bev-er-age *n.* A refreshing liquid.

bev-y *n.* A collection or group.

be-ware *v.* To be cautious.

be-wilder *v.* To confuse.

be-witch *v.* To captivate completely.

bey *n.* A turkish title.

be-yond *prep.* Outside the reach of.

be-zique *n.* A card game.

bi-an-nu-al *adj.* Twice a year.

bi-as *n.* A line cut diagonally.

bib *n.* A cloth tied under the chin to protect from spilling food.

Bi-ble *n.* The holy book of the Old and New Testaments.

bib-li-og-ra-phy *n.* A list of work by a writer.

bib-u-lous *adj.* Inclined to drink.

bi-cen-ten-ni-al *adj.* Happening every 200 years.

bi-ceps *n.* An arm muscle.

bick-er *v.* To quarrel or argue.

bi-cus-pid *n.* A tooth with two roots.

bi-cy-cle *n.* A vehicle propelled by pedals.

bid *v.* To offer a price.

bi-det *n.* A basin for bathing the private parts.

bi-en-ni-al *adj.* Occurring every two years. **-ly** *adv.*

bier *n.* A stand for a coffin.

bi-fo-cal *adj.* Having two different focal lengths.

bi-fur-cate *v.* Divide into two parts. **-cation** *n.*

big *adj.* Very large. **-ger, -gest** *adj.*

big-a-my *n.* Married to two people at the same time.

big-wig *n.* A person of authority.

bike *n.* A bicycle.

bi-ki-ni *n.* A two-piece bathing suit.

bi-lat-er-al *adj.* Having two sides.

bile *n.* A liquid secreted by the liver.

bilge *n.* The hull of a ship.

bi-lin-gual *adj.* Being able to speak two languages.

bil-ious *adj.* A gastric distress.

bill *n.* The amount owed. **-able** *adj.*

bill-fold *n.* A pocket-sized wallet.

bil-liards *n.* A game played on a table.

bil-lion *n.* A thousand million.

bill of lading *n.* A list of merchandise.

bil-low *n.* A large wave.

billy goat *n.* A male goat.

bi-month-ly *adj.* Occurring every two months.

bin *n.* An enclosed place for storage.

bi-na-ry *adj.* Made of two parts.

bind *v.* To hold with rope.

bind-er *n.* A notebook.

bind-er-y *n.* A place where books are bound.

bin-go *n.* A game of chance.

bin-oc-u-lar *n.* A device to bring objects far away into focus.

bi-o-chem-is-try *n.* A chemistry of substances.

bi-ol-o-gy *n.* The science of living organisms.

bi-o-phys-ics *n.* The physics of living organisms.

bi-plane *n.* An airplane with wings on two levels.

bi-po-lar *adj.* Referring to two poles. **-ity** *n.*

birch *n.* A large tree with little leaves. **-en** *adj.*

bird *n.* An egg-laying flying animal.

bird-bath *n.* A basin where birds can bathe.

bird-brain *n.* A person who does not have much sense. **-ed** *adj.*

bird-call *n.* The sound a bird makes.

bird dog *n.* A dog used for hunting birds.

bi-ret-ta *n.* A cap worn by Roman Catholic clergy.

birl *v.* The act of pouring.

birth *n.* The beginning of existence.

birth cer-ti-fi-cate *n.* The record of one's birth.

birth-day *n.* The day a person is born.

birth-mark *n.* A mark on the skin present at birth.

birth-place *n.* The place where one is born.

birth-rate *n.* The ratio of the number of births to a given population.

birth-stone *n.* The stone associated with a month of the year.

bis-cuit *n.* A small piece of bread.

bi-sect *v.* To divide into two parts. **-tor, -ion** *n.*

bi-sex-u-al *adj.* Sexually relating to both sexes.

bish-op *n.* Christian clergyman. **-ric** *n.*

bis-muth *n.* A metallic element.

bi-son *n.* A large buffalo.

bis-que *n.* A creamy soup.

bis-ter *n.* Brown color used for drawing. **-ed** *adj.*

bis-tro *n.* A small club or restaurant.

bit *n.* A tiny amount.

bitch *n.* A female dog.

bite *v.* To cut with the

teeth. **-ting** *adj*,
-ingly *adv*.
bit-ter *adj*. A sharp,
unpleasant taste.
ness *n.*, **-ish** *adj.*,
-ly *adv*.
bit-ter-sweet *n*. A
poisonous woody vine.
bi-valve *n*. A mollusk that
has a hinged two-part
shell. **-vular** *n*.
biv-ou-ac *n*. A temporary
military camp.
bi-week-ly *n*. Occurring
every two weeks.
bi-year-ly *n*. Occurring
every two years.
bi-zarre *adj*. Extremely
strange. **-ness** *n.*,
-ly *adv*.
blab *v*. To reveal a
secret.
blab-ber *v*. To chatter.
black *adj*. Being very
dark in color.
black-ball *n*. A vote to
prevent admission to a
club.
black-board *n*. A slate
board written on with
chalk.
black eye *n*. A bruise
around the eye.
black-head *n*. A small
mass of dirt that clogs
skin pores.
black-out *n*. A temporary
loss of electrical power.
black-snake *n*. A dark
colored snake of the U.S.
black-top *n*. Paving as-
phalt.

black wal-nut *n*. A nut of
tree grown in N. America.
black wid-ow *n*. An extremely poisonous
spider.
blad-der *n*. The sac
that holds urine. **-y** *adj*.
blade *n*. The part of a
knife that cuts.
blame *v*. To find fault in
something that is done.
-ful, -able, -less *adj*.
-lessness *n.*,
-lessly *adv*.
blanch *v*. To remove the
color.
blan-dish *v*. To coax by
flattery. **-ment, -er** *n*.
blank *adj*. To empty.
-ness *n.*, **-ly** *adv*.
blan-ket *n*. A covering
on a bed.
blare *v*. To make a loud
sound.
blar-ney *n*. Talk that is
deceptive.
blas-pheme *v*. To talk
badly about someone.
-ous *adj.*, **-y, -er** *n*.
blast *n*. A strong gust of
air.
blast-off *n*. The launch-
ing of a spaceship.
bla-tant *adj*. Unpleasant.
-tancy *n.*, **-ly** *adv*.
blaze *n*. A bright burst
of fire. **-ing, ed** *v*.
bla-zon *v*. To make
known.
bleach *v*. To remove the
color. **-er** *n*.
bleach-ers *pl., n*. Seat-

ing for spectators.
bleak *adj.* Depressing.
-ness *n.,* **-ly** *adv.*
bleat *n.* The cry of a sheep or goat.
bleed *v.* To lose blood.
bleep *n.* To signal with a loud sound.
blem-ish *n.* A flaw; a defect.
blend *v.* To mix together smoothly. **-er** *n.*
bless *v.* To honor or praise.
bless-ing *n.* A short prayer.
blight *n.* A disease of plants.
blimp *n.* A large aircraft.
blind *adj.* Having no eyesight; window shades **-ness** *n.,* **-ing** *adj.* **-ly, -ingly** *adv.*
blind-fold *v.* To cover the eyes.
blink *v.* To open and close the eyes quickly.
blintz *n.* A very thin pancake.
bliss *n.* Having great happiness. **-ful** *adj.,* **-fulness** *n.*
blis-ter *n.* A swelling of a thin layer of skin. **-y** *adj.*
blithe *adj.* Being carefree. **-ly** *adv.*
blitz *n.* A sudden attack.
bliz-zard *n.* A severe winter storm.
bloat *v.* To swell or puff out.

blob *n.* A small shapeless mass.
block *n.* A solid piece of matter. **-er, -age** *n.*
block-ade *n.* A closure of an area. **-er** *n.*
blond *adj.* A golden color.
blood *n.* A red fluid in the veins circulated by the heart.
blood-shot *adj.* Redness of the eyes.
blood-stream *n.* Blood in the vascular system.
blood vessel *n.* A canal which circulates blood.
bloom *v.* To bear flowers.
bloom-ers *n., pl.* Loose trousers.
bloom-ing *adj.* To grow; to blossom. **-ingly** *adv.*
blos-som *n.* The flower on a plant.
blot *n.* An area that is stained; a spot.
blouse *n.* A woman's shirt.
blow *v.* Current of air. **-er** *n.*
blow-out *n.* A sudden deflation of a tire.
blow-torch *n.* A tool that melts soft metals.
blow-up *n.* An enlargement.
blue *n.* The color of the sky. **-ness** *n.*
blue-berry *n.* An edible berry.
blue jay *n.* A bird having

blue colored feathers.

blue-print n. A reproduction of drawings or plans.

blues pl., n. A style of jazz.

bluff v. To deceive.

blun-der n. An error or mistake. **-ingly** adv., **-er** n.

blunt adj. To be frank and abrupt. **-ness** n., **-ly** adv.

blur v. To smear. **-ry** adj.

blurt v. To speak impulsively.

blush v. To turn red in the face. **-ful** adj.

blus-ter n. Violent and noisy storm. **-ous** adj., **-ingly** adv., **-er** n.

bo-a n. A large non-venomous snake.

boar n. A male pig.

board n. A flat piece of lumber; to get on a train. **-er** n.

board-walk n. A walkway at the beach.

boast v. To brag. **-ful** adj., **-fulness, -er** n., **-ingly** adv.

boat n. A small ship.

boat-swain n. An officer in charge of rigging.

bob v. To cause to move up and down.

bob-bin n. A spool that holds thread.

bob-cat n. A wild-cat.

bob-sled n. A sled with

steering controls.

bod-ice n. The upper section of a dress.

bod-y n. The physical part of a person. **-ied** adj.

body-guard n. A person hired to protect another.

bo-gus adj. Something that is not real.

boil v. To raise the temperature of liquid until it bubbles.

boil-er n. A vessel for heating water for power.

bois-ter-ous adj. Undisciplined. **-ness** n., **-ly** adv.

bold adj. Having courage. **-ness** n., **-ly** adv.

bold-face n. A style of printing. **-d** adj.

bo-le-ro n. A short jacket.

bo-lo-gna n. Smoked sausage.

bol-ster n. A round pillow. **-er** n.

bolt n. A threaded metal pin. **-er** n.

bomb n. A weapon detonated upon impact.

bom-bard v. To attack repeatedly. **-ment** n.

bom-bast n. A very ornate speech. **-ically** adv., **-ic** adj.

bomber n. A military aircraft.

bo-na fide adj. Genuine; authentic.

bond *n.* Something that binds together. **-ed** *adj.*

bone *n.* The connecting tissue of the skeleton.

bon-fire *n.* An open outdoor fire.

bon-net *n.* A woman's hat.

bon-sai *n.* A small ornamental shrub.

bo-nus *n.* Over and above what is expected. **-es** *n., pl.*

bon voyage *n.* A farewell wish.

boo *n.* Disapproval or contempt.

book *n.* Literary work that is written or printed. **-binder** *n.*

book-keep-ing *n.* A person recording transactions of a business.

boom *n.* A deep, resonant sound.

boo-mer-ang *n.* A curved, flat missile.

boon *n.* Something that is pleasant.

boor *n.* A person with little refinement. **-ish** *adj.*

boost *v.* To lift by pushing up.

boost-er *n.* A promoter.

boot *n.* A covering for the foot.

booth *n.* A small compartment.

bo-rax *n.* A cleaning compound.

bor-der *n.* The margin or edge. **-line** *n.*

bore *v.* To make a hole.

bor-ough *n.* A self-governing town.

bor-row *v.* To receive money with the intentions of returning it.

bos-om *n.* A female's breasts.

boss *n.* The supervisor.

bot-a-ny *n.* The science of plants. **-nist** *n.*

botch *v.* To ruin something.

both *adj.* Two in conjunction.

both-er *v.* To pester, harass. **-some** *n.*

bot-tle *n.* A receptacle made of glass.

bot-tom *n.* The lowest part.

bot-u-lism *n.* Food poisoning.

bouil-lon *n.* A clear broth.

boul-der *n.* A large round rock.

boul-e-vard *n.* A broad city street.

bounce *v.* To leap suddenly.

bound-a-ry *n.* The limit or border.

boun-ti-ful *adj.* Abundant.

bounty *n.* Generosity.

bou-quet *n.* A group of cut flowers.

bour-geois *pl., n.* A member of the middle class.

bout *n.* A contest.

bou-tique *n.* A small retail shop.

bow *n.* The front section of a boat.

bow-el *n.* The digestive tract.

bowl *n.* A container for food.

bow-leg *n.* An outward curve of the knee.

box *n.* A small container.

box-car *n.* An enclosed railway car.

box-er *n.* A person who fights professionally.

box of-fice *n.* A place for selling tickets.

boy *n.* A male child.

boy-cott *v.* A means of protest.

brace *n.* A device that supports something.

brace-let *n.* A band on the wrist.

brack-et *n.* A support to hold a shelf.

brad *n.* A small nail.

brag *v.* To talk boastfully. **-gart** *n.*

braid *v.* To interweave.

braille *n.* Printing for the blind.

brain *n.* The nerve tissue enclosed in the cranium. **-less** *adj.*

brake *n.* The device to stop motion.

bran *n.* The husk of cereal grains.

branch *n.* An extension from the trunk of a tree.

bran-dy *n.* An alcoholic liquor.

bras-siere *n.* A woman's undergarment.

brat-wurst *n.* A fresh pork sausage.

brave *adj.* Having courage.

bra-vo *interj.* Expressing approval.

brawl *n.* A noisy argument or fight.

bray *v.* To make a loud cry.

bra-zen *adj.* Made of brass.

breach *n.* Ruptured, or broken.

bread *n.* Leavened food made from a flour and yeast.

breadth *n.* The measurement from side to side.

break *v.* To separate into parts. **-able** *adj.*

break-down *n.* The failure to function.

breast *n.* The milk-producing glandular organs.

breath *n.* The air inhaled and exhaled. **-less** *adj.*

breech *n.* The buttocks.

breeze *n.* A slight gentle wind.

brev-i-ty *n.* A brief duration.

brew *v.* To make beer. **-er** *n.*

bribe *v.* To influence.

brick *n.* A block of baked

clay.

bride *n.* A woman just married.

bride-groom *n.* A man just married.

brides-maid *n.* A woman who attends a bride at her wedding.

bridge *n.* A structure over water.

bri-dle *n.* A harness used to guide a horse.

brief *n.* A concise, formal statement. **-ness** *n.*

brief-case *n.* A case for carrying papers or books.

brig *n.* A prison on a ship.

bri-gade *n.* A military unit.

brig-and *n.* A bandit.

bright *adj.* Brilliant in color. **-ness** *n.*

brim *n.* The edge or rim of a cup. **-ming** *v.*

brine *n.* Salty water.

brink *n.* The upper edge or margin.

bri-oche *n.* A sweet roll.

brisk *adj.* Moving or acting quickly. **-ly** *adv.*

bris-tle *n.* Stiff and coarse.

brit-tle *adj.* Very easy to break. **-ness** *n.*

broach *n.* A tool used for enlarging hole.

broad *adj.* Covering a wide area. **-en** *v.*

broad-cast *v.* To make widely known.

broad-mind-ed *adj.* Fair.

broad-side *n.* The side of a ship.

bro-cade *n.* A silk fabric.

broc-co-li *n.* A green vegetable.

bro-chure *n.* A booklet.

brogue *n.* A strong regional accent.

broil *v.* To cook by direct heat.

broil-er *n.* A part of a stove.

broke *adj.* Penniless.

bro-ken *adj.* Separated into parts.

bro-mide *n.* A sedative.

bron-chi-al *adj.* Pertaining to the bronchi. **-tis** *n.*

bronze *n.* An alloy of tin, and copper.

brooch *n.* A decorative pin.

brood *n.* The young of an animal. **-er** *n.*

brook *n.* A small stream.

broom *n.* An implement for sweeping.

broth *n.* The juices from meat.

brow *n.* The ridge above the eye.

brow-beat *v.* To bully.

brown-ie *n.* A chewy piece of chocolate cake.

bruise *n.* An injury that ruptures small blood vessels.

brush *n.* A device used for grooming hair.

bru-tal *adj.* Cruel treatment. **-ize** v.

bub-ble n. A round hollow object.

bub-ble gum n. Chewing gum with ability to make bubbles.

bu-bon-ic plague n. A highly infectious disease causing death.

buck n. An adult male deer.

buck-et n. A pail for carrying liquids.

buck-eye n. A type of shrub.

buckle v. To warp.

buck-ram n. A fabric stiffened with a glue for the making of book covers.

buck-skin n. The hide of a deer or buck, used as clothing.

buck-wheat n. A grain used for pancakes.

bud n. A flower not developed completely.

budge v. To move slightly.

budg-et n. The total amount of money allocated for expenses.
-ary adj.

buff n. To polish.

buf-fa-lo A wild ox; a bison.

buff-er n. A tool used to polish or shine.

buf-fet n. A table for serving food.

buf-foon n. A clown.
-ish adj., **-ery** n.

bug n. An insect.
-gy adj.

bug-gy n. A small baby carriage.

bu-gle n. A brass instrument. **-er** n.

build v. To erect. **-er** n.

build-ing n. A roofed and walled structure.

bulb n. Electricity for lamps.

bulge n. The swelling of the surface. **-y** adj.

bulk n. A large mass; anything. **-iness** n., **-y** adj.

bulk-head n. A retaining wall.

bull n. The adult male in cattle and other animals.

bull-dog n. A small, rough dog.

bull-doze v. To excavate or dig up land.

bull-dozer n. A machine used for moving earth.

bul-let n. A projectile fired from a gun.

bul-le-tin n. A public notice.

bul-let-proof adj. A condition which doesn't allow a bullet to pass through something.

bull-fight n. A fight between a bull and a man; a Spanish tradition.
-ing, -er n.

bull-finch n. A bird of Europe, kept as a pet.

bull-frog n. A type of a frog, large in size.

bul-lion *n.* Refined gold; gold bars.

bull-pen *n.* A place where the pitcher of a baseball game warms up.

bull ring *n.* An area where a bullfight takes place.

bul-ly *n.* A person who is mean. **-lied** *v.*

bul-rush *n.* Tall marsh grass.

bul-wark *n.* Defense.

bum *n.* A homeless person who begs from others. **-mer** *adj.*

bum-ble-bee *n.* A large hairy bee.

bump *v.* To collide with. **-y** *adj.*, **-iness** *n.*

bump-er *n.* The device on the front of vehicles.

bump-kin *n.* An awkward person.

bump-tious *adj.* Being forward; pushy. **-ness** *n.*

bunch *n.* A group of items or people. **-y** *adj.*

bun-dle *n.* Anything wrapped or held together. **-dled, -dling** *v.*

bung *n.* The stopper used in barrels.

bun-ga-low *n.* A one-story cottage.

bun-gle *v.* To act in a clumsy manner. **-er** *n.*

bun-ion *n.* A painful swelling of the big toe.

bunk *n.* A bed with upper and lower sections for sleeping.

bun-ny *n.* A small rabbit.

bunt *v.* To hit a pitched ball a short distance.

bunt-ing *n.* A hooded blanket for babies.

buoy *n.* A floating object to mark a channel.

buoy-an-cy *n.* The ability to remain afloat.

bur-den *n.* Something that is hard to bear. **-some** *adj.*

bu-reau *n.* A low chest for storing clothes.

bur-glar *n.* A person who steals. **-ize** *v.*

bur-i-al *n.* The act of burying the dead.

bur-lap *n.* A coarse cloth.

bur-lesque *n.* Theatrical entertainment. **-er** *n.*

bur-ly *adj.* Very heavy and strong. **-iness** *n.*, **-ily** *adv.*

burn *v.* To be destroyed by fire. **-ed** *v.*, **-ing** *adj.*

bur-nish *v.* To polish. **-er** *n.*

burr *n.* A rough edge.

bur-ro *n.* A small donkey.

bur-row *n.* A tunnel dug by an animal. **-er** *n.*

burst *adj.* To explode. **-ing** *v.*

bury *v.* To cover; hide.

bus *n.* A large passenger vehicle.

bush *n.* A dense tuft or growth. **-y** *adj.*

bush-el *n.* A unit of dry measurement which equals four pecks.

bush-mas-ter *n.* A large venomous snake.

bush-whack *v.* To ambush someone.

busi-ness *n.* A person's occupation.

bus-kin *n.* A boot extending halfway up the leg.

bus-y *adj.* Full of activity; occupied.

bus-y bod-y *n.* A person concerned with others affairs.

butch-er *n.* A person who slaughters animals.

but-ler *n.* A man servant. **-ship** *n.*

but-ter-fin-gers *n.* A clumsy person. ·

but-tocks *pl., n.* Fleshy parts of the rump.

but-ton *n.* A small disk for closing a garment.

buzz *v.* A low vibrating sound.

byte *n.* Binary digits in computers.

C

C, c The third letter of the English alphabet.

ca-ban-a *n.* A small shelter on the beach.

cab-i-net *n.* A storage unit.

ca-ble *n.* A very heavy rope.

caf-e-te-ri-a *n.* A restaurant with self-service.

ca-lam-i-ty *n.* A misfortune. **-ously** *adv.*

cal-ci-um *n.* An element found in teeth and bones.

cal-cu-late *v.* To estimate something. **-able** *adj.*

calf *n.* The offspring of a domestic cow.

call *v.* To call out; to telephone.

cal-lus *n.* Thickening of the skin.

calm *adj.* An absence of motion.

cal-o-rie *n.* A measurement of food energy.

cam-e-o *n.* A precious gem.

cam-er-a *n.* An apparatus for taking pictures.

camp *n.* A temporary lodging.

cam-pus *n.* The grounds of a college.

can *v.* To be physically or mentally able.

ca-nal *n.* A man-made water channel.

ca-nar-y *n.* A small, colorful songbird.

ca-nas-ta *n.* A card game.

can-cel *v.* To invalidate or annul. **-ation** *n.*

can-cer *n.* A malignant tumor. **-ous** *adj.*

can-di-date *n., pl.* A person seeking an office.

can-dle *n.* A wax tallow

burned to produce light.

ca-nine *adj.* Of the dog family.

can-is-ter *n.* A container to store food in.

can-ker *n.* A sore in the mouth.

can-non *n.* A heavy war weapon.

ca-noe *n.* A light-weight, slender boat. **-ist** *n.*

can-on *n.* The laws of a church.

can-o-py *n.* A cloth covering over a bed.

can-teen *n.* A container for carrying water.

can-ter *n.* A movement that is slower than a gallop.

can-vas *n.* A fabric used in making tents.

can-yon *n.* A deep, narrow gorge.

cap *n.* A covering for the head.

ca-pa-ble *adj.* Having the ability to perform.

cape *n.* A covering for the shoulders.

cap-il-lary *n.* A small vessels that connect.

cap-i-tal *n.* The seat of government.

ca-pit-u-late *v.* To surrender. **-tor** *n.*

cap-size *v.* To overturn in a boat.

cap-sule *n.* A gelatinous case for oral medicine.

cap-tain *n.* The chief leader of a group.

cap-tion *n.* A subtitle.

cap-ti-vate *v.* To hold the attention of someone or thing.

cap-tive *n.* A prisoner.

cap-ture *v.* To take by force. **-er** *n.*

ca-rafe *n.* A wine bottle.

car-a-mel *n.* A chewy candy.

car-at *n.* A unit of weight for gems.

car-a-van *n.* A group of people traveling together.

car-bo-hy-drate *n.* An organic compound.

car-bon *n.* A nonmetallic element. **-ize** *v.*

car-bun-cle *n.* An infection of the skin.

car-bu-re-tor *n.* A device to mix vapor, fuel, and air.

car-ci-no-ma *n.* A malignant tumor.

car-di-ac *adj.* Of the heart.

car-di-gan *n.* A button down sweater.

car-di-ol-o-gy *n.* The study of the heart. **-gist** *n.*

card-sharp *n.* A person who cheats when playing cards.

care *n.* A feeling of concern.

ca-reer *n.* An occupation.

care-free *adj.* Free from all worries.

care-ful *adj.* Exercising

care.

ca-ress *v.* To touch gently.

car-go *n.* Freight.

car-il-lon *n.* A set of tuned bells in a tower.

car-nage *n.* A massacre.

car-ni-val *n.* An amusement show.

car-ol *n* A song.

car-rot *n.* An orange root vegetable.

car-ry *v.* To transport from one place to another.

car-tel *n.* A group of companies organized to control prices, etc.

car-ti-lage *n.* A connective tissue.

car-toon *n.* A funny caricature. **-ist** *n.*

cart-wheel *n.* A sideways handspring.

cas-cade *n.* A waterfall.

case *n.* A particular occurrence.

cash *n.* Money.

cash-ew *n.* An edible nut.

cash-ier *n.* An employee who handles cash.

ca-si-no *n.* A public place for gambling.

cas-ket *n.* A coffin.

cas-sette *n.* A tape used in tape recorders.

cast *v.* To hurl or throw with force. **-way** *adj.*

cast-er *n.* A small set of swiveling rollers.

cas-ti-gate *v.* To punish or criticize severely.

cas-tle *n.* A fort.

cast-off *adj.* To discard or throw away.

ca-su-al *adj.* Informal.

ca-su-al-ty *n.* One who is injured or killed.

cat-a-log *n.* A publication listing of names and addresses.

ca-tas-tro-phe *n.* A terrible disaster.

catch *v.* To capture or seize.

cat-e-go-ry *n.* A grouping of something.

ca-the-dral *n.* A large church.

cat-nap *n.* A short nap.

cat-tle *n., pl.* Farm animals.

cau-cus *n.* The meeting of a political party.

cau-li-flow-er *n.* A vegetable.

caulk *v.* To seal seams against leakage.

cause *v.* To produce a result.

cau-ter-ize *v.* To burn with a hot instrument.

cau-tion *n.* A warning.

cav-al-cade *n.* Horse-drawn carriages.

cav-al-ry *n.* The army troops on horseback.

cave *n.* An underground tomb or chamber.

cav-i-ar *or* **cav-i-are** *n.* The eggs of a large fish.

cav-i-ty *n.* A decayed place in a tooth.

cease v. To stop.

cease-fire v. To stop fighting.

cease-less adj. Endless. **-ly** adv.

ce-dar n. An evergreen tree.

cel-e-brate v. To observe with ceremonies. **-tion** n.

cel-leb-ri-ty n., pl. **-ies** A famous person.

cel-er-y n. A vegetable with an edible stalk.

ce-les-tial adj. Heavenly.

cell n. A small room in a prison.

cel-lar n. An underground area of a house.

cel-lu-lite n. A fatty deposit.

cel-lu-lose n. A carbohydrate.

ce-ment n. A hard construction material.

cem-e-ter-y n. A place for burying the dead.

cen-sor n. A person who examines films. **-ship** n.

cen-sure n. An expression of criticism.

cen-sus n. The count of the population.

cen-ter n. The equal distance from all sides.

cen-tral adj. The center or main part. **-ize** v.

cen-tu-ry n. A period of 100 years.

ce-ram-ic adj. Material made by firing clay.

ce-re-al n. An edible grain; breakfast food.

cer-a-bel-lum n. The lower part of the brain.

cer-e-brum n. The upper part of the brain.

cer-e-mo-ny n. A ritual.

cer-tain adj. To be very sure. **-ly** adv.

cer-tif-i-cate n. A document stating the truth.

cer-ti-fy v. To declare in writing to be true.

ces-sa-tion n. The act of stopping or ceasing.

ces-sion n. The act of giving up rights.

cha-grin n. The feeling of disappointment.

chain n. The connecting links.

chair n. A seat with four legs and a back.

chair-man n. A person presiding at a meeting.

cha-let n. A cottage.

chal-ice n. A drinking goblet.

chalk n. A soft mineral used for writing.

chal-lah n. A loaf of braided bread.

chal-lis n. A lightweight printed cloth.

cham-ber n. A judge's office.

chamber-maid n. A maid at a hotel.

champ n. A champion.

cham-pagne n. A white sparkling wine.

chance n. Accident.

chan-cel n. An area of a

church.

chan-cel-lor *n.* A chief director. **-ship** *n.*

chan-croid *n.* A lesion in the genital area.

chan-de-lier *n.* A large light fixture.

change *v.* To become or make different; alter.

chan-nel *n.* The deepest part of a harbor, lake or river.

chant *n.* A melody sung on the same note.

cha-os *n.* A total disorder.

chap *n., Slang* A fellow.

chap-el *n.* A place to worship.

chap-er-on *n.* A woman who supervises younger women.

chap-lain *n.* A clergyman.

chaps *pl., n.* The leather overpants.

chap-ter *n.* One division or part of a book.

char-ac-ter *n.* A persons quality or trait.

char-coal *n.* A material used for fuel.

chard *n.* An edible white beet.

charge *v.* To give full responsibility to; price.

charg-er *n.* An apparatus to recharge a battery.

char-i-ot *n.* A horse-drawn vehicle.

char-i-ty *n.* The money given to the needy.

cha-ri-va-ri *n.* A playful serenade to newlyweds.

charm *n.* An ability to please; ornament.

chart *n.* A map.

char-ter *n.* An official document.

chase *v.* To run after.

chasm *n.* A deep crack in the earth's surface.

chas-sis *n.* The framework for automobiles.

chaste *adj.* Being pure.

chas-tise *v.* To reprimand.

chat *v.* To converse in a friendly manner.

chat-tel *n.* Movable personal property.

chauf-feur *n.* A person who drives someone.

cheap *adj.* Inexpensive; low in cost.

cheapen *v.* To lessen the value.

cheap-skate *n.* One who won't spend money.

cheat *v.* To break the rules. **-er** *n.*

check *v.* To restrain; examine for correctness.

check-ers *n.* A board game.

cheek *n.* The fleshy part of the face.

cheek-bone *n.* The facial bone below the eyes.

cheer *v.* To give courage to.

cheer-ful *adj.* Having

good spirits.

cheer-leader n. A person who cheers at a sporting event.

cheese n. A food made from the curd of milk.

chee-tah n. A swift-running wildcat.

chef n. A male cook.

cher-ish v. To hold dear.

cher-ry n. A fruit tree bearing red fruit.

cher-ub n. An angel resembling a child.

chess n. A game for two played on a chessboard.

chest-nut n. A tree with edible nuts.

chev-ron n. An insignia or emblem.

chew v. To crush or grind with the teeth.

chick-en n. A domestic fowl.

chick-en pox n. A contagious childhood disease.

chide v. To scold or find fault.

chief n. A person of highest rank; a boss.

chief-tain n. A head of a group, or tribe.

chif-fon n. A sheer fabric.

chif-fo-nier n. A tall chest of drawers.

chig-ger n. An insect.

chi-gnon n. Hair worn on the back of the neck.

child n. A young person of either sex. **-ish** adj.

child-birth n. The act of giving birth.

chill v. To reduce to a lower temperature.

chill-y adj. Very cold condition.

chime n. A set of bells tuned to a scale.

chi-me-ra n. An absurd fantasy.

chim-ney n. A flue for smoke to escape.

chim-pan-zee n. An ape.

chin n. The lower part of the face.

chi-na n. A fine porcelain from China.

chin-chil-la n. A rodent from South America.

chintz n. A printed, glazed cotton fabric.

chintz-y adj. Cheap.

chip n. A small broken off piece; disk used in the game of poker.

chip-munk n. A striped rodent.

chi-ro-prac-tic n. A method of therapy. **-tor** n.

chirp n. The high-pitched sound of a bird.

chis-el n. A tool with a sharp edge to shape.

chiv-al-ry n. The brave qualities of a knight.

chive n. An herb used as flavoring in cooking.

choc-o-late n. The ground cacao nuts. **-y** adj.

choir *n.* An organized group of singers.

chok-er *n.* A short necklace.

cho-les-ter-ol *n.* A fatty substance present in blood cells.

choose *v.* To select or pick out.

chop-sticks *pl., n.* The sticks of wood for eating.

cho-ral *adj.* Sung by a choir or chorus.

cho-rale *n.* A hymn with a simple melody.

chore *n.* A daily task.

cho-re-a *n.* An acute nervous disease.

cho-re-og-ra-phy *n.* A creation of a dance routine in ballets.

chor-is-ter *n.* A member of a choir.

cho-rus *n.* A group of people singing together.

cho-sen *adj.* Preferred above all others.

chow *n., Slang* Food.

chow-der *n.* A soup made with fish or clams.

Christ *n.* Jesus; The Messiah.

chris-ten *v.* To baptize; give a Christian name.

Christ-mas *n.* December 25th; believed to be the birthday of Jesus Christ by Christians.

chrome *n.* Anything plated with chromium.

chron-ic *adj.* To be frequently recurring.

chron-i-cle *n.* A record of events in order.

chuck-hole *n.* A hole in the street.

chuck-le *v.* To laugh quietly. **-er** *n.*

chum *n.* A close friend or pal.

chunk *n.* A thick piece; a lump.

churl *n.* A rude person.

churn *n.* A container for making butter.

chut-ney *n.* A condiment made with fruit.

ci-der *n.* The juice from apples.

ci-gar *n.* Rolled tobacco leaves.

cinch *n.* A strap for holding a saddle.

cin-der *n.* A piece of burned wood.

cin-e-ma *n.* A motion picture.

cin-na-mon *n.* A bark of a tree used for spice.

cir-ca *prep.* Approximate.

cir-cle *n.* A process that ends at its starting point.

cir-cuit *n.* A path where electric current flows.

cir-cu-lar *adj.* To be moving in a circle.

cir-cu-late *v.* To pass from place to place.

cir-cum-cise *v.* To remove skin on the male penis.

cir-cum-fer-ence *n.* The

perimeter of a circle.

cir-cum-scribe *v.* To confine within boundaries.

cir-cum-stance *n.* A fact to consider when making a decision.

cir-cum-stan-tial *adj.* Not essential.

cir-cum-stan-ti-ate *adj.* Provide circumstantial evidence.

cir-cum-vent *v.* To gain advantage. -ion *n.*

cir-cus *n.* A show featuring clowns, and trained animals.

cir-rho-sis *n.* A liver disease.

cir-rus *n.* A white, wispy cloud.

cis-tern *n.* A man-made tank for holding rain water.

cit-a-del *n.* A fortress.

ci-ta-tion *n.* An official summons from a court.

cit-i-zen *n.* A native or naturalized person.

cit-ron *n.* A fruit.

cit-y *n.* A place larger than a town.

civ-et *n.* A cat-like mammal.

civ-ic *adj.* Relating to or of a city.

ci-vil-ian *n.* A person not in the military.

civ-i-li-za-tion *n.* A high level development.

civ-i-lize *v.* To tame.

claim *v.* To hold some-thing to be true.

clair-voy-ance *n.* Visualize objects hidden from the senses.

clam *n.* A freshwater bivalve mollusks.

clam-ber *v.* To climb using both hands and feet.

clam-my *adj.* Being damp, cold, and sticky.

clam-or *n.* A loud noise or outcry.

clamp *n.* A device for holding things.

clan *n.* A group of people who are related.

clan-des-tine *adj.* Done in secrecy.

clang *v.* To make a loud, ringing sound.

clap *v.* To applaud.

clap-board *n.* A board covering for a house.

clap-per *n.* Part of a bell.

clar-i-fy *v.* To become or make clearer.

clar-i-net *n.* A woodwind instrument.

clash *v.* To collide; conflict.

clasp *n.* A hook to hold objects together.

class *n.* A group with common interest.

clas-sic *adj.* Belonging in a certain category.

clas-si-fy *v.* To arrange into the same category.

clause *n.* A group of words part of a complex sentence.

claus-tro-pho-bia *n.* A fear of enclosed places.

clav-i-chord *n.* A keyboard instrument.

clav-i-cle *n.* A bone connecting the breastbone and shoulder blade.

claw *n.* A sharp, curved nail on the foot of an animal.

clay *n.* Pliable earth that hardens when fired.

clean *adj.* Being free from impurities.

cleanse *v.* To make pure or clean. **-er** *n.*

clear *adj.* Not cloudy; able to see easily.

clear-ance *n.* A distance between two objects.

cleav-er *n.* A knife used by butchers.

cler-gy *n.* Women and men religious leaders.

cler-gy-man *n.* A member of the clergy.

cler-i-cal *adj.* Trained for office duties.

clerk *n.* A clerical worker in an office.

cli-ent *n.* A patron; a customer.

cliff *n.* A steep edge or face of a rock.

cli-mate *n.* Weather conditions. **-ic** *adj.*

cli-max *n.* A point of greatest intensity.

climb *v.* To move to a higher location.

clinch *v.* To settle defini-tively.

cling *v.* To hold fast to; to grasp or stick.

clin-ic *n.* A medical establishment.

clock *n.* An instrument that measures time.

clog *v.* To choke up.

clone *n.* An identical reproduction.

close *adj.* Near, as in time; nearly even.

clos-et *n.* A compartment or room for storage.

clot *n.* A thick or solid mass, as of blood.

cloth *n.* A fabric, used to cover a table.

clothe *v.* To provide clothes.

cloud *n.* Something that obscures.

clout *n.* A heavy blow with the hand; influence.

clove *n.* A spice.

clo-ver *n.* A herb with tri-foliolate leaves.

clo-ver-leaf *n.* A junction of highway.

clown *n.* A professional comedian. **-ish** *adj.*

cloy *v.* To make sick with too much sweet-ness.

club *n.* A heavy wooden stick.

clump *n.* A thick cluster.

clum-sy *adj.* To be lacking coordination.

clus-ter *n.* A group of something.

clutch v. To seize and hold tightly.

clut-ter n. A confused mass of disorder.

coach n. A director of athletics, drama, etc.

co-ad-ju-tor n. Assistant.

coal n. A mineral widely used for fuel; ember.

co-a-lesce v. To come together.

co-ali-tion n. A temporary alliance.

coarse adj. Lacking refinement. -ness v.

coast n. A land bordering the sea.

coat n. An outer garment.

coax v. To persuade by gentleness. -ingly adv.

cob n. A male swan; a corncob.

co-balt n. A metallic element resembling iron and nickel.

cob-ble v. To make or repair shoes.

co-bra n. A venomous snake.

cob-web n. A fine thread spun into a web.

co-caine n. A narcotic.

coch-le-a n. A spiral tube of the inner ear.

cock-pit n. A compartment where the pilot and the crew sit.

cock-roach n. A fast running nocturnal insect.

co-co n. The fruit of the coconut palm.

co-coa n. A powder from kernels of the cacao.

co-coon n. A silky, protective case spun by insect larvae.

cod n. A large fish of the North Atlantic.

cod-dle v. To cook just below boiling point.

code n. A set of rules; set of secret words.

co-ed-u-ca-tion n. An educational system for both men and women.

co-erce v. To dominate with force.

co-ex-ist v. To exist together.

cof-fee n. A beverage prepared from ground beans.

cof-fin n. A box for burying a corpse.

cog n. A series of a teeth on the rim of a wheel.

co-gent adj. Forceful.

cog-i-tate v. To think carefully about.

co-gnac n. A fine brandy made in France.

co-hab-it v. To live as husband and wife.

co-here v. To stick or hold together.

co-hort n. A group of people united in one effort.

coif n. A hat worn under a nun's veil.

coil n. A series of connecting rings.

coin *n.* A piece of metal used as money.

co-in-cide *v.* To happen at the same time.

co-in-ci-dence *n.* Two events happening at the same time.

coke *n.* An carbonaceous fuel; cocaine.

cold *adj.* Having a low temperature. **-ness** *n.*

col-i-se-um *n.* A large amphitheater.

col-lab-o-rate *v.* To work with another person.

col-lapse *v.* To fall; to give way.

col-lar *n.* A part of a garment around the neck.

col-late *v.* To assemble in correct sequence.

col-lat-er-al *adj.* Security for a loan.

col-league *n.* One who works in the same profession.

col-lect *v.* To gather or assemble.

col-lide *v.* To come together with impact.

col-lusion *n.* A secret agreement.

co-lon *n.* A punctuation mark (:); section of the large intestine.

colo-nel *n.* An officer in the armed forces.

col-o-ny *n.* A group of emigrants living in a new land.

col-or *n.* A hue or tint.

-ful *adj.*

col-or-a-tion *n.* An arrangement of different colors or shades.

col-or--blind *adj.* Not able to distinguish colors.

col-or-fast *adj.* Color that will not fade.

col-os-sal *adj.* Large or gigantic in size.

colt *n.* A very young male horse. **-ish** *adj.*

col-umn *n.* A decorative, supporting pillar.

col-um-nist *n.* A person who writes a newspaper column.

co-ma *n.* A deep unconscious sleep.

comb *n.* An instrument for arranging the hair.

com-bat *v.* To oppose; to struggle.

com-bi-na-tion *n.* A series of numbers or letters to open locks.

com-bine *v.* To unite; to merge.

com-bus-ti-ble *adj.* Capability of burning.

come *v.* To arrive; to approach.

com-e-dy *n.* A humorous, entertaining performance.

com-et *n.* A celestial body orbiting the sun.

com-fort *v.* To console in time of grief.or fear.

com-fort-er *n.* A heavy quilt; one who comforts.

com-ic *adj.* Characteristic of comedy.

com-i-cal *adj.* Funny.

com-ma *n.* A punctuation mark (,) indicating a break or series.

com-mand *v.* To give orders; to dominate.

com-mem-o-rate *v.* To honor the memory of. **-ive** *adj.*

com-mence *v.* To begin; start.

com-mence-ment *n.* A graduation ceremony.

com-mend *v.* To give praise. **-able** *adj.*

com-men-su-rate *adj.* Equal in duration.

com-ment *n.* A statement of observation.

com-merce *n.* Exchanging of products.

com-mer-cial *adj.* Relating to a product.

com-mis-er-ate *v.* To feel sympathy for someone.

com-mis-sar-y *n.* A store on a military base.

com-mis-sion *n.* The moneys paid sales.

com-mit-tee *n.* The people appointed perform a task or function.

com-mode *n.* A movable washstand.

com-mo-dore *n.* A naval officer.

com-mon *adj.* To be general, ordinary.

com-mu-ni-ca-ble *adj.* Capable of being trans-

mitted, as with a disease. **-ly** *adv.*

com-mu-ni-cate *v.* To make known.

com-mu-ni-ca-tion *n.* An act of transmitting ideas.

com-mun-ion *n.* A mutual sharing of feelings and thoughts.

com-mu-nism *n.* A system of government.

com-mu-ni-ty *n.* A group of people living in the same area.

com-mute *v.* To travel to one's job each day.

com-pact *adj.* To be packed together.

com-pan-ion *n.* An associate. **-ship** *n.*

com-pan-ion-a-ble *adj.* Being friendly. **-ly** *adv.*

com-pa-ny *n.* A gathering of persons for a social purpose.

com-pa-ra-ble *adj.* Being capable of comparison.

com-pare *v.* To note the likenesses of.

com-part-ment *n.* An enclosed area.

com-pass *n.* An instrument to determine geographic direction.

com-pas-sion *n.* Sympathy for someone.

com-pat-i-ble *adj.* Live together harmoniously.

com-pa-tri-ot *n.* A person of the same country.

com-pel *v.* To urge or

force action.

com-pen-dium *n*. A short summary.

com-pen-sate *v*. To make up for; to pay.

com-pete *v*. To engage in a contest.

com-pe-tent *adj*. Having sufficient ability.

com-pe-ti-tion *n*. A trial of skill or ability. **-tive** *adj*.

com-pet-i-tor *n*. One who competes against another.

com-pile *v*. To put together information.

com-plain-ant *n*. A person filing a formal charge.

com-plaint *n*. An expression of dissatisfaction, or resentment.

com-plai-sance *n*. A willingness to please.

com-ple-ment *n*. Something that adds to.

com-plete *adj*. Having all the necessary parts; whole.

com-plex *adj*. To be consisting of intricate parts.

com-pli-ment *n*. An expression of praise.

com-pli-men-ta-ry *adj*. Giving a compliment.

com-ply *v*. To consent.

com-po-nent *n*. A constituent part.

com-port *v*. To conduct oneself in a certain way.

com-pose *v*. To make up from elements or parts. **-er** *n*.

com-pos-ite *adj*. Made from separate elements.

com-po-si-tion *n*. An artistic literary work.

com-post *n*. A fertilizing mixture of vegetable matter.

com-po-sure *n*. Tranquillity.

com-pote *n*. A fruit preserved or stewed in syrup.

com-pound *n*. Combination of two or more parts. **-able** *adj*.

com-pre-hend *v*. To perceive. **-sion** *n*.

com-pre-hen-sive *adj*. Being large in scope.

com-pres-sor *n*. A machine used for compressing air.

com-prise *v*. To be made up of.

com-pro-mise *n*. Settling of differences.

comp-trol-ler *n*. A person who examines accounts.

com-pute *v*. To determine by the use of math.

com-puter *n*. An electronic machine which performs logical calculations.

computerize *v*. To process or store information on a computer.

com-rade *n*. An associate who shares one's interest or occupation.

con *v. Slang* To swindle or trick.

con-cat-e-nate *v.* To join, or link together.

con-cave *adj.* Hollowed and curved inward. **-ly** *adv.*

con-ceal *v.* To keep from sight; to hide. **-ment** *n.*

con-cede *v.* To yield to a privilege; to acknowledge as true. **-ed** *adj.*

con-ceive *v.* To become pregnant; to create a mental image.

con-cen-trate *v.* To give intense thought to.

con-cen-tra-tion *n.* A state of being concentrated.

con-cept *n.* A generalized idea. **-ual** *adj.*

con-cep-tion *n.* A union of sperm and egg.

con-cern *n.* A sincere interest. **-ed** *adj.*

con-cert *n.* A musical performance.

con-cer-to *n.* One or more solo instruments in a composition.

con-ces-sion *n.* An act of conceding.

con-ces-sion-aire *n.* An operator or holder of a concession.

conch *n.* A tropical marine mollusk.

con-cil-i-ate *v.* To win over or to gain a friendship.**-tion** *n.*

con-cise *adj.* Short and to the point.

con-clave *n.* A private or secret meeting to elect a new pope.

con-clude *v.* To bring to an end. **-sion** *n.*

con-com-i-tant *adj.* Accompanying. **-tantly** *adv.*

con-cur *v.* to agree or express approval.

con-cur-rent *adj.* Acting together.

con-cus-sion *n.* A sudden and violent jolt.

con-demn *v.* To find to be wrong. **-able** *adj.*

con-di-tion *n.* A state of existence of a thing.

con-di-tion-al *adj.* Tentative. **-ly** *adv.*

con-di-tioned *adj.* Prepared for a certain process or action.

con-di-tion-er *n.* An application that improves a substance.

con-do-min-i-um *n.* A building in which all units are owned separately.

con-done *n.* To forgive.

con-duct *v.* To lead and direct a band; lead the way.

con-duc-tor *n.* A person who conducts a musical ensemble.

con-duit *n.* A pipe to pass electric wires

through.

cone *n.* A solid body tapered evenly to a point.

con-fab-u-late *v.* To chat informally.

con-fed-er-a-cy *n.* The union of southern states.

con-fer *v.* To consult with another. **-ment** *n.*

con-fer-ence *n.* A meeting for discussion.

con-fess *v.* To admit to.

con-fet-ti *pl., n.* Small pieces of paper thrown during a happy occasion.

con-fide *v.* To entrust a secret to another. **-ing** *adj.*

con-fi-dence *n.* A feeling of self-assurance.

con-fi-den-tial *adj.* Hold as a secret. **-ity** *n.*

con-fig-u-ra-tion *n.* An arrangement of parts or things.

con-fine *v.* To keep within a certain boundary or limit.

con-firm *v.* To establish or support the truth of something. **-able** *adj.*

con-flict *n.* A battle.

con-form *v.* Be similar in form or character.

con-for-ma-tion *n.* The manner in which something is shaped.

con-found *v.* To amaze, to confuse.

con-front *v.* To stand face to face with defiance.

con-fuse *v.* To mislead or bewilder.

con-fu-sion *n.* A state of being confused; disorder.

con-geal *v.* To jell; to solidify.

con-gen-ial *adj.* Having agreeable characteristics.

con-gen-i-tal *adj.* Existing from the time of birth, but not from heredity.

con-gest *v.* Enlarge with an excessive accumulation of blood; to clog, as with traffic. **-tion** *n.*

con-glom-er-ate *n.* A business consisting of many different companies.

con-grat-u-late *v.* To acknowledge an achievement with praise. **-tor** *n.*

con-grat-u-la-tions *pl., n.* An expression of or the act of congratulating.

con-gre-gate *v.* To assemble together in a crowd.

con-gre-ga-tion *n.* A group of people meeting for worship.

Con-gress *n.* A United States legislative body.

con-gru-ent *adj.* Agreeing to conform.

con-ju-gate *adj.* Change the form of a verb; to join in pairs. **-ly** *adv.*

con-junct *adj.* Combined.

con-junc-tion *n.* The act of joining; the state of

being joined.

con-junc-ti-va *n.* The membrane lining of the eyelids.

con-junc-tive *adj.* Connective.

con-jure *v.* To bring into the mind; to appeal or call on solemnly.

con-nect *v.* To join.

con-nec-tion *n.* An association of one person or thing to another.

con-nec-tive *adj.* Capable of connecting; tending to connect.

con-nive *v.* To ignore a known wrong, therefore implying sanction.

con-no-ta-tion *n.* The associative meaning of a word in addition to the literal meaning.

con-note *v.* To imply along with the literal meaning.

con-nu-bi-al *adj.* Having to do with marriage or the state of marriage.

con-quer *v.* To subdue; to win.

con-science *n.* The ability to recognize right and wrong.

con-sci-en-tious *adj.* Honest.

con-scious *adj.* Aware of one's own existence and environment.

con-script *n.* One who is drafted for a service or a job.

con-se-crate *v.* Declare something to be holy.

con-sec-u-tive *adj.* Following in uninterrupted succession. **-ly** *adv.*

con-sen-sus *n.* A collective opinion.

con-sent *v.* To agree; give permission.

con-se-quent *adj.* Following as a natural result or effect. **-ly** *adv.*

con-serv-a-tive *adj.* Opposed to change.

con-ser-va-to-ry *n.* A school of dramatic art or music.

con-serve *v.* Save something from decay, loss, or depletion. **-able** *adj.*

con-sider *v.* Seriously think about; to examine mentally.

con-sid-er-a-ble *adj.* Large in amount or extent; important.

con-sign *v.* To commit to the care of another; to deliver merchandise.

con-sist *v.* Be made up of.

con-sis-ten-cy *n.* A degree of texture, viscosity, or density.

con-sole *v.* To give comfort to someone.

con-sol-i-date *v.* Combine in one or to form a union of; to form a compact mass. **-ation** *n.*

con-so-nant *n.* A sound in speech other than a

vowel. **-ly** adv.

con-sort n. Spouse; companion or partner; agreement.

con-spic-u-ous adj. Noticeable. **-ly** adv.

con-spir-a-cy n. A plan or act of two or more persons to do an evil act.

con-spire v. To plan a wrongful act in secret.

con-sta-ble n. A peace officer.

con-stant adj. Unchanging; steady in action, purpose, and affection.

con-ster-na-tion n. Sudden confusion or amazement.

con-sti-pa-tion n. A condition of the bowels characterized by inability to empty the bowels.

con-stit-u-ent adj. Having the power to elect a representative.

con-sti-tu-tion n. The fundamental laws that govern a nation; structure or composition.

con-strain v. Restrain by physical or moral means. **-ed** adj.

con-straint n. The threat or use of force; confinement.

con-struct v. To create, make, or build.

con-strue v. To interpret; to translate.

con-sul n. An official that resides in a foreign country. **-ship** n.

con-sult v. To seek advice or information from; to compare views. **-ant, -ation** n.

con-sume v. To ingest; to eat or drink; to absorb. **-able** adj. & n.

con-sum-er n. A person who buys services or goods.

con-sum-mate v. To make a marriage complete by the initial act of sexual intercourse.

con-sump-tion n. Fulfillment; the act of consuming.

con-sump-tive adj. Tending to destroy or waste away.

con-tact n. A place, or junction where two or more surfaces or objects touch.

con-ta-gion n. The transmission of a disease by contact.

con-tain v. To include or enclose.

con-tain-er n. Something that holds or carries.

con-tam-i-nate v. To pollute or make inferior.

con-temn v. To scorn or despise.

con-tem-plate v. To ponder. **-tion** n.

con-tempt n. Viewing something as mean, vile, or worthless.

con-temp-tu-ous *adj.* Feeling or showing contempt. **-ly** *adv.*

con-tend *v.* To dispute; to fight; to debate; to argue.

con-tent *n.* Something contained within; subject matter of a book.

con-ten-tion *n.* Competition. **-tious** *adj.*

con-test *n.* A competition; strife; conflict. **-ant** *n.*

con-text *n.* A sentence, or phrase.

con-ti-nent *n.* One of the seven large masses of the earth.

con-tin-ue *v.* To maintain without interruption; to resume. **-ance** *n.*

con-ti-nu-i-ty *n.* Quality of being continuous.

con-tin-u-ous *adj.* Uninterrupted or unbroken. **-ly** *adv.*

con-tort *v.* Severely twist out of shape.

con-tor-tion-ist *n.* An acrobat who exhibits unnatural body positions.

con-tour *n.* The outline of a body, figure, or mass.

con-tra-band *n.* Illegal or prohibited traffic; smuggled goods.

con-tra-cep-tion *n.* A voluntary prevention of impregnation.

con-tract *n.* A formal agreement between two or more parties.

con-trac-tion *n.* A shortening of a word by using an apostrophe (').

con-trac-tile *adj.* Having the power to contract.

con-tra-dict *v.* Express the opposite side or idea. **-tion** *n.*

con-tral-to *n., pl.* **-tos** Lowest female singing voice.

con-tra-pun-tal *adj.* Relating to counterpoint.

con-trast *v.* Note the differences between two or more people, things, etc.

con-tra-vene *v.* To be contrary; to violate.

con-trib-ute *v.* To give something to someone. **-tion** *n.*

con-trol *v.* To have the authority to regulate, direct, or dominate a situation. **-able** *adj.*

con-trol-ler *n.* The chief accounting officer of a business.

con-tro-ver-sy *n.* A dispute; a debate; a quarrel. **-sial** *adj.*

co-nun-drum *n.* A riddle with an answer that involves a pun.

con-va-lesce *v.* To grow strong after a long illness. **-ent** *adj.*

con-vene *v.* To meet or assemble formally.

con-ven-ience *n.* The

quality of being suitable.

con-vent *n.* The local house of a religious order, especially for nuns.

con-ven-tion *n.* A formal meeting; a regulatory meeting between people, or nations.

con-verge *v.* To come to a common point.

con-ver-sa-tion *n.* An informal talk.

con-verse *v.* To involve oneself in conversation with another.

con-vey *v.* To transport; pass information on to someone else.

con-vict *v.* To prove someone guilty.

con-vince *v.* Persuade to believe without doubt.

con-voy *n.* A group of vehicles traveling together.

con-vulse *v.* To move or shake violently.

con-vul-sion *n.* An involuntary muscular contraction.

cook *v.* To apply heat to food; to prepare food.

co-op-er-a-tive *adj.* Willing to cooperate with others.

co-or-di-nate *v.* To be equal in importance, plan a wardrobe.

co-or-di-na-tion *n.* The state of being coordinated.

coot *n.* A bird.

cop *n., Informal* A police officer.

cope *v.* To struggle or contend with something.

cop-ier *n.* A machine that makes copies.

co-pi-lot *n.* An assistant pilot on an aircraft.

co-pi-ous *n.* Large in quantity; abundant.

cop-u-late *v.* To have sexual intercourse.

copy *v.* To reproduce an original.

copy-right *n.* A statutory right to distribute literary work.

cor-al *n.* A small sea creature.

cor-al snake *n.* A venomous snake.

cord *n.* String or twine; an insulated wire.

cor-dial *adj.* Warmhearted and sincere.

cor-don *n.* A circle of ships to guard an area.

cor-du-roy *n.* A durable ribbed cotton fabric.

core *n.* The innermost part of something.

cork *n.* The elastic bark of the oak tree.

cor-ne-a *n.* Membrane of the eyeball.

cor-ner *n.* An angle where surfaces meet.

cor-ner back *n.* A defensive halfback.

cor-ner-stone *n.* The stone that forms part of a building.

cor-net *n.* A brass musical instrument.

corn-row *v.* To braid the hair in rows.

corn-starch *n.* Starch made from corn used to thicken food.

co-rol-la *n.* The petals of a flower.

cor-ol-lary *n.* Something that naturally follows or accompanies.

cor-o-nar-y *adj.* Relating to the arteries of the heart muscles.

cor-po-ral *n.* A non-commissioned officer.

cor-po-rate *adj.* Combined into one joint body.

cor-po-ra-tion *n.* A group of merchants.

corps *n.* A branch of the armed forces.

corpse *n.* A dead body.

cor-pu-lence *n.* Excessive body fat; obesity.

cor-pus-cle *n.* A living cell in the blood.

cor-ral *n.* An enclosure for containing animals.

cor-rect *v.* To make free from fault or mistakes.

cor-rel-a-tive *adj.* Having a mutual relation.

cor-re-spond *v.* To communicate by written words. **-ence** *n.*

cor-ri-dor *n.* Long hall.

cor-ri-gen-dum *n.* An error accompanied by its correction.

cor-ri-gi-ble *adj.* Able to

correct.

cor-rob-o-rate *v.* To support with evidence.

cor-rode *v.* To eat away. **-ion** *n.*

cor-rupt *adj.* Dishonest.

cor-sage *n.* Small bouquet of flowers.

cor-sair *n.* A pirate; a fast moving vessel.

co-ry-za *n.* An acute inflammation of the respiratory system.

co-sign *v.* To sign a document jointly.

co-sig-na-to-ry *n.* One who cosigns a document.

cos-met-ic *n.* Preparation to beautify the face. **-ally** *adv.*

cost *n.* An amount paid or charged for a purchase.

cos-tume *n.* Clothes worn for playing a part or dressing up in a disguise.

cot *n.* Small, often collapsible bed.

cot-tage *n.* Small house.

cot-ton *n.* A fabric created by the weaving cotton fibers.

cot-ton-mouth *n.* A water moccasin snake.

couch *n.* A piece of furniture.

cou-gar *n.* A mountain lion, panther, and puma.

cough *v.* To suddenly expel air from the lungs.

could *v.* Past tense of

can.

could-n't *contr.* Could not.

coun-cil *n.* A group of people assembled for consultation; advisory body. **-man** *n.*

coun-sel *n.* Advice through consultation.

coun-sel-or *n.* A lawyer.

count *v.* To find the total number of units; to name numbers in order.

coun-te-nance *n.* An expression of the face.

coun-ter-act *v.* To oppose; make ineffective.

coun-ter-bal-ance *n.* A weight that balances another; counterpoise.

coun-ter-claim *n.* A contrary claim made to offset another.

coun-ter-feit *v.* To closely imitate or copy.

coun-ter-mand *v.* To reverse a command by issuing a contrary order.

count-ess *n.* A wife of an earl or count.

coun-try *n.* The land of one's birth.

coun-ty *n.* A territorial division.

cou-ple *n.* A pair; a few.

cou-plet *n.* Rhyming lines of poetry.

cou-pon *n.* A form to obtain a discount.

cour-age *n.* A strength to face danger without fear.

cous-in *n.* A child of one's uncle or aunt.

cov-er *v.* To place something on or over.

cow *n.* A mature female of cattle.

cow-ard *n.* One showing great fear or timidity.

co-zy *adj.* Comfortable and warm; snug.

crab *n.* One of numerous crustaceans.

crack *v.* To break without completely separating *n.* addictive form of cocaine.

cra-dle *n.* A small bed for infants.

craft *n.* A special skill or ability.

cramp *n.* A painful contraction of a muscle; abdominal pain.

cran-ber-ry *n.* A tree with tart red berries.

crane *n.* A large bird; machine for lifting heavy objects.

cra-ni-um *n.* The skull.

crank *n.* A device to turn a shaft.

crash *v.* To break noisily; collapse.

crate *n.* A container for shipping or storage.

cra-ter *n.* A depression in a volcano.

crave *v.* Desire intensely.

cra-ven *adj.* Lacking courage.

crav-ing *n.* An intense

longing or desire.

crawl v. To move on hands and knees; progress slowly.

craze v. To become insane.

cra-zy adj. Insane. **-iness** n.

creak v. Squeaking or grating noise.

cream n. The fatty part of milk.

crease n. A line made by folding and pressing.

cre-ate v. To bring something into existence.

cre-a-tion n. Something created.

cre-a-tor n. God.

crea-ture n. A living being.

cre-den-za n. A buffet or sideboard.

cred-i-ble adj. Reasonable grounds for belief.

cred-it n. The money available in a bank; acknowledgment; college unit.

creep v. To advance at a slow pace.

cre-mate v. To reduce to ashes by burning.

cre-scen-do adv. To be gradually increasing in loudness.

cres-cent n. A quarter shape of the moon.

cress n. A plant with edible leaves.

crest n. A top line of a mountain or hill; ridge of a wave or roof.

cre-tin-ism n. A condition of physical stunting and mental deficiency.

cre-tonne n. A cotton or linen cloth.

cre-vasse n. A deep crack in a glacier.

crew n. A group of people that work together.

crick-et n. A leaping insect; a game.

crime n. An act forbidden by law.

crimp v. To pinch in or together.

cringe v. To shrink or recoil in fear.

crin-kle v. To wrinkle.

crip-ple n. One who is partially disabled.

cri-sis n. An uncertain time; turning point of a disease.

crisp adj. Brittle; brisk or cold.

crit-ic n. One who expresses an opinion.

crit-i-cal adj. Tending to criticize harshly. **-ly** adv.

crit-i-cize v. To find fault with.

croc-o-dile n. Large, tropical reptiles.

cro-ny n. Close friend.

crook n. A bend or curve; dishonest person.

croon v. To sing in a gentle, low voice.

crop n. Plants harvested for use or for sale.

cross *n.* An upright post with a crossbar.

cross-breed *v.* Breeding different species.

crotch *n.* An angle formed by the junction of two parts.

crouch *v.* To bend at the knees.

crou-ton *n.* A piece of toasted bread.

crowd *n.* Large group of people together.

crown *n.* A head covering made of precious metal and jewels.

cru-cial *adj.* Extremely important.

cru-ci-fy *v.* To put to death on a cross.

crude *adj.* Lacking refinement.

cruel *adj.* Inflicting suffering. -ty *n.*

cruise *v.* To drive or sail about for pleasure.

crumb *n.* A fragment of bread.

crum-ble *v.* To break into small pieces.

crunch *v.* To chew with a crackling noise.

crush *v.* To squeeze or force to damage.

crust *n.* A hardened exterior of bread; shell of a pie.

crus-ta-cean *n.* Crabs, lobsters, etc.

cry *v.* To shed tears.

crypt *n.* Underground chamber or vault.

crys-tal *n.* Glassware.

crys-tal-lize *v.* To form crystals; coat with crystals.

cub *n.* The young of the lion, wolf, or bear.

cube *n.* A solid with six equal squares.

cubic *adj.* Having three dimensions.

cud-dle *v.* To caress fondly and hold close.

cuff *n.* A lower part of a sleeve or pants.

cui-sine *n.* A style of preparing food.

cul-mi-nate *v.* To reach the highest point.

cul-ti-vate *v.* To improve land by fertilizing and plowing.

cul-ture *n.* A form of civilization, beliefs, arts, and customs.

cum-ber-some *adj.* Being unwieldy.

cun-ning *adj.* Crafty.

cup *n.* A container with handle for drinking.

curb *n.* Control; edge of a street.

curd *n.* Portion of milk for making cheese.

cure *n.* Recovery from a sickness.

cu-ri-ous *adj.* Inquisitive.

curl *v.* Twist into curves.

cur-rant *n.* A small seedless raisin.

cur-ren-cy *n.* The money in circulation.

cur-rent *adj.* Occur in

the present time.

cur-ric-u-lum *n.* Courses offered in a school.

curse *n.* A wish for harm to come to someone or something.

cursor *n.* A computer screen indicator.

cur-sive *n.* Flowing writing.

curt *adj.* Abrupt; rude.

cur-tail *v.* To shorten.

cur-tain *n.* A material that covers a window.

cush-ion *n.* A pillow with a soft filling.

cus-pid *n.* Pointed tooth.

cus-to-dy *n.* The act of guarding; the care and protection of a minor.

cus-tom *n.* An accepted practice of a community or people; the usual manner of doing something. **-ary** *adj.*

cus-tomer *n.* A person with whom a merchant or business person must deal.

cut *v.* To penetrate with a sharp edge, as with a knife.

cute *adj.* An attractive in a delightful way.

cut-lery *n.* Cutting instruments used to prepare food for cooking.

cut-ter *n., Naut.* A fast-sailing vessel with a single mast.

cy-a-nide *n., Chem.* A poison.

cy-cle *n.* A time in which an event occurs repeatedly; a bicycle or motorcycle.

cy-clist *n.* A person who rides a cycle.

cy-clone *n.* A storm with wind rotating about a low pressure center.

cyl-in-der *n.* A long, round body that is either hollow or solid.

cyst *n.* Abnormal sac or vesicle which may collect and retain fluid.

cys-tic fi-bro-sis *n.* A disease of the lungs and pancreas.

czar *n.* Former emperors of Russia.

D

D, d The fourth letter of the English alphabet.

dab *v.* To touch with light, short strokes.

dab *n.*

dab-ble *v.* To play in a liquid with the hands.

dachs-hund *n.* A small dog with a long body.

dad *n., Informal* Father.

dad-dy--long-legs *n.* An insect with very long legs.

daf-fo-dil *n.* A bulbous plant with yellow flowers.

dag-ger *n.* A pointed, short-edged weapon.

dahl-ia *n.* A perennial plant having tuberous roots.

dai-ly *adj.* Occurring or happening every day.

dain-ty *adj.* Having or showing refined taste. **-iness** *n.*

dai-qui-ri *n.* A cocktail made with rum and lime juice.

dair-y *n.* A business that processes milk for resale.

dai-sy *n.* A plant with yellow and white flowers.

dal-ly *v.* To waste time; to dawdle; to flirt.

dam *n.* A barrier to control water level.

dam-age *n.* An injury to person or property. **-able** *adj.*

dame *n.* A mature woman.

damn *v.* To swear or curse; to pronounce as bad, or worthless. **-ation** *n.*

damp *adj.* State between dry and wet. **-ish** *adj.*

dam-sel *n.* A maiden; a young unmarried woman.

dam-son *n.* A tree with an oval purple plum.

dance *v.* To move rhythmically to music.

dan-de-lion *n.* A weed of North America.

dan-druff *n.* A scaly material which forms on the scalp.

dan-dy *n.* An elegantly dressed man. **-ish** *adj.*

dan-ger *n.* Exposure to injury, evil, or loss.

dan-ger-ous *adj.* Unsafe. **-ly** *adv.,* **-ness** *n.*

dan-gle *v.* Hang loosely and swing to and fro.

dank *adj.* Damp; wet and cold. **-ness** *n.*

dan-seuse *n.* A female ballet dancer.

dap-per *adj.* Being stylishly dressed.

dap-ple *v.* To make variegated in color.

dare *v.* Have courage to take a risk; to challenge a person's courage.

dare-devil *n.* A reckless or bold person.

dark *adj.* Having little or no light.

dark-en *v.* To make dark or become dark. **-ish** *adj.*

dar-ling *n.* Someone who is very dear; a favorite person. **-ly** *adv.* **-ness** *n.*

darn *v.* To mend a hole.

dart *n.* A pointed missile.

dash *v.* To move quickly; to finish in haste. **-er** *n.*

da-ta *pl., n.* Facts or figures from which conclusions may be drawn.

data bank *n.* The location in a computer where information is stored.

date *n.* A particular point in time; the exact time at which something happens.

date-line *n.* An imaginary line.

da-tum *n.* A single piece of information.

daub *v.* Coat with grease, or an adhesive substance. **-er** *n.*

daugh-ter *n.* Female offspring.

daughter--in--law *n.* One's son's wife.

daunt *v.* To intimidate or discourage.

dav-it *n.* A small crane on the side of a ship.

daw-dle *v.* To waste time. **-r** *n.*

dawn *n.* The beginning of a new day.

day *n.* The period of time between dawn and nightfall.

day-care *n.* Supervised care for children of working parents.

daze *v.* To stun with a heavy blow or shock. **-dly** *adv.*

D--Day *n., Milit.* June 6, 1944.

dea-con *n.* A clergyman who ranks immediately below a priest.

dead *adj.* Without life; dormant.

dead-line *n.* A time when something must be finished.

dead-ly *adj.* Very dangerous; likely to cause death.

deaf *adj.* Unable to hear; refusing or unwilling to listen.

deal *v.* To pass out playing cards.

deal-er-ship *n.* A franchise to sell a certain item in a specified area.

deal-ing *n., Slang* Involved in the buying and selling of illegal drugs.

dean *n.* The head administrator of a college, or university. **-ship** *n.*

dear *adj.* Greatly cherished. **-ly** *adv.*

death *n.* The permanent cessation of all vital functions. **-ly** *adj.*

death-trap *n.* An unsafe structure.

death-watch *n.* A vigil kept for a person who is dying.

de-ba-cle *n.* A sudden downfall.

de-base *v.* To lower in character or value. **-ment** *n.*

de-bate *v.* To discuss or argue opposing points. **-able** *adj.*

de-bauch *v.* To corrupt. **-ment** *n.*

de-ben-ture *n.* A voucher given as an acknowledgment of debt.

de-bil-i-tate *v.* To make feeble or weak.

deb-it *n.* An item recorded in an account.

de-brief *v.* To question or interrogate to obtain information.

de-bris *n.* Discarded or

scattered trash.

debt *n.* Money or goods owed to someone.

debt-or *n.* A person owing a debt to another.

de-bug *v.* To find and remove a concealed listening device.

de-bunk *v.* To expose false pretensions.

de-but *n.* Someone's first public appearance; a beginning.

deb-u-tante *n.* A young woman making her debut in society.

dec-ade *n.* A period of ten years; a set of ten.

de-ca-dence *n.* A process of deterioration or decay.

de-caf-fein-at-ed *adj.* Having no caffeine.

dec-a-gon *n., Geom.* A polygon with ten sides.

dec-a-gram *n.* A metric weight equal to 10 grams.

de-cal *n.* A design or picture that is transferred.

de-cal-co-ma-ni-a *n.* A process of transferring pictures or designs.

dec-a-li-ter *n.* A metric measure equal to 10 liters.

dec-a-logue *n.* The Ten Commandments.

dec-a-me-ter *n.* A metric measure equal to 10 meters.

de-camp *v.* To break camp; to leave suddenly.

de-cant-er *n.* A decorative bottle for serving wine.

de-cap-i-tate *v.* To cut off the head; to behead.

de-cath-lon *n.* An athletic events of track and field.

de-cay *v.* To rot.

de-cease *v.* To die.

de-ceit *n.* Falseness; deception. **-ful** *adj.*

de-ceive *v.* To mislead by falsehood; to lead into error.

de-cel-er-ate *v.* To decrease in velocity.

de-cen-ni-al *adj.* Occurring once every 10 years; continuing for ten years.

de-cent *adj.* Satisfactory; generous; adequate.

de-cen-tral-ize *v.* To divide the administrative functions.

de-cep-tion *n.* The act of deceiving.

de-cep-tive *adj.* Having the power to deceive.

de-ci-bel *n.* The measurement of sound.

de-cide *v.* To make up one's mind; to settle.

de-cid-u-ous *adj.* Shedding or falling off at maturity.

dec-i-gram *n.* The tenth part of a gram in metrics.

dec-i-li-ter *n.* The tenth part of a liter in metrics.

dec-i-mal *n.* A proper

fraction based on the number 10.

decimal point n. A period to the left of a decimal fraction.

dec-i-mate v. To destroy or kill a large proportion of something.

dec-i-meter n. The tenth part of a meter in metrics.

de-ci-pher v. To decode; to translate from code to text.

de-ci-sion n. A judgment or conclusion; an act of deciding.

deck n. A set of playing cards; a platform.

deck hand n. A member of a ship's crew.

de-claim v. To speak loudly and rhetorically.

de-clare v. To state formally or officially.

de-clas-si-fy v. To make public.

de-clen-sion n. A downward slope; a decline.

de-cline v. To reject or refuse something.

de-cliv-i-ty n. A steep downward slope or surface.

de-coct v. To extract by boiling; to condense.

de-code v. To convert into plain language.

de-com-pose v. To decay.

de-com-press v. To relieve of pressure.

de-con-ges-tant n. An agent that relieves congestion.

de-con-tam-i-nate v. To make free of contamination.

de-con-trol v. To remove all controls.

de-cor n. The style of decorating.

dec-o-rate v. To adorn with fashionable or beautiful things.

dec-o-ra-tion n. The process, or act of decorating.

dec-o-ra-tive adj. Ornamental; suitable for decoration. **-ly** adv.

de-co-rum n. Proper behavior.

de-coy n. An artificial animal to lure game.

de-crease v. To grow less or smaller.

de-cree n. A formal order.

de-crep-it adj. Worn out by old age.

de-cry v. To denounce.

ded-i-cate v. To commit oneself to a certain cause.

de-duce v. To derive a conclusion by reasoning.

de-duct v. To subtract or take away from.

deed n. A notable achievement or feat.

deem v. To judge or consider.

deep *adj.* Extending far below a surface. **-ness** *n.*

deep-en *v.* To become or make deep or deeper.

deep-freeze *v.* To quick-freeze food.

deep--root-ed *adj.* Firmly implanted.

deep-six *v., Slang* To throw overboard; toss out.

deer *n., pl.* **deer** A hoofed ruminant mammal.

deer fly *n.* Bloodsucking flies.

deer-skin *n.* A deer's hide or leather made from it.

de-es-ca-late *v.* To decrease gradually.

de-face *v.* To spoil or mar the surface of something.

de fac-to *adj.* Actually exercising authority.

de-fal-cate *v.* To misuse funds; to embezzle.

de-fame *v.* To slander.

de-fault *v.* To neglect to fulfill an obligation.

de-feat *v.* To win a victory.

de-feat-ism *n.* Accepting defeat as inevitable.

def-e-cate *v.* To discharge feces from the bowels.

de-fect *n.* The lack of perfection; a fault.

de-fec-tive *adj.* Being imperfect; less than normal intelligence.

de-fend *v.* To protect.

de-fend-ant *n.* A person charged in a lawsuit.

de-fense *n.* The action of defending.

de-fer *v.* To delay or postpone. **-ment** *n.*

de-fi-ance *n.* A strong opposition.

de-fi-cient *adj.* Lacking a necessary element.

def-i-cit *n.* A deficiency in amount.

de-flate *v.* To remove air; to collapse. **-flation** *n.*

de-flect *v.* To turn aside; to swerve from a course.

de-flower *v.* To rob one's virginity; to violate.

de-fog *v.* To remove fog from.

de-for-est *v.* To clear of trees.

de-form *v.* To distort the form of; to spoil the natural form of.

de-fraud *v.* To cheat; to swindle.

de-fray *v.* To make payment on something. **-able** *adj.*

de-frost *v.* To cause to thaw out; to remove the ice or frost from.

deft *adj.* Being skillful and neat in one's actions. **-ness** *n.*

de-funct *adj.* Deceased.

de-fuse *v.* To remove the detonator or fuse from; to make less dangerous.

de-fy v. To confront or resist boldly; to dare.

de-gauss v. To neutralize a magnetic field.

de-gen-er-ate v. To decline in quality or value; to become worse.

de-grade v. To reduce in rank; to demote.

de-gree n. The succession of stages or steps; academic title; amount.

de-horn v. To remove the horns from an animal.

de-hu-man-ize v. To deprive of human qualities.

de-hu-mid-i-fy v. To remove moisture from.

de-hy-drate v. To lose moisture or water.

de-ice v. To keep free of ice. **-r** n.

de-i-fy v. To glorify or idealize; raise in high regard.

deign v. To grant.

de-ism n. The belief in the existence of God; but not that he has control.

de-ject v. To lower the spirits; to dishearten.

de-ject-ed adj. Low in spirit. **-ion** n.

de-lay v. To put off until a later time; to defer.

de-le n., Print A mark in typesetting to delete.

de-lec-ta-ble adj. Giving great pleasure.

de-lec-ta-tion n. Enjoy-

ment or pleasure.

del-e-gate n. A representative for another; a deputy or agent.

del-e-ga-tion n. The state of being delegated.

de-lete v. To cancel; to take out. **-letion** n.

del-e-te-ri-ous adj. Harmful; causing physical injury.

delft n. Glazed earthenware.

del-i n., Slang Delicatessen.

de-lib-er-ate v. To say or do something intentionally. **-ness** n.

del-i-ca-cy n. Select or choice food.

del-i-cate adj. Being exquisite and fine in quality.

de-li-cious adj. Enjoyable and pleasant to the taste. **-ly** adv.

de-li-cious n. A variety of red, sweet apples.

de-light n. A great joy or pleasure. **-ful** adj.

de-lim-it v. To set or prescribe the limits.

de-lin-e-ate v. To represent by a drawing.

de-lin-quent adj. Neglecting duty; falling behind in a payment.

del-i-quesce v., Chem. Become liquid by absorbing moisture.

de-lir-i-um n. A temporary mental disturbance.

delirium tremens *n.* An acute delirium resulting from use of alcohol.

de-liv-er *v.* To hand over; assist at a birth of an offspring.

del-phin-i-um *n.* A perennial plant.

de-lude *v.* To mislead the mind; to deceive.

del-uge *v.* To flood with water; to overwhelm.

de luxe *adj.* Elegance or luxury.

delve *v.* To search carefully for information.

de-mag-net-ize *v.* To remove the magnetic properties of.

dem-a-gogue *n.* A person who appeals to the emotions.

de-mand *v.* To ask for in a firm tone; claim as due.

de-mar-cate *v.* To set boundaries or limits.

de-mean *v.* To behave or conduct oneself in a particular manner.

de-mean-or *n.* A person's conduct to others.

de-men-tia *n.* An irreversible deterioration of the mind.

de-mer-it *n.* A defect.

dem-i-god *n.* A mythological, semidivine being.

dem-i-john *n.* A narrow-necked bottle.

de-mil-i-ta-rize *v.* To remove the military characteristics from.

de-mise *n.* A death; a transfer of an estate by lease or will.

dem-i-tasse *n.* A small cup of very strong coffee.

dem-o *n.* A demonstration to show a product.

de-mo-bi-lize *v.* To disband; to release from the military service.

de-moc-ra-cy *n., pl. -cies* A form of government by and for the people.

dem-o-crat *n.* One who believes in social and political equality.

de-mog-ra-phy *n.* The study of the characteristics of human population.

de-mol-ish *v.* To tear down; to raze.

dem-o-li-tion *n.* The process of demolishing.

de-mon *n.* An evil spirit; a devil.

de-mon-e-tize *v.* To deprive the currency of its standard value.

dem-on-strate *v.* To show or prove by evidence. **-tion** *n.*

de-mon-stra-tive *adj.* Able to prove beyond any doubt; conclusive.

de-mor-al-ize *v.* To undermine the morales.

de-mote *v.* To reduce in rank, or grade.

-**motion** n.

de-mur v. To take issue; to object.

de-mure adj. Reserved and modest; coy.

de-murrer n. A plea to dismiss a lawsuit.

den n. A small room.

de-na-ture v. To change the nature of.

den-drol-ogy n. The botanical study of trees.

de-ni-al n. The refusal to comply with a request or truth.

den-i-grate v. To slander.

den-im n. A strong cotton used for jeans.

de-nom-i-nate v. To give a name to; designate.

de-nom-i-na-tion n. A name of a group or classification.

de-nom-i-na-tor n. The bottom half of a fraction.

de-nounce v. To condemn openly; accuse formally.

dense adj. Slow to understand; stupid.

den-si-ty n. Quality of being dense.

dent n. A small surface depression.

den-tal adj. Pertaining to the teeth.

dental hygienist n. A dental professional who provides preventive dental care.

den-tine n. The calcified part of the tooth.

den-ture n. A set of artificial teeth.

de-nude v. To remove all covering; to cause to be naked.

de-ny v. to declare untrue.

de-o-dor-ant n. A product to prevent unpleasant odors.

de-ox-i-dize v. To remove oxygen from.

de-part v. To leave; to go away; to deviate.

de-part-ment n. The distinct division of something.

de-part-men-tal-ize v. To divide into organized departments.

department store n. A large retail store.

de-pend v. To rely on.

de-pend-a-ble adj. Trustworthy. -**bility** n.

de-pend-ent adj. Needing the help of another.

de-pict v. To represent in a picture.

de-pil-a-to-ry n. A chemical which removes hair.

de-plane v. To disembark or leave an aircraft.

de-plete v. To exhaust, empty, or use up.

de-plor-a-ble adj. Very bad; grievous; wretched. -**ly** adv.

de-plore v. To show disapproval of something.

de-ploy v. To place or position according to plans. **-ment** n.

de-po-lit-i-cize v. To remove the political status or aspect from.

de-po-nent n. A person testifying under oath.

de-pop-u-late v. To lower the population by massacre or disease.

de-port v. To banish from a country.

de-pose v. To remove from position or office.

de-pos-it v. To put money in a bank.

dep-o-si-tion n. In law, written testimony given under oath.

de-pos-i-to-ry n. A place for safekeeping.

de-pot n. A railroad station.

de-prave v. To render bad or worse.

dep-re-cate v. To express regret or disapproval; to belittle.

de-pre-ci-ate v. To lessen in value or price.

de-pre-ci-a-tion n. A loss in value from usage.

de-press v. To make gloomy; to lower the spirits.

de-pres-sant adj. To act to lower the nervous activities.

de-press-ed adj. Low in spirits.

de-pres-sion n. A severe decline in business; deep dejection.

de-prive v. To take something away from; to keep from using.

depth n. The distance downward; intensity of sound; comprehension.

depth charge n. An underwater bomb.

dep-u-ta-tion n. A person acting for another.

dep-u-tize v. To appoint as a deputy.

dep-u-ty n. A person designated to act for or assist a sheriff.

de-rail v. To cause a train to run off the rails.

de-range v. To disturb the normal order of.

der-by n. A horse race for 3-year-olds; a stiff hat with narrow brim.

de-reg-u-late v. To remove from regulation or control.

der-e-lict adj. Neglectful; remiss.

der-e-lic-tion n. Voluntary neglect.

de-ride v. To ridicule.

der-i-va-tion n. The process of deriving.

de-rive v. To receive or obtain from a source.

der-mal adj. Relating to or of the skin.

der-ma-ti-tis n., Pathol. Inflammation of the skin.

der-ma-tol-o-gy n. The

medical study of the skin and the diseases. **gist** *n.*

der-o-gate *v.* To take away from; to distract.

der-rick *n.* A machine to lift heavy loads.

der-ri-ere *n.* The buttocks.

des-cant *v.* To play or sing a varied melody.

de-scend *v.* To move from a higher to a lower level.

de-scen-dent *n.* Offspring from another.

de-scen-dant *adj.* Proceeding downward.

de-scent *n.* A slope; lowering in level or status.

de-scribe *v.* To explain in written or spoken words. **-ble** *adj.*

de-scrip-tion *n.* A mental image of something.

de-scry *v.* To catch sight of.

des-e-crate *v.* To violate something sacred.

de-seg-re-gate *v.* To eliminate racial segregation in.

de-sen-si-tize *v.* To make less sensitive.

des-ert *v.* To abandon or forsake.

des-ert *n.* A dry, barren region.

de-ser-tion *n.* The act of deserting or leaving.

de-serve *v.* To be worthy of or entitled to.

des-ic-cate *v.* To preserve food by drying; dehydrate.

de-sid-er-a-tum *n.* A desired and necessary thing.

de-sign *v.* To sketch preliminary outlines; create in the mind.

des-ig-nate *v.* To assign a name or title to; specify.

de-sir-a-ble *adj.* Attractive, or valuable. **-ness** *n.*

de-sire *v.* To long for; to wish.

de-sir-ous *adj.* Having a craving or strong desire.

de-sist *v.* To stop doing something.

desk *n.* Furniture used in school and offices for writing.

des-o-late *adj.* Forlorn; forsaken **-ly** *adv.*

de-spair *v.* To lose or give up hope.

des-per-a-do *n.* A dangerous criminal.

des-per-ate *adj.* Without care; intense.

des-per-a-tion *n.* The state of being desperate.

des-pi-ca-ble *adj.* Hateful; contemptable.

de-spise *v.* To regard with contempt.

de-spoil *v.* Strip of possessions by force.

de-spond *v.* Lose hope, courage, or spirit.

des-pot *n.* An absolute

ruler; a tyrant.

des-sert *n.* Sweet food, as pastry, etc.

des-ti-na-tion *n.* A goal; end of journey.

des-ti-ny *n.* Fate; predetermined course of events.

des-ti-tute *adj.* Impoverished; poor. **-tution** *n.*

de-stroy *v.* To demolish; to kill.

de-stroy-er *n.* One that destroys; small warship.

de-struct *n., Aeros.* The deliberate destruction of a defective missile.

de-struc-ti-ble *adj.* Capable of being destroyed.

de-sul-fur-ize *v.* To remove sulfur from.

des-ul-to-ry *adj.* Something occurring by chance.

de-tach *v.* To unfasten, or separate **-ment** *n.*

de-tail *n.* The part considered separately; task.

de-tain *v.* To keep from proceeding.

de-tect *v.* To find out; to expose or uncover.

de-tec-tive *n.* The person that investigates crimes.

de-ten-tion *n.* Hold in custody.

de-ter *v.* To prevent someone from acting by intimidation. **-ment** *n.*

de-ter-gent *n.* A cleansing agent.

de-te-ri-o-rate *v.* To worsen; to depreciate. **-ration** *n.*

de-ter-mine *v.* To settle or decide conclusively.

de-ter-mined *adj.* Having a fixed purpose.

de-ter-rent *n.* Something which deters. **-ly** *adv.*

de-test *v.* To dislike strongly. **-able** *adj.*

de-throne *v.* To remove from the throne.

det-o-nate *v.* To explode suddenly violently. **-tion** *n.*

det-o-na-tor *n.* A fuse used to detonate an explosive.

de-tour *n.* A deviation from a direct route.

de-tox-i-fy *v.* To free oneself from dependence on drugs or alcohol. **-ication** *n.*

de-tract *v.* To take away from; to divert. **-tion** *n.*

de-train *v.* To leave a railroad train. **-ment** *n.*

det-ri-ment *n.* Damage; injury; loss. **-tal** *adj.*

de-tri-tus *n.* A loose fragments from disintegration.

deuce *n.* Two.

deut-sche mark *n.* A standard monetary unit of Germany.

de-val-u-ate v. To reduce or lessen the value of. **-tion** n.

dev-as-tate v. To destroy; to ruin. **-tion** n.

de-vel-op v. To expand the potentialities; to enlarge; process film.

de-vel-op-er n. A person who builds and sells homes; chemical to process film.

de-vel-op-ment n. A group of homes; improvement.

de-vi-ant adj. Stray from the norm. **-ance** n.

de-vi-ate v. To turn away from prescribed behavior or course.

de-vice n. Something built and used for a specific purpose.

dev-il n. A spirit of evil, the ruler of Hell; Satan; wicked person.

dev-il-ish adj. Resemble or have the characteristics of a devil.

dev-il--may--care adj. Reckless.

dev-il-ment n. A reckless mischief.

dev-il-try n. Malicious mischief; cruelty or wickedness.

de-vi-ous adj. Leading away from the direct course. **-ly** adv.

de-vise v. To form in the mind; contrive; give real estate by will.

de-vi-see n. A person to whom a devise is made.

de-vi-sor n. A person who devises property.

de-vi-tal-ize v. To make weak.

de-void adj. Empty; lacking.

de-voir n. An act or expression of courtesy or respect.

de-volve v. To pass duty or authority on to a successor.

de-vote v. To apply oneself completely to some activity.

de-vot-ed adj. Feeling or showing loyalty. **-ly** adv.

dev-o-tee n. An enthusiastic supporter.

de-vo-tion n. A strong attachment or affection. **-edly** adv.

de-vout adj. Extremely and earnestly religions; showing sincerity. **-ly** adv.

dew n. A moisture condensed from the atmosphere in small drops onto cool surfaces.

dew-claw n. A rudimentary toe in some dogs and other mammals.

dew-lap n. The loose skin under the throat and neck of cattle and certain dogs.

dex-ter-i-ty n. A proficiency or skill in

using the hands or body; cleverness.

deex-ter-ous *adj.* Skillful or adroit in the use of the hands.

di-a-gram *n.* A sketch, plan or outline designed to demonstrate the similarity among parts of a whole.

di-al *n.* A graduated circular plate or face where a measurement is indicated by means of a pointer.

di-a-logue *n.* A conversation involving two or more persons.

di-am-e-ter *n.* A straight line which passes through the center of a circle.

di-a-met-ri-cal *adj.* Along or relating to a diameter.

dia-mond *n.* A very hard highly refractive colorless or white crystalline of carbon used as a gem.

di-a-pa-son *n.* A full range of a voice or an instrument.

di-a-per *n.* A baby's pants of absorbent material.

di-aph-a-nous *adj.* Transparent or translucent.

di-a-phragm *n., Anat.* A muscular wall between chest and abdomen; contraceptive device.

di-ar-rhe-a *n.,Pathol.* A disorder of the intestines.

di-a-ry *n.* A daily record.

di-as-tro-phism *n., Geol.* A processes through which the earth's crust are formed.

di-a-ther-my *n., pl. - mies Med.* A generation of heat in the body tissues.

di-as-to-le *n.* A rhythmical expansion of the heart.

di-a-tom *n.* A various tiny planktonic algae.

di-a-tom-ic *adj.* Having two atoms in a molecule.

di-a-ton-ic *adj., Mus.* Relating to a musical scale having eight tones to an octave.

di-a-tribe *n.* Malicious criticism.

dib-ble *n.* A gardener's pointed tool for planting bulbs.

dice *pl., n.* The small cubes used in a game of chance.

di-chot-o-my *n., pl. - mies* A division into two mutually exclusive subclasses.

dick-er *v.* To haggle or work towards a deal or bargain.

dick-ey *n.* A woman's blouse front worn under a jacket.

di-cot-y-le-don *n.* A plant having two seed

leaves.

dic-tate v. To speak aloud for another to record or transcribe. **-tion** n.

dic-ta-ting ma-chine n. A phonographic machine which records speech.

dic-ta-tor n. A person having absolute authority and supreme governmental powers. **-ship** n.

dic-ta-to-ri-al adj. Tending to dictate.

dic-tion n. An arrangement of words in speaking and writing.

dic-tion-ar-y n. A book containing words, definitions and usages.

dic-tum n. An authoritative utterance.

did v. Past tense of do.

di-dac-tic adj. Inclined to teach excessively.

did-dle v. To cheat; to swindle.

did-n't contr. Did not.

die v. To expire; to stop living.

die cast-ing n. A process of giving an alloy or metal a desired shape.

die-hard n. A stubborn person.

diel-drin n. A highly toxic chemical used as an insecticide.

di-e-lec-tric n., Elect. A non-conductor of electricity.

die-sel n. A vehicle driven by a diesel engine.

diesel engine n. An internal-combustion engine run by an air-fuel mixture.

die-sink-er n. A person who engraves metal dies.

di-et n. A regulated selection of food and drink.

di-e-tet-ics pl., n. A study of diet and regulations of a diet.

di-eth-yl-bes-trol n. A synthetic estrogen to treat menstrual disorders.

di-e-ti-tian n. A diet planner.

dif-fer v. To have different opinions.

dif-fer-ence n. A state, or degree of being different or unlike.

dif-fer-ent adj. Not the same.

dif-fer-en-tia n. A specific difference.

dif-fer-en-tial adj. Showing a difference or differences.

dif-fer-en-ti-ate v. To show, or distinguish the difference.

dif-fi-cult adj. Hard to do, or accomplish; hard to please.

dif-fi-cul-ty n., pl. -ties A quality or state of being difficult.

dif-fi-dent adj. Lacking confidence in oneself;

timid.
-ly *adv.*
dif-frac-tion *n., Phys.* A modification of light rays.
dif-fuse *v.* To spread freely in all directions; to scatter.
dig *v.* To break up the earth.
di-gest *v.* To summarize; change ingested food into usable form.
di-gest-ion *n.* A dissolving food in the stomach.
dig-it *n.* A toe or finger.
dig-i-tal *adj.* Expressed in digits, as for computer use.
dig-i-tal-is *n.* A drug prepared from dried leaves of foxglove.
dig-ni-fied *adj.* Stately; poised.
dig-ni-fy *v.* To give distinction to something.
dig-ni-tary *n., pl.* **-ies** A person of high rank.
dig-ni-ty *n., pl.* **-ties** The quality being excellent.
di-graph *n.* A pair of letters that represents a single sound.
di-gress *v.* To wander.
dik-dik *n.* Small African antelope.
dike *n.* An embankment made of earth, control flood waters.
di-lap-i-dat-ed *adj.* State of decay or disrepair.
di-late *v.* To become larger. **-able** *adj.*

dil-a-to-ry *adj.* Delaying; slow; tardy.
di-lem-ma *n.* A perplexing situation.
dil-et-tante *n.* A superficial interest in something.
dil-i-gent *adj.* Industrious.
dill *n.* An aromatic herb.
di-lute *v.* To reduce concentration.
dim *adj.* Dull.
dime *n.* U. S. coin worth ten cents.
di-men-sion *n.* A measurable extent.
di-min-ish *v.* To make smaller.
di-min-u-en-do *adv.* Gradually lessening in volume.
di-min-u-tive *adj.* Being very small.
dim-ple *n.* A depression in the skin.
din *n.* Loud noise.
dine *v.* To eat dinner.
di-nette *n.* A small dining room.
din-ghy *n., pl.* **-ghies** A small rowboat.
din-ky *adj., Informal* Insignificant or small.
din-ner *n.* Last meal of the day.
di-no-saur *n., Paleon.* Extinct reptiles.
dip *v.* To put into a liquid momentarily.
diph-the-ri-a *n., Pathol.* An acute infectious disease.

di-plo-ma *n.* A document from school.

dip-lo-mat *n.* A government representative.

dip-per *n.* A long-handled cup.

dip-so-ma-ni-a *n.* An insatiable craving for alcohol.

dire *adj.* Dreadful or terrible.

di-rect *v.* To give orders.

di-rec-tion *n.* An act of directing; instruction.

di-rect-ly *adv.* Immediately; at once.

di-rec-tor *n.* The person who manages.

di-rec-to-ry *n., pl.* **-ries** A book listing data.

dirge *n.* A slow mournful song.

dir-i-gi-ble *n.* A lighter-than-air plane.

dirn-dl *n.* A dress with a full skirt.

dirt *n.* The soil or earth.

dirt-y *adj.* Not clean. **-iness** *n.*

dis-a-ble *v.* To incapacitate.

dis-ad-van-tage *n.* An unfavorable condition.

dis-a-gree *v.* To vary in opinion. **-able** *adj.*

dis-al-low *v.* To refuse to allow.

dis-ap-pear *v.* To vanish. **-ance** *n.*

dis-ap-point *v.* To fail to satisfy.

dis-ap-pro-ba-tion *n.* A disapproval.

dis-ap-prove *v.* To refuse to approve.

dis-arm *v.* To make harmless.

dis-ar-range *v.* To disturb the order. **-ment** *n.*

dis-ar-ray *n.* A state of confusion or disorder.

dis-as-sem-ble *v.* To take apart.

dis-as-so-ci-ate *v.* To break away or detach from an association.

dis-as-ter *n.* An event that causes distress.

dis-a-vow *v.* To disclaim or deny.

dis-band *v.* To disperse.

dis-bar *v.* To be expelled from the legal profession. **-ment** *n.*

dis-be-lieve *v.* To refuse to believe.

dis-burse *v.* To pay out money.

disc *or* **disk** *n., Informal* A phonograph record that holds information.

dis-card *v.* To throw out.

dis-cern *v.* To understand.

dis-charge *v.* To release.

dis-ci-ple *n.* A follower.

dis-ci-pline *n.* A train; punishment to correct poor behavior.

dis-claim *v.* To deny interest in or association

with.
dis-close v. To make known **-ure** n.
dis-co n., pl. **-cos** A discotheque.
dis-color v. To alter or change the color of.
dis-com-fit v. To defeat in battle.
dis-com-fort n. An uneasiness; pain.
dis-com-mode v. To inconvenience.
dis-com-pose v. To disrupt composure of.
dis-con-cert v. To upset.
dis-con-nect v. To break the connection of.
dis-con-so-late adj. Unhappy.
dis-con-tent n. A dissatisfaction.
dis-con-tin-ue v. To bring to an end.
dis-cord n. Lacking harmony.
dis-co-theque n. A nightclub.
dis-count v. to sell for lower price than usual.
dis-coun-te-nance v. To look upon with disfavor.
dis-cour-age v. To be deprived of enthusiasm or courage.
dis-course n. A conversation; lengthy discussion.
dis-cour-te-ous adj. Lacking courteous man-

ners.
dis-cov-er v. To make known or visible. **-able** adj.
dis-cred-it v. To cast disbelief on.
dis-creet adj. Tactful; careful of appearances; modest.
dis-crep-an-cy n., pl. **-cies** Difference in facts.
dis-crete adj. Separate; made up of distinct parts.
dis-cre-tion n. The act of being discreet.
dis-crim-i-nate v. distinguish between
dis-cur-sive adj. Covering a wide field of subjects in a quick manner.
dis-cuss v. To talk.
dis-dain v. To ignore; to scorn.
dis-ease n. A sickness; an illness. **-ed** adj.
dis-em-bark v. To unload.
dis-em-body v. To free from the body.
dis-en-chant v. To free from false beliefs.
dis-en-gage v. To set free.
dis-en-tan-gle v. To free from involvement.
dis-fig-ure v. To deform appearance.
dis-fran-chise v. To deprive the legal right.
dis-gorge v. To regurgitate; to pour out.
dis-grace n. A loss of

honor.

dis-guise v. To alter appearance.

dis-gust v. Version.

dish n. An eating utensil.

dis-har-mo-ny n. Discord.

dis-heart-en v. To lose spirit.

di-shev-el v. Disarrange.

dis-hon-est adj. Lacking honesty.

dis-hon-or n. Disgrace.

dis-il-lu-sion v. To disenchant.

dis-in-fect v. To free from infection.

dis-in-gen-u-ous adj. To be lacking frankness.

dis-in-her-it v. To deprive of inheritance.

dis-in-te-grate v. To break into small particles.

dis-in-ter-est-ed adj. Unselfish, or not interested.

dis-join v. To become detached.

dis-like v. To regard with disapproval.

dis-lo-cate v. To put out of place.

dis-lodge v. To remove from.

dis-loy-al adj. Untrue to obligations or duty.

dis-mal adj. Depressing.

dis-man-tle v. To take apart.

dis-may v. Disheartened.

dis-mem-ber v. To cut into pieces.

dis-miss v. To discharge.

dis-mount v. To get down from something.

dis-o-bey v. To refuse or fail to obey.

dis-o-blige v. To act contrary to wishes of.

dis-or-der n. A confussion.

dis-or-gan-ize v. To destroy or break up the unity of something.

dis-own v. To refuse to claim as one's own.

dis-patch v. To send off on a particular destination.

dis-pel v. To drive or away.

dis-pense v. To give out.

dis-perse v. To scatter in various directions.

dis-place v. To change the position of.

dis-play v. To put in view of someone.

dis-please v. To cause disapproval or annoyance of.

dis-pose v. To put in place; arrange.

dis-prove v. To prove to be false.

dis-pute v. To debate or argue.

dis-qual-i-fy v. To deprive of the required conditions.

dis-qui-si-tion n. A formal inquiry.

dis·re·gard v. To neglect.

dis·re·pute n. A state of low esteem.

dis·re·spect n. A lack of respect.

dis·robe v. To undress.

dis·rupt v. To throw into disorder.

dis·sat·is·fy v. To fail to satisfy.

dis·sect v. To cut into pieces.

dis·sem·ble v. To conceal; disguise.

dis·sem·i·nate v. To spread; distribute.

dis·sen·sion n. A difference of opinion.

dis·sent v. To differ in opinion or thought.

dis·ser·ta·tion n. A written essay.

dis·serv·ice n. Ill turn.

dis·sim·i·lar adj. Being different.

dis·sim·u·late v. To dissemble or take apart.

dis·si·pate v. To disperse or drive.

dis·so·ci·ate v. To break association.

dis·solve v. To cause to fade away; to melt.

dis·so·nance n., Mus. A lack of agreement.

dis·suade v. To alter the course of action.

dis·tance n. A separation in time or space.

dis·tant adj. Separate by a specified amount of time or space.

dis·taste v. Feeling aversion to.

dis·tem·per n. A contagious viral disease of dogs.

dis·tend v. To expand.

dis·till v. To extract by distillation.

dis·til·late n. The condensed substance separated by distillation.

dis·tinct adj. Being clearly seen.

dis·tinc·tion n. An act of distinguishing.

dis·tinc·tive adj. Serving to give style or distinction to.

dis·tin·guish v. To recognize as being different.

dis·tort v. To twist or bend out of shape. -tion n.

dis·tract v. To draw or divert one's attention.

dis·trait adj. Being absent-minded.

dis·traught adj. Deeply agitated with doubt or anxiety.

dis·trict n. An administrative or political section of a territory.

dis·turb v. To destroy the tranquillity of; to unsettle mentally. -er n.

ditch n. A trench in the earth.

dive v. To plunge into water headfirst; to submerge.

di-verge v. To move or extend in different directions from a common point.

di-verse adj. Unlike in characteristics.

di-ver-si-fy v. To give variety to something; to engage in varied operations.

di-ver-sion n. The act of diverting from a course or activity.

di-vert v. To undress or strip, especially of clothing or dispossess of property.

di-vide v. To separate into parts; to cause to be apart.

di-vi-sion n. A separation; something which divides or marks off.

div-ot n. A square of turf or sod.

diz-zy adj. Having a whirling sensation in the head.

do-cent n. A teacher at a college or university.

doc-ile adj. Easily led, taught, or managed. **-ity** n.

dock n. A landing slip or pier for ships or boats; a loading area for trucks or trains.

dock-et n. A brief written summary of a document.

doc-tor n. A person trained and licensed to practice medicine.

doc-tor-ate n. The degree, status, or title of a doctor.

doc-trine n. Something taught as a body of principles.

doc-u-ment n. An official paper. **-ation** n.

doc-u-men-ta-ry adj. Relating to or based on documents.

dodge v. To avoid by moving suddenly.

doe n. A mature female deer.

does-n't contr. Does not.

dog n. A domesticated carnivorous mammal.

dog-ged adj. Stubbornly determined.

dog-ma n. A rigidly held doctrine.

dog-mat-ic adj. Marked by an authoritative assertion.

dol-drums pl., n. A period of listlessness.

dole n. The distribution of food or money to the needy.

dole-ful adj. Being filled with sadness.

doll n. Child's toy.

dol-lar n. The standard monetary unit of the U.S.

dol-men n. A prehistoric monument.

do-lor-ous *adj.* Being marked by grief; mournful.

dol-phin *n.* An aquatic mammal.

dolt *n.* A stupid person.

do-main *n.* A territory under one government.

dome *n.* A round shaped roof.

do-mes-tic *adj.* Relating to household.

dom-i-cile *n.* A dwelling place.

dom-i-nant *adj.* State of prevailing.

dom-i-nate *v.* To rule or control someone.

dom-i-no *n.* A small rectangular block with dots on the face.

don *v.* To put on.

don-key *n., pl.* **-keys** A domesticated ass.

do-nor *n.* One who donates or contributes.

don't *contr.* Do not.

doo-dle *v.* To scribble or draw aimlessly.

doom *n.* An unhappy destiny.

door *n.* A means of entrance or exit.

dope *n.* A drug or narcotic.

dor-mant *adj.* Asleep; state of rest.

dor-sal *adj., Anat.* Of or relating to back.

do-ry *n., pl.* **-ries** A small flat-bottomed boat.

dose *n.* A measured amount of medicine take at one time.

dos-si-er *n.* The complete data on a person.

dot *n.* Small round mark.

dote *v.* To show excessive affection.

dou-ble *adj.* Twice as much.

dou-ble--cross *v., Slang* To betray someone.

dou-ble--deck-er *n.* A vehicle with two decks for passengers.

doubt *v.* **-er** *n.* To be uncertain of something. **-er** *n.*

dough *n.* A soft pastry mixture of flour and other ingredients.

dough-nut *or* **donut** *n.* A small cake made of rich, light dough.

douse *v.* To plunge into liquid or throw water on.

dove *n.* Any of numerous pigeons. **-ish** *adj.*

dow-dy *adj.* Not neat or tidy; old-fashioned. **-iest** *adj.*

dow-el *n.* A round wooden object that fastens two joined pieces.

down *adv.* Being from higher to lower.

down-er *n., Slang* A depressant drug; a barbiturate.

doz-en *n.* Twelve of a kind of something.

drab *adj.* Unexciting;

yellow-brown. **-ness** *n.*

draft *n.* A current of air; sketch or plan. *Milit.* A mandatory selection for service. **-ee** *n.*

drag *v.* To pull along by force.

drag-on *n.* A mythical, serpent-like monster.

drain *v.* To draw off liquid gradually.

drake *n.* A male duck.

dram *n.* A small drink; a small portion.

dra-ma *n.* A play recounting a serious story.

drape *v.* To cover or adorn with something.

dras-tic *adj.* Being extreme or severe.

draw *v.* To cause to move toward a position to sketch.

draw-back *n.* An undesirable feature.

draw-bridge *n.* A bridge that is raised or lowered.

drawer *n.* One that draws pictures; a sliding receptacle in furniture.

draw-ing *n.* A picture; process of choosing lots.

drawl *v.* To speak slowly.

dray *n.* A heavy cart used for hauling.

dread *v.* To fear greatly.

dread-ful *adj.* Inspiring dread; awful.

dream *n.* A series of thoughts or images

which occur during sleep or the REM state of sleep.

drea-ry *adj.* Being bleak and gloomy; dull. **-iness** *n.*

dredge *v.* To remove sand or mud from under water. **-er** *n.*

dregs *pl., n.* A sediment of a liquid.

drench *v.* To wet thoroughly.

dress *n.* An outer garment for women and girls. *v.* To put clothes on.

drib-ble *v.* To slobber or drool; to bounce a ball repeatedly.

drift *v.* To be carried along by a current to move about aimlessly.

drill *n.* A tool used in boring holes; the act of training soldiers by repeated exercise.

drink *v.* To take liquid into the mouth and swallow.

drip *v.* To fall in drops. *n.* The sound made by falling drops.

drive *v.* To propel, push, or press onward.

driv-el *v.* To slobber.

driz-zle *n.* A fine, quiet, gentle rain.

droll *adj.* Whimsically comical.

drom-e-dar-y *n.* A one-humped camel.

drone *n.* A male bee; unmanned boat or aircraft.

drool *v.* To let saliva dribble from the mouth.

droop *v.* To hang or bend downward. **-iness** *n.*

drop *n.* A tiny, rounded mass of liquid; smallest unit of liquid measure.

drop *v.* To fall in drops; let fall.

drop-sy *n., Med.* A diseased condition with excessive water in the body.

dross *n.* An impurity forming molten metal.

drought *n.* A prolonged period of dryness.

drove *n.* A herd of cattle.

drown *v.* To die by suffocating in a liquid.

drowse *v.* To doze.

drub *v.* To hit with a stick.

drudge *n.* A person who does menial tasks. **-ry** *n.*

drug *n.* A substance for treatment of disease or illness.

drum *n.* A musical percussion instrument.

drunk *adj.* Intoxicated with alcohol.

drunk-ard *adj.* A person habitually drunk.

drupe *n.* A one seeded fruit, as the peach.

dry *adj.* Free from moisture; having no rain.

dry--clean *v.* To clean fabrics with chemical solvents.

dry goods *n.* Textile fabrics.

du-al *adj.* Made up or composed of two parts.

dub *v.* To confer knighthood upon; nickname.

du-bi-ous *adj.* Causing doubt; unsettled in judgment.

duch-ess *n.* The wife or widow of a duke.

duck *n.* Swimming birds with short necks and legs.

duct *n.* Bodily tube or canal.

duc-tile *adj.* Capable of being shaped.

dud *n., Informal* A bomb or explosive round which fails to detonate; a failure.

dude *n., Informal* A city person vacationing on a ranch.

due *adj.* Owed; payable.

dues *n., pl.* A fee or charge for membership.

du-el *n.* Premeditated combat between two people.

du-et *n.* A musical composition for two.

duf-fel bag *n.* A large cloth bag for personal belongings.

duke *n.* A noble ranking below a prince.

dul-cet *adj.* Melodious.

dul-ci-mer *n.* A musical stringed instrument.

dull *adj.* Having a blunt edge or point; not exciting. **-ness** *n.*

du-ly *adv.* In a proper or due manner.

dumb *adj.* Unable to speak; uneducated. **-ness** *n.*

dumb-bell *n.* A short bar with weights.

dumb-waiter *n.* A small elevator used to convey food or dishes, from one floor to another.

dum-found *v.* To confound with amazement.

dum-my *n.* One who is stupid; a hand in bridge.

dump *v.* To throw down or discard; dispose of garbage.

dump-ling *n.* A mass of dough cooked in soup or stew.

dun *v.* To press a debtor for payment. **dun** *adj.*

dunce *n.* A slow-witted person.

dune *n.* A hill of sand drifted by the wind.

dung *n.* An excrement of animals; manure.

dun-ga-ree *n.* A sturdy, cotton fabric, especially blue denim; pants or overalls made from this material.

dun-geon *n.* A dark, underground prison chamber.

dunk *v.* To dip a piece of food into liquid before eating.

du-o-de-num *n., pl.* The first portion of the small intestine. **-nal** *adj.*

dupe *n.* A person who is easily deceived.

du-plex *n.* An apartment with rooms on two adjoining floors.

du-pli-cate *n.* Identical; exact copy of an original. **-cation** *n.*

du-ra-ble *adj.* Able to continue for a long period of time without deterioration. **-bility** *n.*

du-ra-tion *n.* A period of time during which something lasts or exists.

du-ress *n.* Constraint by fear or force; forced restraint.

dur-ing *prep.* Throughout the time of; within the time of.

dusk *n.* The earliest part of the evening, just before darkness.

dust *n.* Fine, dry particles of dirt.

duty *n.* Something a person must do; a moral obligation.

dwarf *n.* A human being, or animal of a much smaller than normal size. **-ish** *adj.*

dwell *v.* To live, as an inhabitant. **-er** *n.*

dwell-ing *n.* A house or building in which one lives.

DWI *abbr.* Driving while intoxicated.

dwin-dle *v.* To waste away.

dye *v.* To fix a color in or stain materials; color with a dye *n.* a color imparted by a dye.

dying *adj.* Coming to the end of life; about to die.

dy-nam-ic *adj.* Forceful; energic; productive activity or change; of or relating to energy, motion, or force.

dy-nam-ics *n., Phys.* The part of physics dealing with force, energy, and motion and the relationship between them.

dy-na-mo *n.* A machine producing electric current.

dy-na-mite *n.* An explosive composed of nitroglycerin or ammonium nitrate and am absorbent material, usually packaged in stick form.

dy-nas-ty *n.* A succession of rulers from the same family; a family or group which maintains great power, wealth, or position.

dys-en-ter-y *n.* An infection of the lower intestinal tract.

dys-lex-i-a *n.* An impairment in one's ability to read. **-lexic** *adj.*

dys-pep-sia *n.* Indigestion.

dys-pro-si-um *n.* A metallic element.

dys-tro-phy *n.* Various neuromuscular disorders, especially muscular dystrophy.

E

E, e The fifth letter of the English alphabet.

each *adj.* Everyone

each oth-er *pron.* Each in reciprocal action.

ea-ger *adj.* To be marked by enthusiasm. **-ness** *n.*, **-ly** *adv.*

ea-ger bea-ver *n.* An over zealous person.

ea-gle *n.* A large, powerful bird.

ea-gle eye *n.* Excellent vision. **-ed** *adj.*

ea-glet *n.* A baby eagle.

ear *n., Anat.* The hearing organ.

ear-ache *n.* A pain within the ear.

ear-drum *n.* The membrane that separates the external ear from the middle ear.

earl *n.* A British nobleman. **-dom** *n.*

ear-ly *adj.* Before the usual time. **-iness** *n.*

ear-ly bird *n.* A person who arrives early.

ear-mark *n.* On cattle, mark of ownership.

ear-muff *n.* Cover to keep the ears warm.

earn *v.* Payment for work done. **-er** *n.*

ear-nest *adj.* Serious intent. **-ness** *n.*, **-ly** *adv.*

earn-ings *pl., n.* Something earned, such as a salary.

ear-phone *n.* An instrument worn in the ear that transfers sound into the ear.

ear-ring *n.* Something worn in the ear.

ear-shot *n.* The range of hearing something.

earth *n.* Globe, dirt or soil.

earth-bound *adj.* Firmly fixed or attached to or in the earth.

earth-en *adj.* To be made of dirt or earth.

earth-en ware *n.* Dishes made of baked clay.

earth-quake *n.* Shaking in the earth's crust.

earth sci-ence *n.* Study of the earth.

earth-ward *adv.* To move in the direction of the earth.

earth-work *n.* Building or structure made of earth.

earth-worm *n.* Segmented worms found in the ground; used as bait by fishermen.

earth-y *adj.* Composed of soil or earth. **-iness** *n.*

ear-wax *n.* The yellowish waxlike substance that protects the ear from dirt.

ease *n.* Being comfortable. **-ing, -ed** *v.*

ea-sel *n.* Frame used by artists.

ease-ment *n.* The right to cross or used another persons property.

eas-i-ly *adv.* To be very easy in manner. **-ness** *n.*

east *n.* Direction in which the sun rises. **-erly** *adv.*, **-ern** *adj.*

East-er *n.* The Christian celabration that commemorates the resurrection of Jesus Christ.

easy *adj.* Little difficulty. **-iness** *n.*

eat *v.* To chew and swallow food. **-able** *adj.*, **-er** *n.*

eaves *pl., n.* The edge of a roof.

eaves-drop *v.* Act of listening to anothers' conversation without them knowing. **-er** *n.*

ebb *v.* To recede, as the tide.

eb-o-ny *n.* A dark, hard, colored wood.

e-bul-lient *adj.* Enthusiasm.

ec-cen-tric *adj.* State of

being strange.
-cally adv.
ech-e-lon n. A formation of military aircraft.
e-chi-no-derm n. A type of starfish.
ech-o n. Repetition of a sound. -er n.,
-ic adj.
e-clair n. A long pastry filled with whipped cream.
ec-lec-tic adj. Having components from a diverse source.
-cism n., -cally adv.
e-clipse n. A partial blocking of one celestial body by another.
e-col-o-gy n. Scientific study of the environment.
-ical, -ic adj., -ist n.
ec-o-nom-ic adj. Relating to the necessities of life. -cal adj.
ec-o-nom-ics n. The science which treats production of commodities.
e-con-o-mize v. To manage thriftly. -er n.
e-con-o-my n. The management of money.
ec-sta-sy n. A state of intense joy.
ec-stat-ic adj. To be rapturous. -cal n.
ec-u-men-i-cal adj. Referring to worldwide.
-ism n., -cally adv.
ec-ze-ma n. A type of skin condition.

ed-dy n. A water current running against the main current.
edge n. The cutting side of a blade. -ed adj.
edg-y adj. To be nervous. -iness n.
ed-i-ble adj. Fit for consumption.
e-dict n. A public decree.
ed-i-fy v. To instruct someone. -ing adj.,
-cation n.
ed-it v. To prepare for publication. -tor n.
e-di-tion n. A form in which a book is published.
ed-i-to-ri-al n. An article in a newspaper, or magazine. -ly adv.
ed-u-cate v. To supply with training or schooling.
-tor, -tion n.,
-tive, -ed adj.
e-duce v. To call or bring out. -tion n., -ible adj.
eel n. A snake-like fish.
-y adj.
ee-rie adj. State of being weird; scary.
-ness n., -ly adv.
ef-face v. To remove or rub out. -er, -ment n.
ef-fect n. Power to produce a desired result.
ef-fec-tive adj. Producing an expected effect.
-ness n., -ly adv.
ef-fem-i-nate adj. To have woman-like quality.

-ly *adv.*

ef-fer-ent *adj.* Carrying away or outward.

ef-fete *adj.* To be exhausted.

ef-fi-ca-cious *adj.* To be producing a intended effect.

ef-fi-cient *adj.* To be adequate in performance. **-ency** *n.*, -ly *adv.*

ef-fi-gy *n.* An image of a hated person.

ef-flo-res-cence *n.* Slow process of development.

ef-flu-ence *n.* An act of flowing out.

ef-fort *n.* An earnest attempt or achievement. -less *adj.*, -lessness *n.*, -lessly *adv.*

ef-fron-ter-y *n.* Shameless; boldness.

ef-ful-gent *adj.* Shining brilliantly. **-ence** *n.*

ef-fu-sion *n.* An unrestrained outpouring of feeling.

egg *n.* The reproductive cell of female animals.

egg-beat-er *n.* A tool with rotating blades used to mix.

egg-nog *n.* A drink of beaten eggs, sugar, and milk or cream.

egg-plant *n.* A plant with egg-shaped edible fruit.

e-go *n.* Thinking of oneself. **-centricity** *n.*

e-go-ma-ni-a *n.* Self obsession.

e-gre-gious *adj.* A state of being remarkably bad. -ly *adv.*

e-gress *n.* The means of departing.

eight *n.* A cardinal number following seven.

ei-ther *pron.* One or the other.

e-jac-u-late *v.* To eject abruptly. **-tion** *n.*, -tory *adj.*

e-ject *v.* To throw out or to expel. **-ment, -tion, -tor** *n.*

e-lab-o-rate *adj.* Carried out with great detail. -tion *n.*, -ly *adv.*

e-lapse *v.* To slip or to glide away.

e-las-tic *adj.* Being capable of easy adjustment. **-ty** *n.*, **-cally** *adv.*

e-late *v.* To make proud of. **-ed** *adj.*

el-bow *n.* The outer joint of the arm between the upper arm and forearm.

eld-er *n.* The one who is older than others. -ly *adj.*, **-ship** *n.*

e-lect *v.* To choose or select by vote. **-tion** *n.*

e-lec-tric *adj.* Pertaining to electricity. **-cally** *adv.*, -cal *adj.*

e-lec-tri-cian *n.* A person who maintains electric equipment.

e-lec-tric-i-ty *n.* Attract or repel each other; form

of energy.

e-lec-tro-cute *v.* To kill by electric current. **-tion** *n.*

e-lec-tron *n.* Particle with a negative electric charge.

e-lec-tro-type *n.* The plate used in printing.

el-e-gance *n.* A refinement in appearance or manner.

el-e-gy *n.* A poem expressing sorrow for one who is dead.

el-e-ment *n.* Constituent part. **-ally** *adv.*

el-e-men-ta-ry *adj.* Fundamental essential.

el-e-phant *n.* A large mammal having a long, flexible trunk.

el-e-vate *v.* To lift up or raise.

e-lev-en *n.* The cardinal number equal to ten plus one.

elf *n.* An imaginary being.

e-lic-it *v.* To bring or draw out.

e-lim-i-nate *v.* To get rid of or remove. **-nation** *n.*

e-lite *n.* The most skilled members of a group.

elk *n.* The largest deer of Europe.

el-lipse *n.* A closed curve.

elm *n.* Various valuable timber and shade trees.

el-o-cu-tion *n.* The art of effective public speaking.

e-lope *v.* To run away to marry.

el-o-quent *adj.* Power to speak fluently. **-quence** *n.*

else *adj.* To be different; other.

else-where *adv.* In another place.

e-lu-ci-date *v.* To make clear. **-dation** *n.*

e-lude *v.* To evade or avoid.

em *n.* An unit of measure for printed matter.

e-ma-ci-ate *v.* To become extremely thin.

em-a-nate *v.* To come forth.

e-man-ci-pate *v.* To liberate. **-pation** *n.*

e-mas-cu-late *v.* To castrate.

em-balm *v.* To treat a corpse with preservatives to protect from decay.

em-bar-go *n.* A restraint on trade.

em-bark *v.* To set out on a venture.

em-bar-rass *v.* To feel self-conscious; to confuse.

em-bas-sy *n.* The ambassador headquarters.

em-bel-lish *v.* To adorn; to decorate. **-ment** *n.*

em-ber *n.* A piece of glowing coal.

em-bez-zle *v.* To take money fraudulently.

-ment *n.*

em-blem *n.* A symbol of something.

em-bod-y *v.* To give a bodily form.

em-bold-en *v.* To encourage; to make bold.

em-bo-lism *n.* A blockage of a blood vessel.

em-boss *v.* To shape or decorate in relief.

em-brace *v.* To hold or clasp in the arms.

em-bro-cate *v.* To rub with liquid medicine. -cation *n.*

em-broi-der *v.* To decorate with needlework.

em-broil *v.* To throw into confusion.

em-bry-o *n.* An organism in early development stage.

em-cee *n.* A master of ceremonies.

e-mend *v.* To correct or remove faults. -ation *n.*

em-er-ald *n.* A bright-green gemstone.

e-merge *v.* To come into existence. -mersion *n.*

e-mer-gen-cy *n.* A sudden and unexpected situation.

e-mer-i-tus *adj.* Retired from duty with honor.

e-met-ic *adj.* Medicine to induce vomiting.

em-i-grate *v.* To move from one country or region. -tion *n.*

em-i-nent *adj.* To be high in esteem.

em-is-sar-y *n.* A person on a mission.

e-mit *v.* To send forth.

e-mol-lient *n.* A substance used for softening skin.

e-mol-u-ment *n.* Compensation.

e-mote *v.* To show emotion.

e-mo-tion *n.* Feelings of sorrow, hate, and love.

em-pa-thy *n.* Understanding feelings of another person.

em-per-or *n.* The ruler of an empire.

em-pha-sis *n.* The importance attached to anything.

em-pire *n.* Nations governed by a single supreme authority.

em-pir-i-cal *adj.* To be gained from experience.

em-ploy *v.* To engage the service of. -ment *n.*

em-ploy-ee *n.* A person who works for another in return for wages.

em-pow-er *v.* To authorize something.

em-press *n.* The emperor's wife.

emp-ty *adj.* To be containing nothing; vacant.

em-u-late *v.* To imitate. -tion *n.*

e-mul-sion *n.* Light-sensitive coating on photographic paper.

en-a-ble *v.* To supply power to. **-ing** *adj.*

en-act *v.* To make into law.

e-nam-el *n.* A glossy coating on the teeth.

en-camp *v.* To stay in a camp. **-ment** *n.*

en-ceph-a-li-tis *n.* An inflammation of the brain.

en-chant *v.* To put under a spell. **-ment** *n.*

en-cir-cle *v.* To surround.

en-close *v.* To form a circle. **-closure** *n.*

en-co-mi-um *n.* High praise.

en-com-pass *v.* To surround.

en-core *n.* A demand for repeat performance.

en-coun-ter *n.* An unexpected meeting.

en-cour-age *v.* To inspire with courage or hope. **-ment** *n.*

en-croach *v.* To intrude upon. **-ment** *n.*

en-cum-ber *v.* To hinder or burden.

en-cy-clo-pe-di-a *n.* A comprehensive work of knowledge.

end *n.* A terminal point where something is concluded.

en-dan-ger *v.* To expose to danger. **-ment** *n.*

en-dear *v.* To make beloved.

en-deav-or *n.* An attempt to attain or do something.

en-dem-ic *adj.* Peculiar to a particular area.

en-dog-e-nous *adj.* To be growing from within.

en-dorse *v.* To write one's signature on the back of a check. **-ment** *n.*

en-dow *v.* To bestow upon.

en-dure *v.* To undergo; to tolerate. **-ing** *adj.*

en-e-ma *n.* An injection of a liquid into the rectum for cleansing.

en-e-my *n.* A hostile force.

en-er-gy *n.* A vigor; strength.

en-er-vate *v.* To deprive of strength.

en-fee-ble *v.* To weaken.

en-force *v.* To compel obedience. **-ment** *n.*

en-fran-chise *v.* To give a franchise to someone.

en-gage *v.* To employ or hire.

en-gen-der *v.* To exist.

en-gine *n.* A mechanical instrument.

en-gorge *v.* To swallow greedily or quickly.

en-grave *v.* To etch into a surface. **-ing** *n.*

en-gross *v.* To occupy

attention. -ment n.

en-gulf v. To enclose completely.

en-hance v. To make greater or bigger.

e-nig-ma n. Anything puzzling; a riddle.

en-join v. To prohibit.

en-large v. To make greater in size. -ment n.

en-light-en v. To give spiritual guidance to.

en-list v. To sign up for service with the armed forces. -ment n.

en-mesh v. To entangle.

en-mi-ty n. A deep hatred; hostility.

en-no-ble v. To confer the rank of nobility. -ment n.

e-nor-mi-ty n. An enormous, great wickedness.

e-nor-mous adj. To be very great in size.

e-nough adj. Adequate to satisfy demands.

en-rage v. To put into a rage.

en-sem-ble n. A group of complementary parts that are in harmony.

en-sign n. An officer in the navy; a flag.

en-slave v. To put in bondage.

en-snare v. To catch; to trap. -ment n.

en-sue v. To follow.

en-sure v. To make certain.

en-tail v. To have a necessary accompaniment or result.

en-tan-gle v. To complicate. -ment n.

en-ter v. To go or to come into something.

en-ter-prise n. A risky undertaking.

en-ter-tain v. To amuse or delight. -ment n.

en-thrall v. To fascinate.

en-throne v. To place on a throne.

en-thu-si-asm n. An intense feeling.

en-thu-si-ast n. A person full of enthusiasm.

en-thu-si-as-tic adj. To be characterized by enthusiasm. -tically adv.

en-tice v. To arouse desire.

en-tire adj. To be whole; complete. -ly adv., -ness n.

en-ti-tle v. To furnish with a right.

en-ti-ty n. Something that exists alone.

en-tomb v. To place in a tomb.

en-to-mol-o-gy n. Study of insects. -gist n.

en-tou-rage n. The group that surrounds an important person.

en-trails n. The internal parts of the body.

en-trance n. The means or place of entry.

en-trance n. Fascinate. -ment n.

en-trap v. To catch in a trap or a cage.

en-treat v. To make a request.

en-trench v. To fix or sit firmly. -ment n.

en-trust v. To transfer to another for care. -ment n.

en-try n. An opening for entering something.

en-twine v. To twine together.

e-nu-mer-ate v. To count off one by one. -ative adj.

e-nun-ci-ate v. To speak with clarity. -ation n.

en-ve-lope n. A paper case, especially for a letter or other items mailed.

en-vi-a-ble adj. Highly desirable. -ness n.

en-vi-ron-ment n. The physical surroundings. -al adj.

en-vi-rons n. The surrounding neighborhood.

en-vis-age v. To visualize or imagine something.

en-voy n. A diplomatic messenger.

en-vy n. Resentment for other's possessions.

en-zyme n. Proteins produced by living organisms that function in plants and animals.

e-on n. An indefinite period of time.

ep-au-let n. A shoulder ornament, as on a military uniform.

e-phem-er-al adj. To be lasting a very short time. -ly adv.

ep-ic n. A long narrative poem. -cal n.

ep-i-cen-ter n. The middle of an earthquake.

ep-i-cure n. Refined tastes. -ism n., -an adj.

ep-i-dem-ic adj. Something widespread. -cally adv.

ep-i-der-mis n Outer layer of the skin. -ic adj.

ep-i-gram n. A brief pointed remark or observation. -matist n., -matical, -matic adj.

ep-i-lep-sy n. A type of nervous disorder.

ep-i-lep-tic adj. State of having epilepsy.

ep-i-logue n. A type of short speech.

ep-i-sode n. A section of a movie, novel, etc.. -ically adv., -ical, -ic adj.

e-pis-tle n. A type of formal letter.

ep-i-taph n. An inscription. -ist n., -ic adj.

ep-i-thet n. The word used to characterize something. -ical, -ic adj.

e-pit-o-me n. The concise summary of a book. -ize v.

ep-och n. Point in time. -al adj.

ep-ox-y *n.* A type of compound.

eq-ua-ble *adj.* Being fair. **-ness, -bility** *n.*, **-ably** *adv.*

e-qual *adj.* To be of the same measurement. **-ness, -izer** *n.*, **-ly** *adv.*

e-qual-i-tar-i-an *n.* The idea of all men are equal. **-ism** *n.*

e-quate *v.* To consider or make equal.

e-qua-tion *n.* A process of being equal. **-ally** *adv.*, **-al** *adj.*

e-qua-tor *n.* A great imaginary circle around the earth.

e-qua-to-ri-al *adj.* Referring to at or near the equator. **-ly** *adv.*

eq-uer-ry *n.* An officer in charge of the horses of royalty.

e-ques-tri-an *n.* One who rides horses.

e-qui-lat-er-al *adj.* To be equal sided.

e-qui-li-brate *v.* The balancing of something. **-tor, -tion** *n.*

e-qui-lib-ri-um *n.* The state of balance.

e-quine *adj.* Pertaining to or like horse.

e-qui-nox *n.* Twice a year when days and nights are equal in time. **-noctial** *adj.*

e-quip *v.* To furnish with whatever is needed. **-er, -ment** *n.*

eq-ui-ta-ble *adj* Being impartial. **-bly** *adv.*, **-ness** *n.*

eq-ui-ty *n.* Fairness or impartiality.

e-quiv-a-lent *adj.* Being equal. **-ence** *n.*, **-ly** *adv.*

e-quiv-o-cal *adj.* Questionable. **-ness** *n.*, **-cally** *adv.*

e-quiv-o-cate *v.* To use vague language. **-tor, -tion** *n.*

e-ra *n.* A period of time.

e-rad-i-cate *v.* To remove; to take away. **-tive, -able** *adj.*, **-tion, -tor** *n.*

e-rase *v.* Remove something written. **-able** *adj.*, **-bility** *n.*

e-rect *adj.* Vertical position. **-ion** *n.*

er-e-mite *n.* A hermit.

er-go *conj. & adj.* Consequently.

er-mine *n.* Weasel fur.

e-rode *v.* To wear away gradually. **-sion** *n.*

e-rog-e-nous *adj.* Responsive to sexual stimulation.

err *v.* To make a mistake; to sin.

er-rand *n.* A trip to carry a message.

er-rant *adj.* Search of adventure. **-ly** *adv.*

er-rat-ic *adj.* Irregular.

-cal·ly *adv.*

er·ro·ne·ous *adj.* Containing an error. -ness *n.*, -ly *adv.*

er·ror *n.* Done incorrectly; wrong-doing. -less *adj.*

er·satz *adj.* Artificial.

er·u·dite *adj.* Scholarly. -ness *n.*, -ly *adv.*

e·rupt *v.* To burst forth violently with steam, lava, etc. -tiveness, -tion *n.*, -tive *adj.*, -tively *adv.*

es·ca·la·tor *n.* A type of moving stairway.

es·cal·lop *v.* & *n.* Variation of scallop.

es·ca·pade *n.* A prankish trick.

es·cape *v.* To break free from capture. -er *n.*

es·ca·role *n.* Endive leaves, used in salads.

es·carp·ment *n.* A steep slope.

es·chew *v.* To shun or to avoid someone or something. -er *n.*

es·cort *n.* Accompanying another.

es·crow *n.* A written deed placed in the custody of a third party.

e·soph·a·gus *n.* The tube leading to stomach.

es·o·ter·ic *adj.* Confidential. -cally *adv.*

es·pe·cial *adj.* Having a special place.

es·pi·o·nage *n.* Act of spying to obtain secret information.

es·pous·al *n.* Adoption or support, as of a cause.

es·pouse *v.* To give in marriage.

es·prit *n.* The mental liveliness.

es·prit de corps *n.* A group's spirit.

es·quire *n.* A title of courtesy.

es·say *n.* A short composition. -er *n.*

es·sen·tial *adj.* Necessary. -ly *adv.*, -ness, -ity *n.*

es·tab·lish *v.* To make permanent. -er *n.*

es·tab·lish·ment *n.* A place of residence or business.

es·tate *n.* A large piece of land containing a large home.

es·teem *v.* To regard with respect.

es·ti·ma·ble *adj.* Worthy of respect. -ly *adv.*, -ness *n.*

es·ti·mate *v.* To give a approximate opinion. -tion *n.*

es·trange *v.* To disassociate or remove oneself. -er, -ment *n.*

es·tro·gen *n.* The female hormones.

es·tu·ar·y *n.* A wide mouth of a river.

etch *v.* To engrave by using acid. -er, -ing *n.*

e-ter-nal *adj.* Lasting indefinitely. -ly *adv.*

e-ter-ni-ty *n.* An existence without beginning or end.

e-ther *n., Chem.* A type of anesthetic.

e-the-re-al *adj.* Delicate. -ness, -ity *n.*, -ly *adv.*

eth-ic *n.* Moral values.

eth-nic *adj.* A racial group. -cally *adv.*

e-ti-ol-o-gy *n.* The study of causes or origins. -ically *adv.*, -ical *adj.*, -ist *n.*

et-i-quette *n.* The prescribed rules for behavior.

et-y-mol-o-gy *n.* History of a word origin. -ist *n.*, -ical, -ic *adj.*

eu-gen-ics *n.* The study of improving the physical qualities.

eu-lo-gy *n.* A speech that honors a person. -gize *v.*

eu-phe-mism *n.* A substitution for a word.

eu-pho-ny *n.* An agreeable sound of spoken words.

eu-pho-ri-a *n.* A strong feeling of elation.

eu-re-ka *interj.* An expression of triumph.

eu-tha-na-sia *n.* An act of mercy killing.

e-vac-u-ate *v.* To leave a threatened area. -ation *n.*

e-vade *v.* To baffle; to elude.

e-val-u-ate *v.* To examine carefully. -tion *n.*

ev-a-nes-cent *adj.* To be vanishing or passing quickly.

e-van-gel-ism *n.* The preaching of the gospel. -ically *adj.*

e-vap-o-rate *v.* To remove the liquid from water, milk, etc.

e-va-sive *adj.* Being vague. -sion *n.*

e-ven *adj.* Being level.

eve-ning *n.* The time between sunset and bedtime.

e-vent *n.* Something that takes place.

e-ven-tu-al *adj.* Happening in due time.

e-ven-tu-al-i-ty *n.* The conceivable outcome.

ev-er *adv.* At any time.

ev-er-glade *n.* A tract of low, swampy land.

ev-er-green *adj.* A tree that has green foliage.

ev-er-last-ing *adj.* To be lasting forever.

ev-er-more *adv.* At all times to come.

eve-ry *adj.* To be without exceptions.

eve-ry-body *pron.* Every person.

eve-ry-day *adj.* Happening daily.

eve-ry-one *pron.* Every person.

eve-ry-thing *pron.* All things.

eve-ry-where *adv.* At, to everyplace.

e-vict *v.* To put out a tenant. **-tion** *n.*

ev-i-dence *n.* The signs or facts on which a conclusion can be based.

ev-i-dent *adj.* Obvious.

e-vil *adj.* Morally bad or wrong. **-ness** *n.*

e-vince *v.* To indicate clearly. **-cive** *n.*

e-vis-cer-ate *v.* To remove the entrails.

ev-i-ta-ble *adj.* State of being avoidable.

e-voke *v.* To call or summon forth.

ev-o-lu-tion *n.* A gradual process of development. **-ist** *n.*

e-volve *v.* To develop or change gradually. **-ment** *n.*

ewe *n.* A female sheep.

ew-er *n.* A large pitcher or jug.

ex-act *adj.* Accurate in every detail. **-ness** *n.*

ex-acting *adj.* Making severe demands.

ex-act-i-tude *n.* An act of being exact.

ex-ag-ger-ate *v.* To represent something as being greater than what it really is. **-ation** *n.*

ex-alt *v.* To increase the intensity. **-ation** *n.*

ex-am-i-na-tion *n.* A test of knowledge.

ex-am-ine *v.* To observe or inspect; look into.

ex-am-ple *n.* Representative as a sample.

ex-as-per-ate *v.* To make frustrated. **-ation** *n.*

ex-ca-vate *v.* To dig a hole. **-vation** *n.*

ex-ceed *v.* To go beyond the limit. **-ingly** *adv.*

ex-cel *v.* To do better than others.

ex-cel-lence *n.* A quality of being superior.

ex-cel-lent *adj.* Having the best quality.

ex-cel-si-or *n.* Wood shavings.

ex-cept *prep.* Aside from; exclude.

ex-cep-tion *n.* Being excepted; unusual instance.

ex-cerpt *n.* A passage from a book.

ex-cess *n.* An over indulgence. **-ively** *adv.*

ex-ces-sive *adj.* Extreme; more than necessary.

ex-change *v.* To trade.

ex-cise *n.* A tax on a sale of a commodity. **-able** *adj.*

ex-cise *v.* To remove surgically.

ex-cite *v.* To stimulate the emotions. **-ment** *n.*

ex-claim *v.* To utter suddenly. **-ation** *n.*

ex-cla-ma-tion mark *n.* A mark (!) to show strong feeling.

ex-clude *v.* To keep out.

ex-clu-sive *adj.* Selective, not shared.

ex-co-ri-ate *v.* To censure harshly.

ex-cre-ment *n.* A bodily waste.

ex-cre-ta *pl., n.* Excretions from the body.

ex-cru-ci-at-ing *adj.* To be painful; torturous.

ex-cul-pate *v.* To free from wrong doing. **-pation** *n.*

ex-cur-sion *n.* A short trip or journey.

ex-cuse *v.* To grant forgiveness. **-able** *adj.*

ex-e-cra-ble *adj.* To be extremely bad.

ex-e-crate *v.* To detest; hate violently.

ex-e-cute *v.* To put to death; perform. **-cution** *n.*

ex-ec-u-tive *n.* An administrator in an organization.

ex-em-plar *n.* A typical example.

ex-em-pla-ry *adj.* Serving as a model.

em-pli-fy *v.* To be an example.

ex-empt *v.* To free from obligation. **-ion** *n.*

ex-er-cise *n.* Developing oneself; physical training.

ex-ert *v.* To use force.

-ion *n.*

ex-haust *v.* To tire.

ex-hib-it *v.* To display.

ex-hi-bi-tion-ism *n.* Calling attention to oneself.

ex-hil-a-rate *v.* To elate.

ex-hort *v.* To urge by earnest appeal. **-ion** *n.*

ex-hume *v.* To remove from a grave.

ex-i-gen-cy *n.* Necessity.

ex-ig-u-ous *adj.* To be extremely small.

ex-ile *n.* A separation from one's country or home.

ex-ist *v.* To live **-ence** *n.*

ex-is-ten-tial *adj.* To be based on experience.

ex-it *n.* Passageway out.

ex-o-dus *n.* A departure of people.

ex-on-er-ate *v.* To free from blame.

ex-or-bi-tant *adj.* Beyond usual and proper limits.

ex-or-cise *v.* To cast out an evil spirit.

ex-ot-ic *adj.* To be strangely beautiful.

ex-pand *v.* To increase.

ex-panse *n.* A wide, open stretch.

ex-pa-tri-ate *v.* To banish.

ex-pect *v.* To look forward to something.

ex-pec-tant *adj.* To be pregnant.

ex-pec-to-rate *v.* To spit.

ex-pe-di-ent *adj.* Selfish

interests. **-ency** n.

ex-pe-dite v. To speed up progress.

ex-pe-di-tious adj. To be quick; speedy.

ex-pel v. To drive or force out.

ex-pend v. To pay out or use up.

ex-pend-a-ble adj. Available for spending.

ex-pen-di-ture n. The amount spent.

ex-pense n. A consumption of money.

ex-pen-sive adj. High-priced.

ex-pe-ri-ence n. A skill acquired from actual participation.

ex-per-i-ment n. A test to illustrate a truth.

ex-pert n. A person having great knowledge. **-ness** n.

ex-pi-ate v. To atone.

ex-pire v. To come to an end. **-ation** n.

ex-plain v. To make understandable.

ex-plic-it adj. Plainly expressed. **-ly** adv.

ex-plode v. To blow up violently. **-plosion** n.

ex-ploit n. A deed that is notable.

ex-plore v. Travel unfamiliar territory. **-ation** n.

ex-pose v. To reveal.

ex-po-si-tion n. A public exhibition.

ex-pos-tu-late v. To

reason earnestly. **-lation** n.

ex-pound n. Detailed statement.

ex-press v. To verbalize. **-iveness** n.

ex-press-way n. A multilane highway.

ex-pro-pri-ate v. Deprive a person. **-ation** n.

ex-pul-sion n. Act of expelling.

ex-pur-gate v. To remove obscene material from a book. **-gator** n.

ex-qui-site adj. Highly sensitive.

ex-tant adj. Still in existence.

ex-tem-po-rize v. To improvise to meet circumstances.

ex-tend v. To make longer or broader. **-ible** adj.

ex-tent n. The size.

ex-te-ri-or adj. External layer.

ex-ter-mi-nate v. Destroy completely. **-nation** n.

ex-ter-nal adj. Outside; exterior. **-ly** adv.

ex-tinct adj. No longer existing. **-ion** n.

ex-tin-guish v. To put an end to.

ex-tol v. Praise highly.

ex-tort n. Money obtained by threat. **-ion** n.

ex-tra adj. To be over

what is normal.

ex-tract v. To pull out by force. **-ion** n.

ex-tra-dite v. To surrender by extradition.

ex-tra-ne-ous adj. Coming from without. **-ly** adv., **-ness** n.

ex-treme adj. Going far beyond the bounds of moderation. **-ly** adv., **-ness** n.

ex-tro-vert n. Out going person. **-version** n.

ex-trude v. To push or thrust out.

ex-u-ber-ant adj. Full of high spirits. **-ly** adv.

ex-ude v. To trickle forth sweat. **-tion** n.

ex-ult v. Be jubilant. **-ly** adv., **-tion** n.

ex-ur-bi-a n. Well-to-do residential area.

eye n. An organ of sight.

eye-ball n. The ball of the eye.

eye-brow n. The short hairs covering the bony ridge over the eye.

eye-ful n. A total view of something.

eye-glass n. Corrective lens used to assist vision.

eye-hole n. An opening to pass a hook, pin, rope, etc.

eye-lash n. stiff, curved hairs growing from the edge of the eyelids.

eye-let n. A perforation for a hook or cord to fit through.

eye-lid n. Either of two folds of skin and muscle that open and close over an eye.

eye--o-pen-er n. That which opens the eyes. **-ing** adj.

eye-piece n. A combination of lenses of an optical instrument.

eye-sight n. A faculty or power of seeing things or objects.

eye-wit-ness n. A person who has seen something and can testify to it firsthand.

F

F, f The sixth letter of the English alphabet.

fa-ble n. A brief, fictitious story. **-ed** adj.

fab-ric n. A cloth produced from fibers.

fab-ri-cate v. To manufacture. **-tion** n.

fab-u-lous adj. To be incredible; very pleasing. **-ly** adv.

fa-cade n., Arch. The face of a building.

face n. The front surface of the head.

fac-et n. A polished surface of a gemstone.

fa-ce-tious adj. To be humorous. **-ness** n.

fac-ile adj. to be requiring little effort.

fa-cil-i-tate v. To make

easier. **-tion** *n.*

fa-cil-i-ty *n., pl.* **-ies** Doing something.

fac-sim-i-le *n.* An exact copy.

fact *n.* Something that actually occurred or exists.

fac-tious *adj.* Dissension; creating friction.

fac-ti-tious *adj.* The state of being produced artificially. **-ness** *n.*, **-ly** *adv.*

fac-tor *n.* Transacting business for commission.

fac-to-ry *n., pl.* **-ies** A place where goods are manufactured.

fac-tu-al *adj.* To be consisting or containing facts. **-ly** *adv.*

fac-ul-ty *n., pl.* **-ies** A natural ability; instructors.

fad *n.* A temporary fashion. **-ness** *n.*

fade *v.* To lose brightness.

fag-ot *or* **fag-got** *n.* A bundle of twigs for fuel.

fail *v.* Not to succeed. **-ure** *n.*

fail--safe *adj.* System to prevent equipment failure.

faint *adj.* Little strength or vigor. **-ness** *n.*, **-ly** *adv.*

fair *adj.* Light in coloring; not stormy. **-ness** *n.*

fair-y *n., pl.* **-ies** An imaginary being.

fair-y tale *n.* A story about fictitious creatures.

faith *n.* A belief and trust in God. **-ful** *adj.*, **-fulness** *n.*

fake *adj.* To be false appearance. **-er** *n.*

fal-con *n.* A bird of prey. **-ry** *n.*

fall *v.* To drop down; to collapse.

fal-la-cy *n., pl.* **-ies** A deception.

fal-low *n.* The plowed ground; light brown in color.

false *adj.* To be incorrect; untrue. **-ness** *n.*, **-ly** *adv.*

false-hood *n.* The act of lying.

fal-set-to *n.* A high singing voice, usually male.

fal-si-fy *v.* To misrepresent. **-fication** *n.*

fal-ter *v.* Uncertain in action. **-ingly** *adv.*, **-er** *n.*

fame *n.* The public esteem. **-ed** *adj.*

fa-mil-iar *adj.* To be well-acquainted. **-ly** *adv.*

fa-mil-i-ar-i-ty *n., pl.* **-ties** The knowledge of something.

fam-i-ly *n.* Related by blood or marriage.

fam-ine *n.* The scarcity of food.

fam-ish *v.* To starve. **-ed** *adj.*

fa-mous *adj.* To be well-known. **-ly** *adv.*

fan *n.* A device for putting air into motion.
-**ner** *n.*, -**like** *adj.*

fa-nat-ic *n.* One moved by enthusiasm.
-**cally** *adv.*

fan-cy *n.* A whimsical notion or idea. -**ied** *adj.*,
-**iness** *n.*, -**ily** *adv.*

fan-fare *n.* A loud trumpet flourish.

fang *n.* A pointed tooth or tusk.

fan-ta-sia *n.* A composition according to composer's fancy.

fan-ta-size *v.* To create mental pictures.

fan-tas-tic *adj.* To be wildly fanciful.
-**calness** *n.*, -**cally** *adv.*

fan-ta-sy *n.*, *pl.* -**ies** A creative imagination.

far *adv.* At a distance.

farce *n.* A theatre comedy. -**cical** *adj.*,
-**cically** *adv.*

fare *n.* A fee paid for transportation.
-**er** *n.*

fare-well *n.* A good-by.

far--fetched *adj.* To be highly improbable.

far-i-na-ceous *adj.* To be composed of starch.

farm *n.* The land used for agriculture. -**ing** *adj.*,
-**er** *n.*

farm-house *n.* A homestead on a farm.

far--off *adj.* To be distant; remote.

far--out *adj.* To be very unconventional.

far-ra-go *n.* A confused mixture.

far--sighted *adj.* See things at a distance clearly. -**ness** *n.*,
-**ly** *adv.*

far-ther *adv.* At a more distant point.
-**most** *adj.*

far-thest *adj.* The greatest distance.

fas-ci-nate *v.* To captivate. -**tion** *n.*,
-**ingly** *adv.*

fast *adj.* To be swift; rapid. -**ness** *n.*

fast-back *n.* A car with a downward slope.

fast-en *v.* To join something else.
-**ing**, -**er** *n.*

fas-tid-i-ous *adj.* To be delicate; refined.
-**ness** *n.*

fat *adj.* Obese; plump.
-**ness** *n.*, -**ly** *adv.*

fat-al *adj.* Causing death.
-**ist** *n.*, -**ly** *adv.*

fa-tal-i-ty *n.* A death caused by a disaster or accident.

fat cat *n.*, *Slang* A powerful and wealthy person.

fate *n.* A predetermined events. -**ful** *adj.*

fa-ther *n.* The male parent. **Father** A priest.
-**ly** *adj.*, -**hood** *n.*

fath-om *n.* A length

equal to six feet.
 -less *adj.*
fa-tigue *n.* An extreme tiredness.
fat-u-ous *adj.* To be silly and foolish.
 -ness *n.*, **-ly** *adv.*
fau-cet *n.* A valve to draw liquids from a pipe.
faugh *interj.* An exclamation of contempt.
fault *n.* An impairment or defect; weakness.
 -iness *n.*, **-ily** *adv.*
faux pas *n.* A false step.
fa-vor *n.* A helpful act.
fa-vor-a-ble *adj.* To be advantageous. **-ness** *n.*,
 -bly *adv.*
fa-vor-ite *n.* Preferred above all others.
 -itism *n.*
fawn *n.* A young deer.
faze *v.* To disconcert.
fe-al-ty *n.* An allegiance owed to a feudal lord.
fear *n.* An anticipation of danger. **-fully** *adv.*,
 -fulness *n.*
fear-less *adj.* To be brave.
 -ness *n.*, **-ly** *adv.*
fea-si-ble *adj.* To be able to be accomplished.
 -ness *n.*, **-bly** *adv.*
feast *n.* A meal; banquet.
feat *n.* A notable achievement.
feath-er *n.* A protective covering of birds.
feath-er-weight *n.* A light weight boxer.

fea-ture *n.* An appearance or shape of the face. **-less** *adj.*
feb-ri-fuge *n.* A medicine to reduce fever.
feb-rile *adj.* Being feverish.
fe-ces *pl. n.* An excrement. **-cal** *adj.*
feck-less *adj.* To be ineffective; weak.
fe-cund *adj.* To be productive. **-ity** *n.*
fed-er-al *adj.* Agreement between states or groups. **-ism** *n.*
fed-er-ate *v.* To unite in a union.
fed-er-a-tion *n.* The two or more states joining a confederacy.
fe-do-ra *n.* A soft felt hat.
fed up *adj.* An extremely annoyed.
fee *n.* A fixed charge.
fee-ble *adj.* To be lacking strength; weak.
 -ness *n.*, **-bly** *adv.*
fee-ble mind-ed *adj.* To be mentally deficient.
 -ness *n.*
feed *v.* To supply with food. **-er** *n.*
feel *v.* To perceive through touch.
 -ing *n.*, **-ingly** *adv.*
feet *n.* A plural of foot.
feint *n.* A deceptive movement.
fe-lic-i-tate *v.* To wish happiness to. **-tation** *n.*
fe-line *adj.* To be relat-

ing to cats. **-ity** n.,
-ly adv.

fell v. Past tense of fall.

fel-low n. A boy or man.

fel-low-ship n. The common interests.

fel-ly n. The rim of a wooden wheel.

fel-on n. The person who committed a felony.

fel-o-ny n. A serious crime. **-ious** adj.,
-iousness n.,
-iously adv.

felt n. An unwoven fabric.

fe-male n. The sex that produces ova.

fem-i-nine adj. To be pertaining to the female sex. **-ness** n., **-ly** adv.

fem-i-nism n. A movement granting equal rights to women.
-tic adj.

fen n. A low, marshy land.

fence n. The boundary or barrier. **-er** n.

fend v. To offer resistance.

fen-nel n. An herb from the parsley family.

fe-ral adj. Not tame.

fer-men-ta-tion n. The decomposition of organic compounds.

fe-ro-cious adj. Extremely savage.
-ness n., **-ly** adv.

fer-ret n. A small, red-eyed polecat. **-er** n.

fer-rous adj. To be containing iron.

fer-rule n. A cap at the end of a walking cane.

fer-ry n. A boat for transporting people, vehicles.

fer-tile adj., Biol. Ability to reproduce.
-tility n., **-ly** adv.

fer-til-ize v. To make fertile. **-able** adj.

fer-vent adj. Ardent; very hot. **-vency** n.,
-ly adv.

fer-vid adj. Fervent to an extreme degree.
-ly adv., **-ness** n.

fer-vor n. A great emotional warmth.

fes-cue n. A type of tough grass.

fes-ter v. To generate pus.

fes-ti-val n. A celebration. **-vity** n.

fes-toon n. A garland of flowers.

fet-a n. Greek cheese.

fetch v. To go after and return with. **-er** n.

fetch-ing adj. To be very attractive.

fete n. A festival or feast.

fet-id adj. A condition of having a foul odor.
-ness n., **-ly** adv.

fet-ish n. An object with magic powers.
-ism n., **-istic** adj.

fet-ter n. A chain to prevent escape.

fe-tus *n.* An unborn organism carried within the womb.

feud *n.* A quarrel between families. **-al** *adj.*

few *adj.* Small in number.

fi-as-co *n.* A complete failure.

fi-at *n.* A positive order or decree.

fib *n.* A trivial lie. **-er** *n.*

fi-ber *n.* A piece of synthetic material. **-ed** *adj.*

fi-ber-board *n.* A pliable building material.

fi-ber-glass *n.* A flexible, nonflammable material.

fi-ber op-tics *pl., n.* The light transmitted through flexible glass rods.

fick-le *adj.* Changeable. **-ness** *n.*

fic-tion *n.* An imaginary or created. **-ally** *adv.*, **-al** *adj.*

fic-ti-tious *adj.* Nonexistent; imaginary. **-ness** *n.*, **-ly** *adv.*

fid-dle *n.* A type of violin. **-er** *n.*

fi-del-i-ty *n.* The loyalty; faithfulness.

fidg-et *v.* To move nervously. **-iness** *n.*, **-y** *adj.*

fief *n.* A feudal estate.

field *n.* A piece of cultivated land.

fiend *n.* An evil spirit. **-ish** *adj.*, **-ishness** *n.*, **-ishly** *adv.*

fierce *adj.* Violent in nature. **-ness** *n.*, **-ly** *adv.*

fier-y *adj.* To be composed of fire. **-iness** *n.*, **-ily** *adv.*

fi-es-ta *n.* A religious holiday.

fife *n.* An instrument similar to a flute.

fif-teen *n.* The cardinal number equal to 14 + 1.

fifth *n.* One of five equal parts.

fif-ty *n.* The cardinal number equal to 5 X 10.

fig *n.* A tree bearing edible fruit.

fight *v.* To argue or quarrel. **-ing** *n.*

fight-er *n.* A person who fights. *Milit.* Fast plane.

fig-ment *n.* An invention or fabrication.

fig-u-ra-tive *adj.* Containing a figure of speech. **-ness** *n.*, **-ly** *adv.*

fig-ure *n.* A symbol which represents a number. **-er** *n.*, **-less** *adj.*

fig-ure-head *n.* One with leadership but no real power.

fil-a-ment *n.* A very finely spun fiber or thread. **-ous** *adj.*

fil-bert *n.* An edible nut of the hazel tree.

filch *v.* To steal. **-er** *n.*

file *n.* A device for storing papers; grinding tool.

fi-let mi-gnon *n.* A tender cut of beef.

fil-i-buster *n.* An attempt to hinder legislative action.

fil-i-gree *n.* An ornamental wire of gold and silver.

fill *v. & n.* To supply fully; satisfy a need; put into.

fil-lip *n.* Snap of the finger.

film *n.* A photosensitive paper used in photography.

film-strip *n.* A strip of film for still projection on a screen.

fil-ter *n.* A device used to purify.

fil-th *n.* Dirty or foul. **-y** *adj.*, **-iness** *n.*

fin *n.* An extension of the body of a fish for swimming. **-like** *adj.*

fi-na-gle *v.*, *Slang* To trick. **-er** *n.*

fi-nal *adj.* Coming to the end. **-ize** *v.*

fi-na-le *n.* the final scene in a play.

fi-nal-ist *n.* The last person in a contest.

fi-nance *n.* The science of monetary affairs.

fin-an-cier *n.* An expert in large financial affairs.

find *v.* To come upon unexpectedly. **-er** *n.*

fine *adj.* To be superior in skill. **-ness** *n.*, **-ly** *adv.*

fin-er-y *n.* Elaborate clothes.

fi-nesse *n.* The tact in handling a situation.

fin-ger *n.* One digit of the hand.

fin-ger bowl *n.* The bowl for cleansing the fingers.

fin-ger-print *n.* A form of identification.

fin-ick-y *adj.* Hard to please.

fi-nis *n.* The end.

fin-ish *v.* To reach the end; conclude. **-ing** *n.*, **-ed** *adj.*

fi-nite *adj.* Having limits. **-ness** *n.*

fir *n.* An evergreen tree.

fire *n.* A chemical reaction of burning. **-er** *n.*

fire-arm *n.* A small weapon.

fire-bug *n.* One who enjoys setting fires.

fire drill *n.* The practice escaping fires.

fire es-cape *n.* A structure used for emergency exit from a building.

fire-fly *n.* A winged insect that glows at night.

fire-man *n.* The person employed to extinguish fires.

fire-plug *n.* A hydrant for supplying water.

fire tow-er *n.* A forest fire lookout station.

firm *adj.* Solid; compact. **-ness** *n.*, **-ly** *adv.*

fir-ma-ment *n.* The expanse of the heavens; the sky.

first adj. To be ahead of all others.

first aid n. An emergency medical care.

fish n., pl. **-es** A cold-blooded aquatic animal. **-man** n.

fish-y adj. Suspicious.

fis-sion n. An act of splitting into parts.

fis-sure n. A narrow crack in a rock.

fist n. A tightly closed hand. **-ful** n.

fit adj. Proper size; good health; competent. **-ting** adj., **-ness** n., **-ly** adv.

five n. The cardinal number equal to 4 + 1.

fix v. To mend; repair. **-er** n., **-ed** adj.

fix-a-tion n. An act of being fixed.

fix-ture n. A part or appendage of a house.

flag n. A banner of a country.

flag-el-lant n. The whipping for sexual pleasure. **-lation** n.

flag-rant adj. To be notorious; evil.

flair n. A dashing style.

flak n. An anti-aircraft fire.

flake n. A piece peeled off surface. **-y** adj., **-ness** n.

flame n. A burning vapor from a fire. **-ingly** adv., **-ing** adj.

fla-min-go n. A tropical wading bird.

flank n. The fleshy part of the hip. **-er** n.

flan-nel n. The woven wool fabric.

flap-per n. A woman of the 1920's.

flare v. To blaze with a bright light.

flare-up n. A sudden outburst.

flash v. To burst into a bright fire. **-iness** n.

flash-back n. A preview of past events.

flash-light n. A battery powered lantern.

flash-y adj. Tastelessly showy. **-iness** n., **-ily** adv.

flask n. A glass container.

flat adj. No curvature; level. **-ten** v., **-ness** n.

flat-car n. A railroad car.

flat-ter v. To praise favorably. **-tery** n.

flat-u-lent adj. Gas in the intestines. **-ly** adv.

flat-ware n. The eating utensils.

flaunt v. To display showily. **-ing** n., **-ingly** adv.

fla-vor n. The distinctive taste. **-ing** n., **-less** adj.

flaw n. The defect or

blemish.

flaw-less *adj.* To be without defects.

flax *n.* A plant yielding linseed oil.

flea *n.* A blood-sucking parasitic.

flea mar-ket *n.* A place to sell used goods and antiques.

fleck *n.* A spot or streak.

fledg-ling *n.* A young bird.

flee *v.* To run away.

fleece *n.* The wool covering a sheep. **-ed** *adj.*

fleet *n.* A number of warships.

flesh *n.* A tissue of the human body. **-iness** *n.*, **-ly** *adv.*

fleur-de-lis *n.,pl.* **fleurs-de-lis** The heraldic emblem.

flex *v.* To contract a muscle.

flex-ible *adj.* Bendable; pliable. **-bly** *adv.*

flick *n.* A quick snapping movement.

flick-er *v.* To burn unsteadily. **-ing** *n.*

flight *n.* A scheduled airline trip. **-less** *adj.*

flight-y *adj.* Fickle. **-iness** *n.*, **-ily** *adv.*

flim-flam *n.* A swindle; hoax.

flim-sy *adj.* Lacking strength. **-iness** *n.*

flinch *v.* To wince from pain. **-ingly** *adv.*

fling *v.* To throw or toss.

flip *v.* To turn or throw suddenly.

flip-pant *adj.* Impudence. **-ancy** *n.*

flirt *v.* To make romantic overtures. **-er** *n.*

flit *v.* To move abruptly. **-ter** *n.*

float *n.* Suspend on water. **-er** *n.*

flock *n.* A group of animals.

floe *n.* A large mass of floating ice.

flog *v.* To beat hard with a whip. **-ger** *n.*

flood *n.* An overflow of water. **-er** *n.*

flood-light *n.* An intense artificial light.

floor *n.* Level base of a room. **-ing** *n.*

flop *v.* Fall down clumsily. **-per** *n.*

flop house *n.* Run down hotel.

flop-py disk *n.* Flexible plastic disk to store computer data.

flo-ra *n.* Plants in a specific region.

flo-ral *adj.* Pertaining to flowers.

flor-id *adj.* Covered with flowers. **-ity** *n.*

flo-rist *n.* A seller of flowers.

floss *n.* A thread to clean between teeth. **-y** *adj.*

flo-til-la *n.* A fleet of vessels.

flot-sam *n.* The debris from sunken ships.

floun-der *v.* To struggle clumsily.

flour *n.* A ground meal of wheat. **-y** *adj.*

flour-ish *v.* To thrive; prosper. **-ing** *adj.*

flout *v.* To show open contempt for. **-er** *n.*

flow *v.* To move freely.

flow-er *n.* A cluster of petals. **-ed** *adj.*

fluc-tu-ate *v.* To shift irregularly. **-tion** *n.*

flue *n.* A pipe for escaping smoke.

flu-ent *adj.* Facile in speech. **-ly** *adv.*
-cy *n.*

flu-id *n.* Flowing liquid.
-ness *n.*, **-ly** *adv.*

fluke *n.* A stroke of luck.
-y *adj.*

flunk *v.*, *Slang* To fail a test. **-y** *n.*

flush *v.* To flow out suddenly.

flus-ter *v.* To become nervous. **-ed** *adj.*

flute *n.* A woodwind instrument. **-ist** *n.*,
-ed *adj.*

flut-ter *v.* Flap irregularly.
-y *adj.*, **-ingly** *adv.*

fly *v.* To travel by air.

fly-wheel *n.* A rotating wheel to regulate speed.

foal *n.* A young horse.

foam *n.* A mass of bubbles.
-iness *n.*, **-y** *adj.*

fo-cus *n.* A point at which rays converge.
-er *n.*

fod-der *n.* The feed for livestock.

foe *n.* An enemy.

fog *n.* A mass of condensed water.
-iness *n.*

foil *v.* To prevent from being successful.

fold *v.* To double or lay one part over another.

fo-li-age *n.* The leaves of plants.

fo-li-o *n.* A folder for loose papers.

folk *n.* An ethnic group of people.

folk lore *n.* The beliefs, customs of a people.

fol-li-cle *n.* Small cavity.
-cular *adj.*

fol-low *v.* To come after; pursue. **-ing** *adj.*,
-er *n.*

fol-ly *n.* An instance of foolishness.

fo-ment *v.* To rouse; incite. **-ation** *n.*

fond *adj.* Cherish with affection. **-ly** *adv.*

fon-dle *v.* To caress affectionately. **-er** *n.*

font *n.* A fountain for holy water.

food *n.* A substance used to sustain life and growth.

fool *n.* A person lacking

sense. **-ish** *adv.*

foot *n.* The lower part of leg; 12 inches.

foot-bridge *n.* The bridge for pedestrians.

foot-hill *n.* A low hill at the base of a mountain.

foot-ing *n.* A stable position.

foot-loose *adj.* Having no ties.

foot-note *n.* The note of reference at bottom of page.

foot-work *n.* A use of the feet.

for *prep.* On behalf of someone; in favor of.

for-age *n.* Food for cattle; seek food.

for-bid *v.* To prohibit by law.
   -den *adj.*, **-ingly** *adv.*

force *n.* Energy; power; strength. **-ful** *adj.*,
   -er *n.*

for-ceps *n.* forceps *pl.* The tongs used in surgery.

ford *n.* A shallow place in water. **-able** *adj.*

fore *adj. & adv.* Toward the front; golfer's warning.

fore-bode *v.* Warning in advance. **-ing** *n.*

fore-cast *v.* To predict in advance. **-er** *n.*

fore-close *v.* To recall a mortgage in default.
   -sure *n.*

fore-fa-ther *n.* An ances-

tor.

fore-go *v.* To go before.

fore-go-ing *adj.* Previous.

fore-gone *adj.* To be finished or gone.

fore-ground *n.* The part of picture nearest viewer.

fore-hand *n.* A stroke in tennis. **-ed** *adj.*,
   -edness *n.*

fore-head *n.* A part of the face.

for-eign *adj.* Outside one's country. **-er** *n.*

fore-man *n.* An overseer.

fore-most *adj. & adv.* The first in rank or order.

fore-noon *n.* Between sunrise and noon.

fore-see *v.* To see beforehand. **-er** *n.*

fore-shad-ow *v.* To warn beforehand. **-er** *n.*

fore-sight *n.* Looking forward. **-edness** *n.*,
   -ed *adj.*

for-est *n.* The land covered with trees.
   -er *n.*

fore-stall *v.* To prevent by prior measures.

for-est ran-ger *n.* An officer protecting a public forest.

fore-tell *v.* To predict.
   -er *n.*

for-ev-er *adv.* Without end.

fore-warn *v.* To warn in advance.

fore-word *n.* An introductory statement.

for-feit *n.* Something taken away. **-ture** *n.*

forge *n.* Furnace to heat metals. **-able** *adj.,* **-er** *n.*

for-get *v.* To lose the memory of. **-fully** *adv.,* **-er** *n.,* **-ful** *adj.*

for-give *v.* To excuse; pardon. **-able** *adj.,* **-ness** *n.*

for-go *v.* To give up. **-er** *n.*

fork *n.* The utensil used for eating. **-ed** *adj.*

for-lorn *adj.* Abandoned; hopeless. **-ness** *n.,* **-ly** *adv.*

form *n.* A shape; contour.

for-mal *adj.* Based on conventions. **-ly** *adv.,* **-ism** *n.*

for-mat *n.* A general layout of a publication.

for-ma-tion *n.* A given arrangement.

for-ma-tive *adj.* Being developed.

for-mer *adj.* Previous. **-ly** *adv.*

for-mi-da-ble *adj.* Extremely strong. **-bly** *adv.,* **-ness** *n.*

for-mu-la *n.* Set of rules; infant's food.

for-mu-late *v.* To express in formula. **-tion** *n.*

for-ni-ca-tion *n.* The sexual intercourse be-

tween unmarried people.

for-sake *v.* To abandon; give up. **-enly** *adv.,* **-en** *adj.*

for-swear *v.* To renounce. **-er** *n.*

fort *n.* A fortified structure.

forte *n.* An activity one excels in.

forth *adv.* Forward in order.

forth-right *adj.* Direct; frank. **-ness** *n.*

for-ti-fy *v.* To strengthen. **-ier** *n.*

for-ti-tude *n.* The strength of mind.

fort-night *n.* Every two weeks.

for-tress *n.* A fort.

for-tu-i-tous *adj.* To be by chance. **-tuity** *n.,* **-ly** *adv.*

for-tu-nate *adj.* Having good fortune. **-ly** *adv.*

for-tune *n.* A large amount of money.

for-ty *n., pl.* **-ies** The cardinal number equal to four times ten.

fo-rum *n.* A judicial assembly.

for-ward *adj.* Toward a place.

fos-sil *n.* The remains of an animal.

fos-ter *v.* To give parental care to.

foul *adj.* To be spoiled; offensive.

found *v.* To establish; set

up.

foun-da-tion n. A base of building; make up base.

found-ling n. An abandoned infant.

fount n. A fountain.

foun-tain n. A natural spring of water.

four n. The cardinal number that equals 3 + 1.

four-score adj. A four times twenty.

four-teen n. The cardinal number that equals 13 + 1.

fowl n. A bird used as food or hunted as game.

fox n. A wild animal.

fox-hound n. A large hunting dog.

fox--trot n. A ballroom dance.

fox-y adj. To be sly or crafty.

foy-er n. The lobby entrance.

fra-cas n. A noisy quarrel.

frac-tion n. A small part of; quantity less than a whole number.

frac-ture n. A broken bone.

frag-ile adj. To be easy to break; frail.

frag-ment n. A detached part. **-arily** adv.

fra-grant adj. Having a sweet odor.

frail adj. Delicate; weak.

frame v. To enclosed border for a picture.

fran-chise n. The license to market a company's goods.

frank adj. To be sincere and straightforward. **-ness** n.

frank-furt-er n. A smoked sausage; hot dog.

frank-in-cense n. An aromatic gum resin.

fran-tic adj. Lose emotional control. **-ly** adv.

fra-ter-nal adj. Pertaining to brothers. **-nity** n.

fraud n. A deception for unlawful gain. **-ulently** adv.

fray n. A brawl, or fight.

freak n. A capricious event.

freck-le n. A dark, sun-induced spots. **-kly** adj.

free adj. Under no obligation; to be without charge. **-dom** n.

free lance n. Services without commitments to any one employer.

free trade n. A trade between nations which is unrestricted.

free-way n. A tollfree highway.

freeze v. To become solid ice. **-ing** n.

freez-er n. An insulated box for storing food.

freight n. A mode of shipping cargo.

freight-er *n.* A cargo ship.

French fries *pl., n.* Strips of potatoes fried in deep fat.

fren-zy *n.* A state of extreme excitement.

fre-quent *adj.* To be happening often. **-ly** *adv.*

fres-co *n.* The art of painting on moist plaster.

fresh *adj.* Newly made; not stale. **-ness** *n.*

fric-tion *n.* A conflict or clash.

friend *n.* A close companion. **-ship** *n.*

frig-ate *n.* A square-rigged warship.

fright *n.* A feeling of alarm.

fright-en *v.* To scare; terrify.

frig-id *adj.* Very cold.

frill *n.* decorative ruffle.

fringe *n.* & *v.* Ornate edging.

frisk *v.* To skip about; search for weapons. **-iness** *n.*

frit-ter *v.* To squander or waste.

friv-o-lous *adj.* Trivial; silly. **-ness** *n.*

frock *n.* A loose-fitting dress.

frog *n.* An aquatic, leaping amphibian.

frol-ic *n.* Playful, carefree. **-some** *adj.*

from *prep.* Starting at a particular place.

front *n.* A forward surface of an object.

fron-tier *n.* An unexplored area.

frost *n.* The ice crystals on a cold surface.

frost-bite *n.* An injury due to exposure to cold.

frost-ing *n.* The icing for a cake.

froth *n.* A mass of bubbles; foam.

frown *v.* To contract the eyebrow in displeasure.

fro-zen *adj.* Covered with or made into ice.

fru-gal *adj.* Thrifty; economical. **-ness** *n.*

fruit *n.* Edible berries, apples, etc.

frus-trate *v.* To keep from attaining a goal; thwart. **-tion** *n.*

fry *v.* To cook in hot fat.

fuch-sia *n.* A tropical plant.

fudge *n.* A soft cooked chocolate candy.

fuel *n.* A combustible matter used to produce energy or heat.

fu-gi-tive *adj.* Fleeing from arrest.

fugue *n., Mus.* A musical composition.

ful-fill *v.* To carry out; to satisfy. **-ment** *n.*

full *n.* The largest amount.

fum-ble *v.* To mishandle.

fume *n., often* **fumes** An irritating smoke or gas; show anger.

fu-mi-gate *v.* To exterminate vermin or insects.

func-tion *n.* An occupation; duty.

fund *n.* A source of money and supplies.

fun-da-men-tal *adj.* Basic or essential. **-ly** *adv.*

fu-ner-al *n.* A services for a dead person.

fun-gus *n., pl.* **-gi** *or* **-guses** The spore-bearing plants. **-gal** *adj.*

fun-nel *n.* A hollow cone utensil for pouring liquid.

fur-bish *v.* To make bright by rubbing; renovate.

fu-ri-ous *adj.* Angry; fit of rage.

furl *v.* To roll up and secure something.

fur-lough *n.* The permission to be absent from duty.

fur-nish *v.* To equip or outfit.

fur-ni-ture *n.* The beds, lamps, sofas, chairs, etc.

fu-ror *n.* A violent anger; rage.

fur-row *n.* A long, narrow trench in the ground.

fur-tive *adj.* Obtained underhandedly; stolen; done in secret.

fu-ry *n., pl.* **-ies** An uncontrolled anger; turbulence; an angry or spiteful person.

fuse *n.* The electrical safety device; device to detonate explosives.

fu-sil-lage *n.* The central section of an airplane that contains the wings and tail.

fu-sil-lade *n.* A quick discharge of firearms.

fu-sion *n.* A blended together by heat.

fus-tian *n.* A sturdy stout cotton cloth.

fu-tile *adj.* Being of no avail.

fu-ture *n.* The time yet to come.

fuzz *n.* A mass of loose fibers.

G

G, g The seventh letter of the English alphabet.

gab *v., Slang* To talk or chat idly. **-ber** *n.*

gab-ar-dine *n.* A type of material.

gab-ble *v.* To speak incoherently. **-bler** *n.*

gad *v.* To wander about restlessly. **-der** *n.*

gad-a-bout *n., Slang* One who seeks excitement.

gad-fly *n.* A fly which is large in size.

gadg-et *n., Slang* A tool used for various jobs.

gaff *n.* A hook used for large fish.

gaffe *n.* A mistake.

gag *n.* A cloth covering the mouth; joke.

gai-e-ty *n.* Being happy; fun.

gain *v.* Acquired possession; put on weight. **-er** *n.*

gain-say *v.* To deny; contradict.

gait *n.* A manner of moving on foot. **-ed** *adj.*

gal *n., Slang* A girl.

ga-la *n.* A festive celebration.

gal-ax-y *n., pl.* **-ies** *Astron.* The large systems of stars.

gale *n., Meteor.* A powerful wind.

gall *n.* A sore due to rubbing.

gal-lant *adj.* Attentive to women.

gal-le-on *n.* Sailing ship.

gal-ler-y *n.* Exhibit hall.

gal-li-vant *v.* To roam about.

gal-lon *n.* Liquid measurement equal to four quarts.

gal-lop *n.* Horse's gait.

gal-lows *n.* Framework used for executions.

gall-stone *n.* A hard mass in the gall bladder which should not be there.

ga-losh *n.* The waterproof overshoes.

gam-ble *v.* To take a chance. **-bling** *n.*

gam-bol *v.* To be leaping around.

game *n.* A contest; hunt for animals for sport or food. **-ness** *n.*

gam-in *n.* A homeless child.

gam-ut *n.* A whole range of anything.

gan-der *n.* Male goose.

gang *n.* A group of people.

gang-ster *n.* A member of a criminal gang.

gan-net *n.* Sea bird.

gap *n.* Wide crack.

gape *v.* To open the mouth wide.

gar *n.* Elongated fish.

ga-rage *n.* A building for parking or repairing cars.

garb *n.* Clothing.

gar-bage *n.* Trash.

gar-ble *v.* To mix up or confuse.

gar-gan-tu-an *adj.* Of enormous size.

gar-goyle *n.* A waterspout.

gar-ish *adj.* Gaudy.

gar-land *n.* A wreath of flowers.

gar-lic *n.* A strong smelling plant.

gar-ment *n.* An article of clothing.

gar-nish *v.* To decorate.

gar-ret *n.* A room in an attic.

gar-ri-son *n.* A military post.

gar-ter *n.* A band to hold a stocking in place.

gas *n., pl.* **-es** A combustible mix. **-eous** *adj.*

gash *n.* Long deep cut.

gas-o-line *n.* The automobile fuel.

gasp *v.* Labored breathing.

gas-tron-o-my *n.* The art of good eating.

gate *n.* A movable opening in a wall.

gath-er *v.* To bring or come together. **-ing** *n.*

gauche *adj.* Socially awkward.

gaud-y *adj.* Not in good taste. **-ness** *n.*

gauge *n.* An instrument used for measuring.

gaunt *adj.* Thin in appearance. **-ness** *n.*

gaunt-let *n.* Long glove.

gav-el *n.* Mallet to call for order.

gawk *v.* To gape; to stare stupidly.

gay *adj.* Merry.

ga-zelle *n.* Graceful antelope.

ga-zette *n.* Newspaper.

Gei-ger coun-ter *n.* An instrument to measure radiation.

gei-sha *n.* Japanese dancing girl.

geld *v.* To castrate or spay.

gel-id *adj.* Cold; frigid.

gem *n.* A precious stone.

gen-darme *n.* French policeman.

gene *n., Biol.* A hereditary characteristics.

gen-er-al *adj.* Affecting the whole group.

gen-er-al prac-ti-tion-er *n.* A doctor who treats all medical problems.

gen-er-ate *v.* To bring into existence.

gen-er-a-tion *n.* An individuals born in the same era.

ge-ner-ic *adj.* Characteristic of a whole group. **-ally** *adv.*

gen-er-ous *adj.* Sharing freely. **-osity** *n.*

ge-net-ic *adj.* The origin of something.

gen-ial *adj.* Kind; cheerful. **-ness** *n.*

ge-nie *n.* A supernatural creature.

gen-i-tals *pl., n.* An external sexual organs.

gen-ius *n.* An exceptional intellectual ability.

gen-teel *adj.* Well-bred; polite. **-ness** *n.*

Gen-tile *n.* Non-Jewish person. **-ness** *n.*

gen-tle-man *n.* Man of noble birth.

gen-tle-wom-an *n.* Woman of noble birth.

gen-u-flect *v.* To bend down on one knee. **-tion** *n.*

gen-u-ine *adj.* Real; authentic. **-ness** *n.*

ge-nus *n.* Group of animals.

ge-o-cen-tric *adj.* Referring to the earth's center. **-cally** *adj.*

ge-o-chem-is-try *n.* Study of chemical changes with the crust of the earth. **-ist** *n.*, **-ical** *adj.*

ge-ode *n.* A stone with crystals in the middle of the stone.

ge-og-ra-phy *n., pl. -hies* A science of earth's natural population. **-ical, -ic** *adj.*, **-pher** *n.*

ge-ol-o-gy *n., pl. -ies* A science of the earth. **-ist** *n.* **-ic, -ical** *adj.*

ge-om-e-try *n.* Mathematics. **-tric** *adj.*

ge-o-ther-mal *adj.* Dealing with the earth's internal heat.

ger-bil *n.* An animal in rodent family.

ger-i-at-rics *n.* Dealing with old age diseases; branch of medicine. **-cian, -rist** *n.*

germ *n.* A microscopic organism.

ger-mane *adj.* Considered or discussed.

Ger-man mea-sles *n.* A type of virus.

Ger-man shep-herd *n.* A large black dog used by the police.

ger-mi-cide *n.* An agent to destroy germs. **-al** *adj.*

ger-mi-nate *v.* To grow; to develop. **-tion** *n.*

ger-on-tol-o-gy *n.* A study of growing older. **-gist** *n.*

ger-und *n., Gram.* Verb form.

ges-tic-u-late *v.* To make expressive gestures. **-tor, -tion** *n.*, **-tory, -tive** *adj.*

get *v.* To come into possession of.

get--to-geth-er *n.* A small gathering.

gey-ser *n.* A natural hot spring.

ghast-ly *adj.* Terrifying. **-iness** *n.*

gher-kin *n.* A small pickle.

ghost *n.* An appearance of a spirit. **-ly** *adj.*, **-liness** *n.*

ghost-writ-er *n.* A person who writes for another.

gi-ant *n.* A supernaturally large.

gib-bon *n.* A long-armed Asian ape.

gibe *v.* To ridicule. **-ingly** *adv.*, **-er** *n.*

gid-dy *adj.* The sensation of whirling. **-iness** *n.*, **-ily** *adv.*

gift-ed *adj.* Talented.

gi-gan-tic *adj.* Huge.

gig-gle *v.* To laugh.

-gly *adv.*, -er *n.*

gig-o-lo *n.* A man kept by a woman.

gild *v.* To coat with layer of gold.

gim-mick *n.* A trick.

gin *n.* An alcoholic liquor.

gin-ger *n.* A tropical plant.

gin-ger ale *n.* A soft drink.

gin rum-my *n.* A card game.

gi-raffe *n.* A long-necked mammal.

gird *v.* To encircle; to get ready for action.

gir-dle *n.* A woman's undergarment.

girl *n.* A female child.
-ish *adj.*, -hood *n.*

gist *n.* A main substance.

give *v.* To make a present of; to bestow.
-er *n.*

gla-cier *n.* A large mass of ice.

glad-den *v.* To make happy.

glam-our *n.* A charm.
-rous *adj.*, -ousness *n.*

glance *v.* Quick look.

gland *n., Anat.* A body organ.

glare *v.* To stare angrily.
-iness *n.*, -y *adj.*

glass *n.* A transparent material for windows.

glau-co-ma *n., Pathol.* A disease of the eye.

glaze *n.* A smooth finish on ceramic.

gleam *n.* A beam of light.

glean *v.* To collect bit by bit.

glee *n.* Merriment.
-fully *adv.*, -ful *adj.*

glen *n.* A secluded valley.

glib *adj.* Spoken easily.
-ness *n.*, -ly *adv.*

glide *v.* To move with little effort.

glid-er *n.* A swing in a metal frame.

glimpse *n.* Momentary look.

glitch *n.* Minor mishap.

glob-al *adj.* Involving the whole world. -ly *adv.*

globe *n.* A spherical object.

globe--trot-ter *n.* A world traveler. -ing *adj.*

gloom *n.* A partial darkness. -iness *n.*, -y *adj.*

glory *n., pl.* -ies A praise or honor.
-rious *n.*, -rify *v.*

glos-sa-ry *n.* A list of words and meaning.

glow *v.* Having a warm, ruddy color.
-ing *adj.*, -er *n.*

glue *n.* The adhesives for bonding items.

glum *adj.* Being moody.
-mest, -mer *adj.*

glut *v.* To overeat.

gnash *v.* To grind the teeth.

gnat *n.* Small insect.

gnaw *v.* To eat away. **-ingly** *adv.*

gnu *n.* A South African antelope.

go *v.* To proceed; to pass, as time.

goal *n.* A purpose; aim.

goat *n.* A cud-chewing mammal. **-like, -ish** *adj.*

gob *n.* A lump of something; a sailor.

gob-ble *v.* To eat food greedily.

gob-let *n.* A stemmed drinking glass.

God *n.* The Supreme Being.

go--get-ter *n.* An aggressive person.

gog-gle *n.* Protective glasses.

gold *n.* A soft, yellow metal.

gon-do-la *n.* A flat-bottomed boat.

gon-er *n., Slang* Close to death; beyond help.

gong *n.* A heavy metal disk.

gon-or-rhe-a *n.* Type of venereal disease.

good *adj.* Desirable; favorable.

good--for--noth-ing *n.* A person of little worth.

goof-y *adj.* Silly.

go-pher *n.* A burrowing rodent.

gore *v.* To stab or to pierce something.

gorge *n.* A ravine; a deep hole.

gor-geous *adj.* To be dazzling.

go-ril-la *n.* A large jungle ape.

go-ry *adj.* To be covered with blood.

gos-ling *n.* A young goose.

gos-pel *n.* The teachings of Christ.

gos-sa-mer *n.* The fine strands of a spider's web.

gos-sip *n.* An idle, malicious talk.

gouge *n.* A chisel with a blade.

gou-lash *n.* A stew.

gour-met *n.* One who knows good food and drink.

gov-ern *v.* To rule or to control. **-able** *adj.*

gov-ern-ment *n.* An administration of affairs of a nation.

gov-er-nor *n.* A chief executive of any state.

gown *n.* A woman's formal dress.

grab *v.* To snatch or take something.

grace *n.* A charm of movement. **-fully** *adv.*

gra-cious *adj.* To be full of compassion.

grade *v.* To level or slope ground; arrange by steps.

gra-da-tion *n.* An advance by regular degrees.

grad-u-al *adj.* To be changing slowly.

grad-u-ate *v.* To complete a course of study.

graf-fi-to *n.* The drawings on a wall.

graft *v.* To transplant skin to another area of the body.

grail *n.* A cup used by Christ at the Last Supper.

grain *n.* A kernal of wheat, etc.

gram *n.* A metric weight.

gram-mar *n.* The study of words and language. **-matical** *adj.*

gran-a-ry *n.* A building for storing grain.

grand *adj.* To be large in size or extent.

grand-child *n.* The child of one's son or daughter.

gran-di-ose *adj.* To be impressive; grand.

grand mal *n., Pathol.* A form of epilepsy.

grand-par-ent *n.* A parent of one's mother or father.

grand-stand *n.* A raised seat.

gran-ite *n.* A coarse grained hard rock.

gra-no-la *n.* Rolled oats.

grant *v.* To allow; to consent to.

gran-u-late *v.* To form into crystals.

grape *n.* Type of juicy, edible berries.

grape-fruit *n.* A large citrus fruit.

graph *n.* A diagram showing figures.

graph-ic *adj.* Full detail. **-cal** *adj.*

graph-ite *n.* A form of black carbon.

grap-ple *n.* An instrument with iron claws.

grasp *v.* To seize and to grip firmly.

grass *n.* The green plants for a lawn.

grate *v.* To shred on a rough surface.

grate-ful *adj.* To be appreciative.

grat-i-fy *v.* To give pleasure to. **-fication** *n.*

grat-is *adv. & adj.* Free.

gra-tu-i-ty *n.* A gift given for a service.

grave *n.* A burial place; serious. **-ly** *adj.*

grav-el *n.* Loose rock.

grav-i-tate *v.* To be drawn by an irresistible force. **-tation** *n.*

gra-vy *n.* The juices exuded by cooking meat.

graze *v.* To feed on growing grasses.

grease *n.* A melted animal fat. **-y** *adj.*, **-iness** *n.*

greed-y *adj.* Excessively eager to gain something. **-iness** *n.*, **-ily** *adv.*

green--eyed *adj.* To be jealous.

green-house *n.* A structure for growing plants.

green thumb *n.* A skill for making plants thrive.

greet *v.* To welcome. **-er, -ing** *n.*

gre-gar-i-ous *adj.* Associating with others; sociable. **-ness** *n.*, **-ly** *adv.*

grem-lin *n.* A mischie ous elf.

gre-nade *n.* A small explosive device.

grey-hound *n.* A breed of swift-running dogs.

grid *n.* A system of parallel lines for charts, etc.

grid-dle *n.* A flat pan for cooking.

grid-i-ron *n.* A football field.

grief *n.* A deep sadness.

griev-ance *n.* A complaint of unfair treatment.

grim *adj.* Forbidding appearance; dismal. **-ness** *n.*, **-ly** *adv.*

grime *n.* The dirt coating a surface. **-y** *adj.*

grin *v.* To smile broadly. **-ner** *n.*

grind *v.* To sharpen; to rub together. **-er** *n.*

grip *n.* Firm hold; grasp.

gripe *v.* To complain. **-er** *n.*

gris-tle *n.* The cartilage of meat.

grits *pl.*, *n.* Coarsely ground hominy.

groan *v.* To sound of disapproval or pain.

-er *n.*

go-cer-y *n., pl.* **-ies** The store which sells foodstuffs.

grog-gy *adj.* To be dazed; not fully conscious. **-iness** *n.*, **-ily** *adv.*

groom *n.* A person who tends horses; man about to marry.

groove *n.* A long, narrow channel. **-er** *n.*

grope *v.* To feel about blindly.

gross *adj.* Excessively large; lack of refinement. **-ness** *n.*, **-ly** *adv.*

gro-tesque *adj.* Bizarre.

grouch *n.* An irritable person. **-iness** *n.*

ground hog *n.* A woodchuck.

ground-work *n.* A foundation; base.

ground ze-ro *n.* The point of detonation of atomic bomb.

group *n.* A collection of people.

grou-per *n.* A large fish.

group-ie *n., Slang* A follower of a rock group.

grov-el *v.* To act with humility.

grow *v.* To increase in size.

grub *v.* To dig up by the roots.

grudge *n.* The feeling of ill will.

grue-some *adj.* To be

causing horror.

gruff *adj.* To be rough in manner.

grump-y *adj.* Moody.

grunt *n.* The guttural sound of a hog. **-er** *n.*

guar-an-tee *n.* An assurance of the durability of products; vouch for.

guard *v.* To shield from danger.

guard-i-an *n.* One legally assigned the care of the person. **-ship** *n.*

guer-ril-la *n.* Member of an irregular military force.

guess *v.* To form an opinion on incomplete knowledge. **-ing** *n.*

guid-ed mis-sile *n.* An unmanned missile controlled by radio signals.

guilt *n.* Feeling ashamed.

guin-ea pig *n.* A domesticated rodent.

guise *n.* An outward appearance.

gui-tar *n.* A musical instrument.

gulf *n.* A large area of ocean or sea.

gull *n.* A web-footed sea bird.

gul-li-ble *adj.* To be easily cheated.

gulp *v.* To swallow rapidly in large amounts.

gum *n.* A sticky substance; tissue around the teeth.

gum-bo *n.* A thick soup.

gun *n.* Portable firearm.

gun pow-der *n.* An explosive powder.

gup-py *n.* Tropical fish.

gush *v.* To flow with sudden force.

gust *n.* A sudden violent rush of wind.

gus-to *n.* A hearty enjoyment.

gut-ter *n.* A channel for carrying off surface water.

guy *n., Slang* A man.

guz-zle *v.* To drink greedily.

gym-na-si-um *n.* A building equipped for indoor sports.

gy-ne-col-o-gy *n.* The study of female reproduction organs. **-ist** *n.*

gyp-sum *n.* A plasterboard.

gy-rate *v.* To rotate around a fixed point.

gy-ro-scope *n.* A spinning wheel.

H

H, h The eighth letter of the English alphabet.

ha-be-as cor-pus *n.* An order to produce prisoner in court.

hab-er-dash-er *n.* A person dealing in mens clothing. **-y** *n.*

ha-bil-i-ment *n.* Characteristic clothing of rank.

hab-it *n.* A pattern of behavior.

hab-i-ta-tion *n.* The place of residence.

hab-it--form-ing *adj.* To be producing physiological addiction

ha-bit-u-al *adj.* To be acting according to habit. **-ly** *adv.*, **-ness** *n.*

ha-bit-u-ate *v.* To familiarize. **-tion** *n.*

hack *v.* Irregular blows; to cough.

hack-le *n.* The hair on the back of a dog.

hack-saw *n.* A saw in a narrow frame for cutting metal.

had *v.* Past tense of have.

had-n't *cont.* Had not.

haft *n.* The handle of a weapon.

hag-gle *v.* To bargain on prices. **-er** *n.*

hag-i-og-ra-phy *n.* A biography of saints.

hail *n.* A precipitation of small ice. **-er** *n.*

hair *n.* A pigmented filaments that grow from the skin of most mammals. **-y** *adj.*, **-iness** *n.*

hair-brush *n.* A brush for grooming the hair.

hair-cloth *n.* A wiry, stiff fabric of horsehair.

hair-dress-er *n.* One who works on hair.

hair--raising *adj.* To be causing fear or horror.

hair-spring *n.* A fine, coiled spring.

hake *n.* A marine fish related to the cod.

hal-berd *n.* A type of medieval weapon.

hal-cy-on *adj.* To be calm and tranquil.

hale *adj.* Healthy.

half *n.* Two equal parts.

half-back *n.* The position played in the game of football.

half--wit *n.* Mentally disturbed person. **-ed** *adj.*

hall *n.* A passageway. **-way** *n.*

hal-i-but *n.* An edible flat fish.

hal-ite *n.* A large crystal of salt.

hal-i-to-sis *n.* Bad breath.

hall *n.* A large room for the holding of meetings.

hal-le-lu-jah *interj.* Used to express joy.

hall-mark *n.* An official mark on something genuine.

hal-low *v.* To sanctify. **-ed** *adj.*

hal-lu-ci-na-tion *n.* An illusion. **-tory** *adj.*

hal-lu-ci-no-gen *n.* A type of drug that causes hallucinations. **-ic** *adj.*

ha-lo *n.* An aura of glory.

hal-o-gen *n.* A nonmetallic element. **-ous** *adj.*

halt *v.* To stop. **-ingly** *adv.*, **-ing** *adj.*

hal-ter *n.* A strap for leading an animal.

halve *v.* To divide into two equal parts.

hal-yard *n.* A type of rope used to lift sails.

ham *n.* The meat of a hog's thigh. **-my** *adj.*

ham-burg-er *n.* Ground beef.

ham-let *n.* A little town or group of houses.

ham-mer *n.* The tool used to strike forcefully.

ham-mer-head *n.* A large shark of warm water.

ham-mock *n.* A type of hanging bed.

ham-per *v.* To interfere or to bother with.

ham-ster *n.* A rodent with large cheek pouches.

ham-string *n.* The two tendons located at the back of the human knee.

hand *n.* The lower part of the arm. **-ful** *n.*, **-ed** *adj.*

hand-bag *n.* A type of woman's purse.

hand-ball *n.* A type of court game.

hand-bill *n.* A hand-distributed advertisement for something.

hand-book *n.* A small reference book.

hand-cuff *v.* To put on handcuffs.

hand-ful *adj.* The most a hand will hold or contain.

hand-gun *n.* A gun that can be held and fired with one hand.

hand-i-cap *n.* A type of physical disability. **-ped** *n.*, **-per** *n.*

hand-i-craft *n.* A skill done with the hands.

hand-ker-chief *n.* A cloth for wiping the nose.

han-dle *v.* To touch, pick up, or hold. **-er** *n.*, **-ing** *v.*

han-dle-bar *n.* The curved bar of a bicycle that is used to guide it.

hand-made *adj.* To be made by the hands or a hand process.

hand-maid-en *n.* A girl who is a servant to someone.

hand--me--down *n.* A used article that is passed from one person to another.

hand-out *n.* Food or other item that is given freely to someone.

hand--pick *v.* To select for a purpose. **-ed** *adj.*

hand-rail *n.* A rail that is used as support.

hand-shake *n.* The grasping of hands between to people.

hand-some *adj.* To be very good-looking. **-ness** *n.*, **-ly** *adv.*

hand-spring *n.* An acrobatic feat.

hand--to--hand *adj.* In close touch or at close

range.

hand-stand *n.* Standing on the hands with feet in the air.

hand-work *n.* The work done by the hands.

hand-writ-ing *n.* A cursive writing.

hand-y *adj.* To be helpful or useful.

hang *v.* Suspended.
-**able** *adj.*

hang-ar *n.* An aircraft building.

han-ger *n.* A device from which something may be hung.

hang-nail *n.* The loose skin from the root of a fingernail.

hand-up *n.* An emotional problem.

hank *n.* A piece of hair, thread or yarn.

han-ker *v.* Craving something. **-ing, -er** *n.*

han-som *n.* A two-wheeled vehicle that is pulled by a horse.

Ha-nuk-kah *n.* An eight-day Jewish holiday.

hap-haz-ard *adj.* To be occurring by accident.
-ly *adv.*, **-ness** *n.*

hap-less *adj.* unfortunate; unlucky.
-ly *adv.*

hap-pen *v.* To discover by chance.

hap-pen-ing *n.* A spontaneous performance.

hap-pen-stance *n.*

Something that occurs by chance.

hap-pi-ness *n.* A quality of being content.

hap-py *adj.* Contentment.
-ier *adj.*, **-iness** *n.*

hap-py--go--luck-y *adj.* To be not worried about what may happen.

ha-ra--ki-ri *n.* Japanese suicide ritual.

ha-rangue *n.* A lecture.
-ment *n.*, **-ed** *v.*

ha-rass *v.* To disturb or annoy. **-ment, -er** *n.*

har-bin-ger *n.* A sign of coming events.

har-bor *n.* An anchorage for ships. **-er** *n.*

hard *adj.* To be difficult; solid texture.
-ness *n.*

hard-back *adj.* A book bound with a firm back.

hard--bit-ten *adj.* Tough by hard experiences.

hard--boiled *adj.* To be cooked in a shell to a hard state.

hard--core *adj* To be very tough in nature; unyielding.

hard copy *n.* The printed data from a computer.

hard-en *v.* To become physically or mentally tough.

hard-head-ed *adj.* A stubborn character.

hard-heart-ed *adj.* To be unfeeling.

har-di-hood n. Daring.

hard-ly adj. Very little.

hard-nosed adj. State of being stubborn.

hard palate n. A bony palate of the mouth roof.

hard-pan n. A hard clay-like subsoil.

hard-ship n. A type of difficult condition.

hard-ware n. The metal household utensils.

har-dy adj. To be bold and robust. **-ily** adv.

hare n. Type of mammal related to rabbits.

hare-brained adj. To be foolish or silly.

har-em n. A residence of sultan's wives.

hark v. To listen closely.

har-le-quin n. A pantomime comic character.

har-lot n. A prostitute. **-ry** n.

harm n. Physical damage or injury. **-ful** adj., **-ness** n.

harm-less adj. To be without harm. **-ly** adv., **-ness** n.

har-mon-ic adj. To be concordant. **-ly** adv.

har-mon-i-ca n. A small rectangular musical instrument. **-cally** adv.

har-mo-ni-ous adj. To be pleasing to the ear. **-ly** adv.

har-mo-ny n. In tune. **-ize** v., **-ious** adj.

har-ness n. The gear that is used to guide a horse.

harp n. A type of string instrument. **-ist** n., **-er** n.

har-poon n. A large spear used to kill large whales and animals.

har-py n. A type of greedy person.

har-ri-dan n. A vicious woman.

har-row n. A tool for breaking up soil.

har-row-ing adj. To cause emotional or mental distress.

har-ry v. To harass.

harsh adj. To be disagreeable. **-ness** n., **-ly** adv.

hart n. A type of fully grown male deer.

har-um--scar-um adj. State of being dangerous or reckless.

har-vest n. Act of gathering a crop. **-er** n.

has--been n. A person who has passed the time of greatest achievement.

hash n. A meat that has been cooked with vegetables.

hasp n. A hinged fastener.

has-sle n. A quarrel or an argument.

has-sock n. A cushioned foot-stool.

haste n. Speed; quickness.

has-ten v. To move with

speed.

hast-y *adj.* To be swift; to be rapid. **-ily, adv.,** *-iness n.*

hat *n.* The covering for the head.

hatch *v.* To bring forth, as an egg.

hatch-er-y *n.* The place or building for hatching eggs.

hatch-et *n.* Type of small ax.

hatch-way *n.* Opening in a ship's deck.

hate *v.* To dislike intensely. **-ful** *adj.,* **-er** *n.*

haugh-ty *adj.* To be or state of being arrogantly proud. **-tily** *adv.,* **-tiness** *n.*

haul *v.* To pull or draw with force.

haul-age *n.* A process or act of hauling.

haunch *n.* The hip.

haunt *v.* To visit frequently. **-ed** *adj.*

haunt-ing *adj.* To be hard to forget.

have *v.* To hold or own.

ha-ven *n.* A safe secure place.

hav-er-sack *n.* A bag for carrying supplies.

hav-oc *n.* A mass confusion.

hawk *n.* A predatory birds. **-ish** *adj.,* **-ness** *n.*

hawk *n.* A large bird of prey. **-sh** *adj.*

haw-ser *n.* A type heavy cable for towing.

hay *n.* An alfalfa.

hay fe-ver *n.* An acute allergy.

hay-fork *n.* A hand tool used to move hay.

hay-loft *n.* An upper loft in a barn.

hay-mow *n.* A large mound of stored hay.

hay-stack *n.* A type of hay stored outdoors.

hay-wire *adj.* To be emotionally out of control.

haz-ard *n.* A risk. **-ous** *adj.,* **-ously** *adv.,* **-ousness** *n.*

haze *n.* A mist.

ha-zel *n.* A tree with edible nuts; a reddish-brown color.

haz-y *adj.* To be lacking clarity; vague.

H-bomb *n.* hydrogen bomb.

head *n.* The upper part of the body. **-ing** *n.*

head-ache *n.* A pain centered in the head.

head-band *n.* A cloth worn around the head.

head-board *n.* A frame standing at the head of a bed.

head-dress *n.* An ornamental head covering usually worn during special ceremonies.

head-first *adv.* Having the head in a forward position.

head-gear *n.* A covering for the head.

head-ing *n.* A title that acts as a beginning.

head-land *n.* A cliff projecting into the water.

head-less *adj.* Having no head.

head-line *n.* A caption or summarizing words.

head-most *adj.* To be foremost.

head-mas-ter *n.* The school principal.

head-piece *n.* A covering for the head.

head-quar-ters *pl., n.* The center of operations.

head-set *n.* A pair of headphones.

head-stall *n.* A part of a bridle that goes over a horse's head.

head start *n.* An advance start.

head-stone *n.* A marker at the head of a grave.

head-strong *adj.* State of being obstinate.

head-waiter *n.* A type of person who supervises a restaurant.

head-wat-ers *n.* The source of a river.

head-y *adj.* State of being headstrong. **-iness** *n.*

heal *v.* To restore to good health. **-er** *n.*, **-able** *adj.*

health *n.* The physical well-being. **-ful** *adj.*

health-y *adj.* A state of good health. **-ily** *adv.*, **-iness** *n.*

heap *n.* A large quantity.

hear *v.* To perceive by the ear. **-er** *n.*

hear-ing *n.* The range by which sound can be heard.

hear-ing aid *n.* A device used to amplify sound.

heark-en *v.* To listen carefully.

hear-say *n.* A rumor.

hearse *n.* A type of vehicle for transporting the dead.

heart *n.* A blood pumping body organ.

heart-ache *n.* An emotional grief.

heart at-tack *n.* An acute malfunction of the heart which may result in death.

heart-beat *n.* The pulsation of the heart.

heart-break *n.* A great sorrow; deep grief. **-ing** *adv.*

heart-brok-en *adj.* To be grieved deeply.

heart-burn *n.* A burning sensation in the esophagus and stomach.

heart-felt *adj.* To be deeply felt.

hearth *n.* The floor of a fireplace.

heart-land *n.* An important central region.

heart-less *adj.* To have

or to show no sympathy.
-ness *n.*, **-ly** *adv.*

heart-rend-ing *adj.* To be causing great distress.

heart-sick *adj.* To be profoundly dejected.

heart-throb *n.* A type of tender emotion.

heart--to--heart *adj.* State of being sincere to someone or to something.

heart--warm-ing *adj.* A feeling of warm sympathy.

heart-wood *n.* No longer active center part of a tree.

heart-y *adj.* To be nourishing or good. **-iness** *n.*

heat *n.* A degree of warmth. **-ed** *adj.*

hea-then *n.* One without religion.

heat light-ning *n.* The electric flashes from the sky without thunder.

heat stroke *n.* A collapse or a person or animal caused by heat.

heave *v.* To lift forcibly.

heaves *n.* The lung disease of horses.

heav-en *n.* The paradise above earth. **-ly** *adj.*

heav-y *adj.* To be of great weight.

heavy--du-ty *adj.* To be designed for hard use.

heavy--heart-ed *adj.* To be sad; depressed.

heavy--set *adj.* State of having a stocky build.

He-brew *n.* The language of Israel.

heck-le *v.* To badger or annoy. **-ler** *n.*

hec-tic *adj.* To be intensely rushed.

he'd *conj.* He had; he would.

hedge *n.* The boundary of shrubs. **-r** *n.*

hedge-row *n.* A dense row of bushes.

he-don-ism *n.* An entire devotion to pleasure.

heed *v.* To pay attention.

heel *n.* The back part of the human foot.

heft-y *adj.* State of being bulky.

he-gem-o-ny *n.* The leadership or dominance.

he-gi-ra *n.* A journey to flee an undesirable situation.

heif-er *n.* A young cow.

height *n.* A degree of tallness.

height-en *v.* To increase height

hei-nous *adj.* To be extremely wicked. **-ness** *n.*

heir *n.* The inheritance of something.

heir-ess *n.* The female heir to something or to money that has been left by another.

heir-loom *n.* A family

possession that is handed down to each generation.

heist *v.* To steal; to take from.

hel-i-cop-ter *n.* An aircraft propelled by rotors.

hel-i-port *n.* An area for helicopters to land and take off.

he-li-um *n.* A light non-flammable gas.

hell *n.* An abode of damned souls. **-ish** *adj.*

he'll *contr.* He will.

helm *n.* A steering wheel for a ship. **-sman** *n.*

hel-met *n.* A protective covering for the head.

helms-man *n.* One who guides a ship.

help *v.* To assist or aid. **-ful** *adj.*

help-ing *n.* A single serving of food.

help-less *adj.* To be lacking strength.

help-mate *n.* A partner.

hel-ter--skel-ter *adv.* Confused manner.

helve *n.* The handle of an axe.

hem *n.* The finished edge of fabric. **-ming** *v.*

he--man *n.* A man marked by strength.

he-ma-tol-o-gy *n.* The science dealing with blood.

hem-i-sphere *n.* One half of earth.

hem-lock *n.* A type of evergreen tree.

he-mo-phil-i-a *n.* An inherited blood disease of spontaneous bleeding.

hem-or-rhage *n.* An excessive bleeding. **-d** *v.*

hem-or-rhoid *n.* The swollen anal tissue. **-al** *adj.*

he-mo-stat *n.* An agent that stops bleeding.

hemp *n.* An Asian herb. **-en** *adj.*

hem-stitch *n.* The ornamental sewing stitch.

hen *n.* The mature female bird.

hence-forth *adv.* From this time on.

hench-man *n.* A loyal and faithful follower. **-ship** *n.*

hen-peck *v.* Persistent nagging.

hep-a-rin *n.* The substance found in liver tissue prolonging the clotting of blood.

he-pat-ic *adj.* Of or like the liver.

hep-a-ti-tis *n.* An inflammation of the liver.

her-ald *n.* The news announcer.

her-ald-ry *n.* The art of tracing genealogies.

herb *n.* The plant used for seasoning.

her-ba-ceous *adj.* To be with herbs.

herb-age *n.* A grass

used especially for grazing.

her-bi-cide *n.* An agent used to kill weeds.

her-biv-o-rous *adj.* -To be feeding on plant life.

her-cu-le-an *adj.* To be of unusual size.

herd *n.* The number of cattle kept together. **-er** *n.*, **-sman** *n.*

here *n.* At the particular place or point.

here-af-ter *adv.* From now on.

he-red-i-tar-y *adj.* To be passing from an ancestor to a legal heir. **-ily** *adv.*, **-iness** *n.*

here-in *adv.* In or into this place.

here-of *n* The belief that conflicts with orthodox religious beliefs.

her-e-sy *n.* An opinion contrary to orthodox a opinion.

her-i-tage *n.* The property that is inherited.

her-maph-ro-dite *n.* The person having both male and female reproductive organs.

her-met-ic *adj.* To be tightly sealed.

her-mit *n.* One who lives in seclusion.

her-ni-a *n.* A rupture. **-tion** *n.*

he-ro *n.* One with exceptional courage. **-ism** *n.*

her-o-in *n.* An addictive narcotic.

her-o-ism *n.* A heroic behavior.

her-on *n.* A bird with a long slender bill, legs and neck.

her-pe-tol-o-gy *n.* The scientific study of reptiles.

her-ring *n.* A type of valuable food fish.

her-ring-bone *n.* A pattern of slanting parallel lines.

hes-i-tant *adj.* To be lacking certainty.

hes-i-tate *v.* To pause; to be doubtful.

hew *v.* To make or shape with.

hex *n.* One held to bring bad luck.

hex-a-gon *n.* Shape having six sides and six angles. **-al** *adj.*

hi-a-tus *n.* A lapse in time.

hi-ba-chi *n.* A portable grill used for cooking.

hi-ber-nate *v.* To sleep during winter. **-nation** *n.*

hi-bis-cus *n.* A plant with large flowers.

hic-cup *n.* A spasm in the throat.

hick-o-ry *n.* North American tree.

hi-dal-go *n.* Spanish nobleman.

hid-den *adj.* To be concealed. **-ness** *n.*

hide *v.* To keep out of

sight. **-er** *n.*

hi-er-o-glyph-ic *n.* A pictorial symbol representing.

high *adj.* To be extending upward.

high-ball *n.* An alcoholic drink.

high-bred *adj.* To be from superior breeding.

high-brow *n.* One claiming to have superior knowledge.

high-er--up *n.* A person with more authority.

high-fa-lu-tin *adj.* To be extravagant in manner.

high fi-del-i-ty *n.* The reproduction of sound.

high fre-quen-cy *n.* A band from three' to thirty magacycles.

high--hand-ed *adj.* State of being overbearing. **-ness** *n.*

high jump *n.* The jump in height in athletics.

high-light *v.* To give emphasis to.

high-ness *n.* A state of being high.

high--pres-sure *adj.* To be using persuasive methods.

high rise *n.* An extremely tall building.

high-road *n.* The main road.

high--spir-it-ed *adj.* To be energetic. **-ly** *adv.*, **-ness** *n.*

high--strung *adj.* To be very excitable.

high--test *adj.* To be relating to gass with a high octane number.

high-way *n.* The main and wide road.

hi-jack *v., Slang* To seize while in transit. **-er** *n.*

hike *v.* To take a lenghty walk.

hi-lar-i-ous *adj.* State of being cheerful; very funny. **-ly** *adv.*, **-ness** *n.*

hill *n.* An elevation of land.

hill-bil-ly *n.* A country person usually from the backcountry.

hill-ock *n.* A small mound.

hill-side *n.* The side or slope of a hill.

hill-top *n.* The highest point of a hill.

hilt *n.* The handle of a sword.

him *pron.* The objective case of the pronoun he.

hind *n.* The female deer after the third year.

hin-der *v.* To interfere; to obstruct.

hin-drance *n.* An act of state of being hindered.

hind-most *adj.* To be farthest in back or behind.

hind-sight *n.* The comprehension of something after it has happened.

hinge *n.* The device which allows a door to

open.

hint *n.* An indication or suggestion. **-er** *n.*

hip *n.* The projecting part thigh.

hip-bone *n.* Bone which forms a lateral half of the pelvis.

hip joint *n.* The joint between the hipbone and thighbone.

hip-po-pot-a-mus *n.* A large, aquatic mammal.

hire *v.* To service of another for pay.

his *adj.* The pronoun of he.

His-pan-ic *adj.* To be relating to the cultures of Spain.

hir-sute *adj.* To be covered with hair.

hiss *n.* The sound of the letter s made by forcing air pass the upper teeth. **-er** *n.*

his-ta-mine *n.* The substance in plant tissue.

his-tol-o-gy *n.* The study of tissues.

his-tor-i-cal *adj.* To be of the past.

his-to-ry *n.* The past events.

his-tri-on-ics *n.* The theatrical arts.

hit *v.* To strike with force.

hitch *v.* To fasten or tie. **-er** *n.*

hitch-hike *v.* To travel by obtaining rides from passing drivers. **-er** *n.*

hive *n.* The habitation for honeybees.

hith-er *adv.* To this place.

hives *pl., n.* The itchy welts on the body.

hoar *adj.* Having gray hair.

hoard *n.* Something stored for future use. **-er** *n.*, **-ing** *n.*

hoarse *adj.* To be of a gruff, voice. **-ness** *n.*, **-ly** *adv.*

hoar-y *adj.* To be old or ancient.

hob-ble *v.* To walk with a limp.

hob-by *n.* An activity for pleasure.

hob-by-horse *n.* The child's rocking horse.

ho-bo *n.* A tramp; vagrant.

hock *n.* The leg joint of an animal.

hock-ey *n.* A game played on ice.

hoe *n.* A tool for weeding.

hog *n.* A large pig.

hog-gish *adj.* To be selfish. **-ness** *n.*, **-ly** *adv.*

hogs-head *n.* A large barrel.

hog-wash *n.* Any nonsense.

hoist *v.* To haul or raise up. **-er** *n.*

hold *v.* To grasp.

hold-ing *n.* The personal property.

hold-up *n.* A robbery at gun point.

hole *n.* An opening in a solid mass.

hol-i-day *n.* The day of celebration.

ho-li-ness *n.* A state of being holy.

hol-ler *v.* To shout loudly.

hol-low *adj.* Having space within. **-ness** *n.*

hol-o-caust *n.* The total destruction.

hol-o-graph *n.* A hand-written document.

hol-ster *n.* The case designed to hold a pistol or gun.

ho-ly *adj.* To be charac-terized by power.

hom-age *n.* Great respect or honor.

home *n.* Someone's residence.

home-bod-y *n.* One who prefers to stay at home.

home-com-ing *n.* An act of returning to one's home.

home e-co-nom-ics *n.* The principles of home management.

home-ly *adj.* To have plain features. **-liness** *n.*

home-made *adj.* To be made at home and not purchased.

home plate *n.* An area where a batter stands.

home-sick *adj.* Yearning for home. **-ness** *n.*

home-word *n.* A work assigned by a teacher or instructor that is to be completed at home.

hom-i-cide *n.* A person killed by another. **-cidal** *adj.*

hom-i-ly *n.* A sermon.

hom-i-ny *n.* The kernels of hulled and dried corn.

ho-mo-ge-ne-ous *adj.* Of the same nature. **-ly** *adv.*, **-ness** *n.*

ho-mog-e-nize *v.* To process milk.

ho-mol-o-gous *adj.* To be related in structure or origin.

hom-o-nym *n.* A word that has the same sound as another but a different meaning.

hon-cho *n.* The main person in charge.

hon-est *adj.* Not lying, or cheating. **-ly** *adv.*

hon-ey *n.* A sweet, sticky substance made by bees.

hon-ey-bee *n.* Bees living in colonies and producing honey.

hon-ey-comb *n.* A struc-ture of was made by bees to store hone.

honey-moon *n.* A trip taken by newly-married couple. **-er** *n.*

honey-suck-le *n.* A vine with highly fragrant flowers.

honk *n.* The harsh sound made by a goose.

hon-or *n.* A high regard or respect.

honor-able *adj.* To be worthy of honor. **-ably** *adv.*

hon-or-if-ic *adj.* To be conveying honor.

hood *n.* A covering for the head.

-hood *suff.* Quality or state of.

hood-lum *n.* A young, destructive kid.

hoo-doo *n.* A jinx.

hood-wink *v.* To deceive. **-er** *n.*

hoof *n.* A covering of a mammals foot. **-ed** *adj.*, **-er** *n.*

hook-er *n.* A prostiitute.

hook-worm *n.* A parasitic intestinal worm.

hoop *n.* A circular band.

hoop-la *n.* A noise and excitement.

hop *v.* To take short leaps on one foot.

hope *v.* To wish for something.

hope-ful *adj.* To be full of hope. **-ly** *adv.*, **-ness** *n.*

horde *adj.* Referring to a large crowd.

ho-ri-zon *n.* The line which the earth and sky meet.

hor-i-son-tal *adj.* To be parallel to the horizon. **-ly** *adv.*

hor-mone *n.* An internal secretion.

horn *n.* A musical instrument.

hor-net *n.* Various wasps that inflict a sever sting.

hor-o-scope *n.* The zodiac signs.

hor-rid *adj.* To be horrible.

hor-ror *n.* An extreme fear.

hors d'oeu-vre *n.* The appatizer served before dinner.

horse *n.* A large hoofed mammal.

horse chest-nut *n.* Trees with chestnut-like fruit.

horse-fly *n.* A large fly that annoys horses and other animals.

horse-hide *n.* The leather made from a horse's hide.

horse-man *n.* A person who rides horseback.

horse sense *n.* Common sense.

horse-shoe *n.* The metal plate that is attached to the hoof of a horse to give protection.

horse-shoe crab *n.* A marine arthropod having a rounded body and stiff pointed tail.

hor-ti-cul-ture *n.* Tending to a garden.

hose *n.* A tube for carrying fluids.

ho-sier-y *n.* A stocking; socks.

hos-pice *n.* A lodging for travelers.

hos-pi-ta-ble *adj.* To be treating guests with generosity. **-bly** *adv.*

hos-pi-tal *n.* A place for medical care.

hos-pi-tal-i-ty *n.* Hospitable treatment.

host *n.* One who entertains guests.

hos-tage *n.* A person held as security kidnapping.

host-ess *n.* The woman who greets.

hos-tile *adj.* To be antagonistic.

hos-til-i-ty *n.* Very deep-seated hatred.

hot *adj.* Having excessive heat.

hot-el *n.* A place for lodging.

hot-house *n.* A heated greenhouse.

hot line *n.* A direct telephone line.

hot plate *n.* A portable electric plate for cooking.

hound *n.* Type of long-eared dogs.

hour *n.* 60 minutes.

hour-ly *adj.* Referring to every hour.

house *n.* A living quarters for families.

house-boat *n.* A boat containing comforts of home.

house-bro-ken *n.* The animals that have been trained to excret in a proper place.

house-hold *n.* The family members.

house-holder *n.* The owner of a house.

house-keeper *n.* A person paid to clean and care for anothers home. **-keeping** *n.*

how *adv.* In what manner or way.

how-dy *interj.* A greeting.

how-ev-er *adv.* To be in whatever manner.

how-it-zer *n.* A short cannon.

howl *v.* To utter a loud sound.

howl-er *n.* One that howls.

hua-ra-che *n.* A sandal.

hub *n.* The center of a wheel.

hub-bub *n.* An uproar.

hub-cap *n.* A removable covering for a wheel and axle.

hud-dle *n.* A group or crowd together.

hue *n.* A color; a shade.

huff *v.* To breathe heavily.

hug *v.* To embrace. **-ger** *n.*

huge *adj.* To be of great size, or extent. **-ly** *adv.,* **-ness** *n.*

hu-la *n.* The dance of Hawaii.

hulk *n.* A heavy, bulky ship.

hulk-ing *adj.* To be awkward.

hull *n.* An outer cover of fruit.

hum *v.* To sing with the lips closed.

hu-man *adj.* To be relating to mankind.

hu-mane *adj.* To be marked by compassion for others.

hu-man-i-ty *n.* A quality of being human.

hum-ble *adj.* To be unpretentious.

hum-bug *n.* A fraud.

hu-mid *adj.* State of being slightly wet or damp.

hu-mid *adj.* To be characterized by moisture.

hu-mil-i-ate *v.* To reduce one's dignity or pride.

hum-mock *n.* A rounded hill of snow or dirt.

hu-mor *n.* Something amusing.

hump *n.* A rounded lump.

hunch *n.* A strong intuitive feeling.

hun-dred *n.* The cardinal number equal to 10 X 10.

hun-ger *n.* The strong need for food.

hunk *n.* A large portion or piece of something.

hunk-y--do-ry *adj.,*

Slang To be very satisfactory; all right.

hunt *v.* To chase, search or hunt for food.

hunts-man *n.* A person who hunts.

hur-dle *n.* a barrier used to jump over in a race.

hurl *v.* To throw with great force.

hur-rah *interj.* To express approval.

hur-ri-cane *n.* A tropical storm with high winds.

hur-ri-cane lamp *n.* A lamp having a protective glass chimney that sheilds the fire from wind.

hur-ry *v.* To move with haste; to proceed or act in a hastily manner.

hurt *n.* A physical or emotional pain.

hur-tle *v.* To rush; to move rapidly.

hus-band *n.* A married man.

hush *v.* To make quiet; to silence; to still.

hush--hush *adj.* To be very confidential; secret.

hush-pup-py *n.* A cornmeal and onion mixture formed into a ball a deep fried.

hush *v.* To become quiet, calm.

husk-y *adj.* To be burly or robust.

hus-sy *n.* A brazen woman; mischievous girl.

hus-tle *v.* To move hurriedly along; *Slang* to obtain or sell by questionable means or tactics. **-r** *n.*

hut *n.* A shack; dwelling; cabin; or temporary housing.

hutch *n.* A compartment for storage.

hy-a-cinth *n.* A type of bulbous plant.

hy-brid *n.* Two animals of different species.

hy-drant *n.* A valve from which water is drawn.

hy-drau-lic *adj.* To be operated, by means of water. **-cal** *adj.*

hy-dro-gen *n.* A highly flammable gas.

hy-dro-pho-bi-a *n.* A fear of water.

hy-dro-plane *v.* To skim over water.

hy-dro-ponics *n., pl.* The method of growing plant rooted in chemical solutions instead of soil. **-ponic** *adj.*

hy-dro-scope *n.* An optical instrument that enables an observer to see object under the surface of water.

hy-dro-stat *n.* An electical device that detects the presence of water.

hy-e-na *n.* A type of carnivorous mammal.

hy-grom-e-ter *n.* An instrument that measures the degree of moisture in the atmosphere.

hy-men *n.* A membrane partically closing the enternal vaginal orifice.

hymn *n.* A song giving praise to God. **-al** *n.*

hype *v.* To stimulate.

hy-per-ac-tive *adj.* To be abnormally active.

hy-per-ten-sion *n.* An abnormally high blood pressure. **-sive** *adj.*

hy-phen *n.* A mark (-) show connection between two words.

hy-phen-ate *v* To join by a hyphen. **-ation** *n.*

hyp-no-tism *n.* An act of inducing hypnosis.

hyp-no-tize *v.* To be dazzled; put into a hyponic state.

hy-po-chon-dri-a *n.* A mental depression.

hys-ter-ia *n.* An uncontrolled emotional outburst. **-ical** *adj.*

hys-ter-ic *n.* A person suffering from hysteria.

hys-ter-i-cal *adj.* Emotionally out of control.

hys-ter-o-gen-ic *v.* To produce hysteria.

hys-ter-ot-o-my *n.* A surgery that involves opening the uterus.

I

I, i The ninth letter of the English alphabet.

I *pron.* A person speaking or writing. *n.* The self.

i-amb *or* **i-am-bus** *n.* A metrical foot consisting of a short or unstressed syllable followed by an accented syllable.

ibes *n.* A wild goat living in high mountain areas.

ice *n.* Solidly frozen water.

ice age *n.* A period in time of widespread glaciation.

ice bag *n.* A waterproof bag used to hold and apply coldness to the body.

ice-berg *n.* A thick mass of floating ice.

ice-break-er *n.* A ship used to clear ice from channels.

ice cap *n.* A covering of ice and snow.

ice cold *adj.* Very cold.

ice cream *n.* A frozen desert made from cream, sugar and eggs.

ice-fall *n.* A waterfall that has frozen.

ice fog *n.* A fog containing particles of ice.

ice pick *n.* A pointed tool used for breaking ice.

i-ci-cle *n.* A hanging spike of ice.

ic-ing *n.* The frosting on cakes.

icky *adj.* Distasteful; offensive to the senses.

i-con *n.* An idol.

i-cy *adj.* Relating to cold.

I'd *contr.* I had; I should; I would.

i-de-a *n.* A thought; design; a plan of action.

i-de-al *n.* A concept; standard of beauty or perfection. **-ness** *n.*

i-de-al-ism *n.* A tendency to view things in an ideal form and not for what they really are.

ide-al-ize *v.* To give an ideal value to. **-ization** *n.*

ide-ate *v.* To from an idea of.

i-den-ti-cal *adj.* Being the same; having the same origin or cause. **-ly** *adv.*, **-ness** *n.*

i-den-ti-fy *v.* To recognize identity. **-able** *adj.*

i-den-ti-ty *n.* A state of recognizing.

i-de-ol-o-gy *n.* A body of ideas that infuences a culture.

id-i-o-cy *n.* A mental deficiency.

id-i-om *n.* A form of expression.

id-i-om-at-ic *adj.* Peculiar to a certain style.

id-i-o-syn-cra-sy *n.* A peculiarity. **-cratic** *adj.*

id-i-ot *n.* A mental deficiency; ignorant person. **-cally** *adv.*

i-dle *adj.* Inactive. **-ness** *n.*

i-dol *n.* A symbol.

i-dol-a-try *n.* A worship of idols.

idol-ize v. To admire to excess. **-ization** n.

if conj. In case or condition that something happens.

if-fy adj. Uncertain.

ig-loo n. Eskimo dwelling.

ig-ne-ous adj. Relating to fire.

ig-nite v. To start a fire.

ig-no-ble adj. Being dishonorable. **-ness** n., **-bly** adv.

ig-no-min-i-ous adj. Characterized by shame. **-ly** adv., **-ness** n.

ig-no-mi-ny n. Disgraceful; personal humiliation.

ig-no-ra-mus n. One who acts ignorantly towards other people.

ig-no-rant adj. Lacking education. **-ly** adv., **-ness** n.

ig-nore v. To not pay attention; refuse to notice.

i-gua-na n. An American lizard.

ill adj. Not healthy; sick.

I'll contr. I will.

ill--ad-vised adj. Lack of sufficient counseling. **-ly** adv.

ill--bred adj. Ill-mannered; raised incorrectly.

il-le-gal adj. Contrary to law; unlawful. **-ly** adv., **-ity** n.

il-leg-i-ble adj. Unreadable; not legible. **-bly** adv. **-ness, -ity** n.

il-le-git-i-mate adj. Born out of wedlock. **-ly** adv., **-cy** n.

ill--fat-ed adj. Unlucky; unfortunate.

il-lic-it adj. Not permitted by law. **-ly** adv.

il-lit-er-ate adj. Uneducated. **-acy** n.

ill--na-tured adj. Unpleasant disposition.

ill-ness n. A sickness.

il-log-i-cal adj. Not having much sense or logic. **-ic** n.

ill tem-per n. To be moody. **-edly** adv., **-edness** n., **-ed** adj.

il-lu-mi-nate v. To give light. **-ing** adj., **-tor** n.

il-lu-sion n. A false reality.

il-lus-trate v. To explain. **-tion** n.

il-lus-tri-ous adj. Being celebrated. **-ness** n., **-ly** adv.

ill will n. Hostile feelings.

I'm contr. I am.

im-age-ry n. The mental pictures.

im-ag-ine v. To form a mental picture.

im-bal-ance n. A lack of functional balance.

im-be-cile n. A mental deficiency. **-ity** n.,

-ly *adv.*

im-bibe *v.* To drink; to take in. **-er** *n.*

im-i-tate *v.* To copy the actions of another. **-tator** *n.*

im-i-ta-tion *n.* A copy; counterfeit; not the real thing. **-al** *adj.*

im-mac-u-late *adj.* Impeccably clean; no blemish, error or flaw. **-ly** *adv.*, **-ness** *n.*

im-ma-ture *adj.* Not fully grown; unfinished. **-ness** *n.*, **-ly** *adv.*

im-mea-sur-able *adj.* Being unable to measure. **-ly** *adv.*, **-ness** *n.*

im-me-di-ate *adj.* Acting at once. **-ness** *n.*, **-ly** *adv.*

im-mense *adj.* Exceptionally large. **-ness** *n.*, **-ly** *adv.*

im-merse *v.* To put into a liquid. **-sion** *n.*

im-mi-grate *v.* To leave one country and settle in another. **-tor** *n.*

im-mi-nent *adj.* About to happen. **-nence** *n.*

im-mo-bile *adj.* Not moving. **-lize** *v.*, **-lity** *n.*

im-mod-est *adj.* Lacking modesty. **-ty** *n.*, **-ly** *adv.*

im-mor-al *adj.* Sinful. **-ity** *n.*

im-mor-tal *adj.* Exempt from death.

im-mov-a-ble *adj.* Not capable of being moved. **-bly** *adv.*, **-bility** *n.*

im-mune *adj.* Not affected.

imp *n.* Mischievous child.

im-pact *n.* A sudden force. **-tion** *n.*

im-pac-ted *adj.* Being wedged together.

im-pair *v.* To diminish in quality. **-ment, -er** *n.*

im-pale *v.* To pierce with a sharp point. **-er** *n.*

im-pal-pa-ble *adj.* Not perceptible to touch. **-bly** *adv.*, **-bility** *n.*

im-part *v.* To make known.

im-par-tial *adj.* Unbiased. **-ly** *adv.*, **-ity** *n.*

im-passe *n.* A road with no exit.

im-pas-sioned *adj.* Filled with passion.

im-pas-sive *adj.* Being unemotional. **-ness** *n.*, **-ly** *adv.*

im-pa-tient *adj.* Being unwilling to wait. **-ly** *adv.*, **-tience** *n.*

im-peach *v.* To charge with misconduct in public office. **-ment** *n.*

im-pec-ca-ble *adj.* Having no flaws. **-ly** *adv.*, **-bility** *n.*

im-pede *v.* To slow down the progress.

im-ped-i-ment *n.* One that stands in the way.

im-pel *v.* To drive forward.

im-per-fect *adj.* Not perfect. **-ness** *n.*, **-ly** *adv.*

im-pe-ri-al *n.* An empire of emperor. **-ly** *adv.*

im-per-il *v.* To endanger. **-ment** *n.*

im-per-ma-nent *adj.* Being temporary. **-ly** *adv.*

im-per-son-al *adj.* No personal reference. **-ly** *adv.*

im-per-son-ate *v.* To imitate. **-tor, -tion** *n.*

im-per-ti-nent *adj.* Being overly bold. **-ly** *adv.*

im-per-turb-a-ble *adj.* To be calm. **-ly** *adv.*

im-per-vi-ous *adj.* Incapable of being affected. **-ness** *n.*, **-ly** *adv.*

im-pe-ti-go *n.* A contagious skin disease.

im-pet-u-ous *adj.* Being impulsive. **-ness** *n.*, **-ly** *adv.*

im-pe-tus *n.* A driving force.

im-pinge *v.* To strike or collide. **-er, -ment** *n.*

imp-ish *adj.* Mischievous.

im-plac-a-ble *adj.* Not capable of being appeased. **-ly** *adv.*, **-ness** *n.*

im-plant *v.* To set in firmly. **-er** *n.*

im-plau-si-ble *adj.* Unlikely. **-bility** *n.*, **-ly** *adv.*

im-ple-ment *n.* A utensil or tool. **-ation** *n.*, **-tal** *adj.*

im-pli-cate *v.* To involve.

im-plic-it *adj.* Being without doubt. **-ness** *n.*, **-ly** *adv.*

im-plore *v.* To plead urgently. **-ation** *n.*

im-ply *v.* To express indirectly.

im-po-lite *adj.* Rude. **-ness** *n.*, **-ly** *adv.*

im-port *v.* To bring in goods from another country. **-er** *n.*, **-able** *adj.*

im-por-tance *n.* A significance.

im-por-tant *adj.* Having value.

im-por-tune *v.* To repeat requests. **-er** *n.*

im-pose *v.* To burden on another. **-ter** *n.*

im-pos-ing *adj.* Being awesome. **-ly** *adv.*

im-pos-si-ble *adj.* Not capable of happening. **-ly** *adv.*, **-bility** *n.*

im-post *n.* A tax or duty.

im-pos-tor *n.* A false identity.

im-po-tent *adj.* Having no power. **-ly** *adv.*

im-pound *v.* To seize and keep. **-age** *n.*

im-pov-er-ish *v.* To make poor. **-ment** *n.*

im-prac-ti-cal *adj.* Unwise to put into effect.
-**able** *adj.*

im-preg-nate *v.* To make pregnant. -**tor** *n.*

im-press *v.* To apply with pressure.
-**ible** *adj.*, -**er** *n.*

im-pres-sion *n.* A feeling retained in the mind.
-**ist** *n.*

im-pres-sion-a-ble *adj.* Being easily influenced.
-**bly** *adv.*

im-pris-on *v.* To put in prison. -**ment** *n.*

im-promp-tu *adj.* Planning or preparation.

im-prop-er *adj.* Unsuitable. -**ness** *n.*,
-**ly** *adv.*

im-prove *v.* To make or become better.
-**able** *adj.*, -**ment** *n.*

im-pro-vise *v.* To make up something. -**er** *n.*

im-pru-dent *adj.* Unwise. -**ly** *adv.*

im-pu-dent *adj.* Disrespectful. -**ly** *adv.*

im-pugn *v.* To cast doubt on. -**er** *n.*

im-pulse *n.* A spontaneous urge. -**sion** *n.*

im-pul-sive *adj.* Being uncalculated.

im-pure *adj.* Being not pure; unclean. -**ness** *n.*,
-**ly** *adv.*

in-ac-tive *adj.* Out of current use. -**ity** *n.*,
-**ly** *adv.*

in-ad-e-quate *adj.* Being not adequate. -**ly** *adv.*

in-ad-ver-tent *adj.* Being unintentional. -**ly** *adv.*

in-ane *adj.* Without sense. -**ness** *n.*,
-**ly** *adv.*

in-an-i-mate *adj.* Not having life.

in-ar-tic-u-late *adj.* Unable to speak. -**ness** *n.*,
-**ly** *adv.*

in-au-gu-rate *v.* To put into office.

in--be-tween *adj.* Being intermediate.

in-cal-cu-la-ble *adj.* Indeterminate. -**bly** *adv.*

in-can-des-cent *adj.* Giving off light when heated. -**ly** *adv.*,
-**cence** *n.*

in-can-ta-tion *n.* A recitation of magic or spells.

in-ca-pac-i-tate *v.* To disable.

in-car-cer-ate *v.* To place in jail. -**tion** *n.*

in-cen-di-ary *adj.* Causing fires.

in-cense *v.* To make angry.

in-cep-tion *n.* Beginning.

in-ces-sant *adj.* Being continuous. -**ly** *adv.*

in-cest *n.* The intercourse between related people. -**uousness** *n.*,
-**uous** *adj.*,

inch *n.* A unit of measurement.

in-ci-dent *n.* An event.

in-ci-den-tal *adj.* Occurring as a result.
-**ly** *adv.*

in-cin-er-ate *v.* To burn up. -**tor** *n.*

in-cip-i-ent *adj.* Just beginning. -**ly** *adv.*

in-ci-sion *n.* A surgical cut.

in-cite *v.* To provoke to action. -**er, -ment** *n.*

in-clem-ent *adj.* Being stormy or rainy.
-**ly** *adv.*, -**ency** *n.*

in-cli-na-tion *n.* An attitude.

in-cline *v.* To slant.
-**er** *n.*

in-clude *v.* To contain.
-**sion** *n.*, -**able** *adj.*

in-cog-ni-to *adv. & adj.* One's identity hidden.

in-co-her-ent *adj.* Lacking order. -**ly** *adv.*,
-**ence** *n.*

in-come *n.* The money received for work.

in-com-ing *adj.* To be coming in.

in-com-pat-i-ble *adj.* Being not suitable.
-**bly** *adv.*, -**bility** *n.*

in-com-pe-tent *adj.* Being not able.
-**ly** *adv.*

in-com-plete *adj.* Being not finished.
-**tion, -ness** *n.*
-**ly** *adv.*

in-con-gru-ous *adj.* Disagreeing. -**ness** *n.*,
-**ly** *adv.*

in-con-sid-er-ate *adj.* To be thoughtless.
-**ness** *n.*, -**ly** *adv.*

in-con-spic-u-ous *adj.* Not readily seen or noticed. -**ness** *n.*,
-**ly** *adv.*

in-con-ti-nent *adj.* Uncontrolled. -**ly** *adv.*

in-con-ven-ience *v.* To bother.

in-cor-po-rate *v.* To form a legal corporation.
-**tor, -tion** *n.*

in-cor-ri-gi-ble *adj.* Incapable of being corrected. -**bly** *adv.*

in-crease *v.* To make or become larger.
-**ingly** *adv.*, -**able** *adj.*

in-cred-i-ble *adj.* Unbelievable. -**bly** *adv.*,
-**ness** *n.*

in-cred-u-lous *adj.* Disbelieving. -**ly** *adv.*,
-**ness** *n.*

in-cre-ment *n.* An increase. -**tal** *adj.*

in-crim-i-nate *v.* To involve in a crime.
-**tor, -tion** *n.*
-**tory** *adj.*

in-cu-bate *v.* To warm and hatch eggs.
-**tion** *n.*

in-cul-pate *v.* To incriminate. -**tion** *n.*

in-cum-bent *adj.* Resting on something else.
-**ly** *adv.*, -**cy** *n.*

in-cur *v.* To become liable.

in-cu-ri-ous *adj.* Lacking interest.

in-debt-ed *adj.* Obligated to another. **-ness** *n.*

in-de-cent *adj.* Morally offensive to good taste. **-ly** *adv.*, **-cy** *n.*

in-de-ci-sion *n.* An inability to make up one's mind.

in-dec-o-rous *adj.* To be lacking good taste.

in-deed *adv.* Most certainly.

in-def-i-nite *adj.* Unclear **-ness** *n.*, **-ly** *adv.*

in-del-i-ble *adj.* Not able to be erased. **-bly** *adv.*, **-ness** *n.*

in-del-i-cate *adj.* Tactless. **-ly** *adv.*, **-ness** *n.*

in-dem-ni-ty *n.* A security against hurt, or loss.

in-dent *v.* To set in from the margin.

in-de-pend-ence *n.* Being independent. **-cy** *n.*

in--depth *adj.* Detailed.

in-de-scrib-a-ble *adj.* Surpassing description. **-ness, -bility** *n.*, **-bly** *adv.*

in-dex *n.* A list for aiding reference. **-er** *n.*

in-di-cate *v.* To point out. **-tion** *n.*

in-dict *v.* To accuse of an offense. **-tor, -ter** *n.*,

-able *adj.*

in-dif-fer-ent *adj.* Being impartial. **-ly** *adv.*, **-ist** *n.*

in-dig-e-nous *adj.* Living naturally in an area. **-ness** *n.*, **-ly** *adv.*

in-di-gent *adj.* Being impoverished. **-ly** *adv.*

in-di-ges-tion *n.* A discomfort in digesting food. **-tive** *adj.*

in-dig-nant *adj.* Being filled with indignation. **-ly** *adv.*

in-dig-ni-ty *n.* Something that offends one's pride.

in-di-go *n.* The blue dye obtained.

in-di-rect *adj.* Not taking a direct course. **-ness** *n.*, **-ly** *adv.*

in-dis-creet *adj.* Lacking discretion. **-ly** *adv.*

in-dis-pen-sa-ble *adj* Necessary.

in-dis-posed *adj.* Being mildly ill.

in-di-vid-u-al *adj.* A single human being. **-ly** *adv.*

in-di-vis-i-ble *adj.* Not able to be divided.

in-doc-tri-nate *v.* To instruct in a doctrine. **-tor** *n.*

in-do-lent *adj.* Lazy.

in-duce *v.* To cause to occur.

in-duct *v.* To admit as a new member.

in-dulge *v.* To give into the desires.

in-dus-tri-ous *adj.* Working steadily and hard.

in-dus-try *n.* A branch of manufacturing.

in-e-bri-ate *v.* To intoxicate.

in-ef-fi-cient *adj.* Wasteful of time.

in-ept *adj.* Not suitable.

in-eq-ui-ty *n.* Unfairness.

in-ert *adj.* Not able to move.

in-ev-i-ta-ble *adj.* Not able to be avoided.

in-ex-pe-ri-ence *n.* Lack of experience.

in-ex-pli-ca-ble *adj.* Not capable of being explained.

in-ex-tre-mis *adv.* At the point of death.

in-ex-tri-ca-ble *adj.* Too complex to resolve.

in-fal-li-ble *adj.* Not capable of making mistakes.

in-fa-my *n.* Evil notoriety.

in-fan-cy *n.* The time of being an infant.

in-fant *n.* A baby.

in-fan-ti-cide *n.* The killing of an infant.

in-fan-try *n.* A foot soldiers.

in-fat-u-ate *v.* To foolishly love.

in-fect *v.* To contaminate.

in-fer *v.* To conclude by reasoning.

in-fer-ence *n.* A conclusion based on facts.

in-fe-ri-or *adj.* Located under or below.

in-fer-nal *adj.* Like, or relating to hell.

in-fer-no *n.* A place suggestive of hell.

in-fest *v.* To over so as to be harmful.

in-fil-trate *v.* To pass through gradually.

in-fi-nite *adj.* Immeasurably large.

in-fin-i-tes-i-mal *adj.* Immeasurably small.

in-firm *adj.* Physically weak.

in-flame *v.* To set on fire.

in-flam-ma-tion *n.* A localized redness in response to an injury.

in-flate *v.* To fill with gas or air.

in-fla-tion *n.* An increase in the monetary supply.

in-flect *v.* To vary the tone of the voice.

in-flex-i-ble *adj.* Not subject to change.

in-flict *v.* To cause to be suffered.

in-flu-ence *n.* A power to produce effects.

in-flu-en-za *n.* An acute, infectious viral disease.

in-flux *n.* The things coming in.

in-for-ma-tive *adj.* To be providing information.

in-frac-tion *n.* A violation of a rule.

in-fringe v. To encroach.

in-fu-ri-ate v. To make very angry.

in-gen-ious adj. Showing great ability.

in-gen-u-ous adj. Frank and straightforward.

in-gest v. To take or put food into the body.

in-got n. A mass of cast metal shaped in a bar.

in-grained adj. Deep-seated.

in-grate n. One who is ungrateful.

in-grat-i-tude n. A lack of gratitude.

in-gre-di-ent n. A part of anything.

in-grown adj. Growing into the flesh.

in-hab-it v. To reside in.

in-hale v. To breathe into the lungs.

in-her-ent adj. Forming an essential element.

in-her-it v. To receive something by a will.

in-hib-it v. To hold back.

in-hu-mane adj. Lacking compassion or pity.

in-im-i-cal adj. Harmful opposition.

in-im-i-ta-ble adj. Incapable of being matched.

in-iq-ui-ty n. A grievous violation of justice.

in-i-tial n. The first letter of a name or word.

in-i-ti-ate v. To begin or start.

in-i-ti-a-tive n. An action of taking the first step.

in-ject v. To force a drug into the body through a blood vessel with a hypodermic syringe.

in-junc-tion n. An authoritative command or order.

in-jure v. To cause physical harm.

in-ju-ri-ous adj. Causing injury, damage or hurt.

in-ju-ry n. The damage or harm inflicted.

in-jus-tice n. A violation of another person's rights.

ink n. Any of variously colored liquids or paste.

ink-ling n. A slight suggestion or hint.

ink-y adj. Resembling ink in color; dark; black.

in-land adj. Located in the interior of a country.

in--law n. A relative by marriage.

in-let n. A bay or stream that leads into land.

in-mate n. A person who is confined in a prison.

inn n. A place of lodging.

in-nate adj. Inborn and not acquired.

in-ner adj. Situated or occurring inside.

in-ner-most *adj.* Most intimate.

in-ning *n.* One of nine divisions of a regulation baseball game.

in-no-cent *adj.* Free from sin, or moral wrong.

in-noc-u-ous *adj.* Having no harmful qualities.

in-no-vate *v.* To begin something new.

in-nu-en-do *n.* An indirect or oblique comment.

in-nu-mer-a-ble *adj.* Too much to be counted.

in-oc-u-late *v.* To protect against disease by vaccination.

in-op-er-a-ble *adj.* Incapable of being treated.

in-or-di-nate *adj.* Exceeding proper or normal limits.

in-or-gan-ic *adj.* Not having living organisms.

in-put *n.* The data put in a computer.

in-quest *n.* A legal investigation into the cause of death.

in-quire *v.* To ask a question.

in-quir-y *n.* A request or question for information.

in-qui-si-tion *n.* An investigation.

in-quis-i-tive *adj.* Curious; probing.

in-sane *adj.* Serious mental disorder.

in-san-i-tar-y *adj.* Not hygienic and dangerous to one's health.

in-scribe *v.* To engrave on a surface.

in-scru-ta-ble *adj.* Difficult understand.

in-sect *n.* A tiny animal such as ant, flea, etc.

in-sec-ti-cide *n.* A substance for killing insects.

in-se-cure *adj.* Feeling of being unsafe.

in-sem-i-nate *v.* To make pregnant.

in-sen-si-ble *adj.* Incapable of feeling.

in-sep-a-ra-ble *adj.* Incapable of being separated.

in-sert *v.* To put in place.

in-shore *adj.* Near the shore.

in-side *n.* A space that lies within.

in-sid-i-ous *adj.* Deceitful.

in-sight *n.* The hidden nature of things.

in-sig-ni-a *n.* A badge or emblem.

in-sin-cere *adj.* Being hypocritical.

in-sin-u-ate *v.* To suggest something by giving a hint.

in-sip-id *adj.* To be lacking flavor.

in-sist *v.* To demand or assert.

in-so-far *adv.* To such an extent.

in-sol-u-ble *adj.* Incapable of being dis-solved.

in-sol-vent adj. Being unable to meet debts.

in-som-ni-a n. A chronic inability to sleep.

in-spect v. To examine very carefully for flaws.

in-spire v. To guide by a divine influence.

in-sta-bil-i-ty n. Lacking stability.

in-stall v. To put in position for service.

in-stall-ment n. The payments due at specified intervals.

in-stance n. An illustrative example.

in-stant n. A very short time.

in-stan-ta-ne-ous adj. Being instantly.

in-stead adv. Lieu of that just mentioned.

in-sti-gate v. To provoke someone.

in-still v. To introduce by gradual instruction.

in-stinct n. An unlearned action.

in-sti-tute v. To establish.

in-sti-tu-tion n. An organization which performs a particular job.

in-struct v. To impart knowledge.

in-struc-tor n. The one who instructs.

in-stru-ment n. A device used to produce music.

in-stru-men-tal-ist n. A person who plays music.

in-sub-or-di-nate adj. Not obedient.

in-suf-fi-cient adj. Being inadequate.

in-su-late v. To prevent loss of heat or sound.

in-su-lin n. The hormone released by the pancreas.

in-sult v. Abuse verbally.

in-su-per-a-ble adj. Not able to be overcome.

in-sur-ance n. The protection against loss, or ruin.

in-sur-mount-a-ble adj. Being incapable of being overcome.

in-sur-rec-tion n. An open revolt.

in-sus-cep-ti-ble adj. Being immune.

in-tact adj. Remaining whole.

in-take n. An act of absorbing.

in-tan-gi-ble adj. Indefinite to the mind.

in-te-gral adj. Being essential and part of a whole.

in-te-grate v. To open to people of all races.

in-teg-ri-ty n. Honesty.

in-tel-lect n. The power to understand.

in-tel-li-gence n. The capacity to comprehend meaning.

in-tend v. to have a plan

in mind.

in-tense *adj.* Profound.

in-ten-si-fy *v.* To make more intense.

in-ten-si-ty *n.* Being intense.

in-ten-sive care *n.* A hospital care for a gravely ill patient.

in-tent *n.* The purpose of a goal.

in-ten-tion *n.* The plan of action.

in-ten-tion-al *adj.* Deliberately.

in-ter *v.* Place in a grave.

in-ter-act *v.* to act on each other or with each other.

in-ter-breed *v.* To crossbreed.

in-ter-cede *v.* To argue or plead on another's behalf.

in-ter-cept *v.* To interrupt the path or course.

in-ter-ces-sion *n.* An entreaty or prayer on behalf of others.

in-ter-com *n.* A two-way communication system.

in-ter-com-mu-ni-cate *v.* To communicate with each other.

in-ter-course *n.* A mutual exchange between persons.

in-ter-dict *v.* To forbid by official decree.

in-ter-est *n.* A curiosity about something.

in-ter-face *n.* A com-

mon boundary between adjacent areas.

in-ter-fere *v.* To get in the way.

in-ter-ga-lac-tic *adj.* Being between galaxies.

in-ter-im *n.* The time between events.

in-te-ri-or *adj.* Away from the coast or border.

in-ter-ject *v.* to go between other parts or elements.

in-ter-jec-tion *n.* An exclamation to express emotion.

in-ter-lace *v.* To intertwine.

in-ter-lock *v.* Join closely.

in-ter-lope *v.* To intrude the rights of others.

in-ter-lude *n.* A period of time that occurs in and divides some longer process.

in-ter-me-di-ar-y *n.* A mediator.

in-ter-me-di-ate *adj.* Situated in the middle.

in-ter-min-gle *v.* To become mixed together.

in-ter-mis-sion *n.* A temporary break between events.

in-ter-mit-tent *adj.* To be coming at intervals.

in-tern *n.* A medical school graduate.

in-ter-nal *adj.* Pertaining to the inside.

in-ter-na-tion-al *adj.* Involving two or more nations.

in-ter-nist *n.* A specialist in internal medicine.

in-ter-pose *v.* To put between parts.

in-ter-pret *v.* To convey the meaning.

in-ter-ra-cial *adj.* Affecting different races.

in-ter-re-late *v.* To have a mutual relationship.

in-ter-ro-gate *v.* To question formally.

in-ter-rupt *v.* To break in on conversation.

in-ter-sect *v.* To divide.

in-ter-sec-tion *n.* A place of crossing.

in-ter-sperse *v.* To scatter.

in-ter-twine *v.* To unite by twisting together.

in-ter-ur-ban *adj.* Among connecting urban areas.

in-ter-val *n.* The time between two points or object.

in-ter-vene *v.* To come between something.

in-ter-view *n.* A meeting arranged for one person to question another.

in-ter-weave *v.* To weave together.

in-tes-tate *adj.* Having made no valid will.

in-tes-tine *n.* A section of the stomach.

in-ti-mate *adj.* Close friendship.

in-tim-i-date *v.* To frighten.

in-to *prep.* The inside.

in-tol-er-ant *adj.* Not able to endure.

in-tone *v.* To chant.

in-tox-i-cate *v.* To make drunk.

in-tra-cel-lu-lar *adj.* Being within a cell.

in-tra-cra-ni-al *adj.* Being within the skull.

in-tra-mu-ral *adj.* Taking place within a school.

in-tra-mus-cu-lar *adj.* Being within a muscle.

in-tra-state *adj.* Being within a state.

in-tra-ve-nous *adj.* Being within a vein.

in-trep-id *adj.* Being courageous.

in-tri-cate *adj.* Complex.

in-trigue *v.* To arouse interest.

in-trin-sic *adj.* Inherent.

in-tro-duce *v.* To make acquainted.

in-tro-vert *n.* A very shy person.

in-trude *v.* To come in without being asked.

in-tu-i-tion *n.* Having insight.

in-un-date *v.* To overwhelm someone.

in-ure *v.* To accept something undesirable.

in-vade *v.* To enter by force.

in-va-lid *n.* A disabled person.

in-val-i-date *v.* To nullify.

in-val-u-able *adj.* Being priceless.

in-var-i-a-ble *adj.* Being constant.

in-vei-gle *v.* To win over by flattery.

in-vent *v.* To create by original effort.

in-ven-tion *n.* The process of inventing.

in-ven-to-ry *n.* A list of items.

in-verse *adj.* To be reversed in order.

in-vert *v.* To turn upside down.

in-ver-te-brate *adj.* Lacking a backbone.

in-vest *v.* Purchase of stocks to obtain profit.

in-ves-ti-gate *v.* To examine carefully.

in-vig-o-rate *v.* To give strength.

in-vin-ci-ble *adj.* Incapable of being defeated.

in-vi-o-la-ble *adj.* Being safe from assault.

in-vi-o-late *adj.* Not harmed.

in-vis-i-ble *adj.* Not open to view.

in-vite *v.* To request the presence.

in-vit-ing *adj.* Tempting.

in-voice *n.* An itemized list of merchandise.

in-voke *v.* To call upon for aid.

in-vol-un-tar-y *adj.* Not done by choice.

in-volve *v.* To include as a part.

in-vul-ner-a-ble *adj.* To be immune to attack.

in-ward *adj.* Being toward the inside, center.

i-o-dine *n.* A grayish-black, corrosive, poisonous element.

i-on *n.* An electrically charged atom.

i-on-ize *v.* To convert completely into ions.

i-ras-ci-ble *adj.* Easily provoked to anger.

i-rate *adj.* Raging angry.

ir-i-des-cent *adj.* Shifting hues of color.

i-ris *n.* The pigmented part of the eye.

irk *v.* To annoy.

i-ron-bound *adj.* Bound with iron.

i-ron-clad *adj.* Covered with protective iron plates.

i-ron-stone *n.* A heavy, white, glazed pottery.

ir-ra-di-ate *v.* To subject to ultraviolet light.

ir-ra-tion-al *adj.* Unable to reason.

ir-rec-on-cil-a-ble *adj.* Not able or willing to be reconciled.

ir-re-deem-a-ble *adj.* Not capable of being recovered.

ir-re-duc-i-ble *adj.* Not having the capabilities of reduction.

ir-ref-ra-ga-ble *adj.* Cannot be refuted.

ir-re-fut-able *adj.* Cannot be disproved.

ir-reg-u-lar *adj.* Not according to the general rule.

ir-rel-e-vant *adj.* Not related to the subject matter.

ir-re-lig-ious *adj.* Lacking in religion.

ir-re-mov-a-ble *adj.* Not removable.

ir-rep-a-ra-ble *adj.* Unable to be repaired.

ir-re-place-a-ble *adj.* Unable to be replaced.

ir-re-press-i-ble *adj.* Impossible to hold back.

ir-re-proach-a-ble *adj.* To be blameless.

ir-re-sist-i-ble *adj.* Completely fascinating.

ir-res-o-lute *adj.* Lacking firmness.

ir-re-spec-tive *adj.* Being regardless.

ir-re-spon-si-ble *adj.* Lacking in responsibility.

ir-re-triev-a-ble *adj.* Unable to be recovered.

ir-rev-er-ence *n.* A lack of reverence.

ir-rev-o-ca-ble *adj.* Unable of being turned in the other direction.

ir-ri-gate *v.* To water the land or crops artificially.

ir-ri-ta-ble *adj.* Easily annoyed.

ir-ri-tate *v.* To annoy or bother.

ir-rupt *v.* Burst or rush in.

is *v.* Third person, singular, present tense of the verb to be.

is-land *n.* A piece of land completely surrounded by water.

isle *n.* A small island.

is-n't *contr.* Is not.

i-so-late *v.* To set apart from the others.

i-so-la-tion-ism *n.* A national policy of avoiding political economic alliances.

i-so-therm *n.* A line on a map linking points that have the same temperature.

i-so-tope *n.* An element form.

i-so-trop-ic *adj.* Same value in all directions.

is-sue *n.* An act of giving out.

isth-mus *n.* A land which connects two larger pieces of land.

it *pron.* Used as a substitute for a specific noun.

i-tal-ic *adj.* Style of printing type in which the letters slant.

i-tal-i-cize *v.* To print in italics.

itch *n.* A skin irritation which causes a desire to scratch.

-ite *suffix* Native or inhabitant.

i-tem *n.* A separately-noted unit included in a category.

i-tem-ize *v.* To specify by item.

it-er-ate *v.* To repeat.

i-tin-er-ant *adj.* Traveling from place to place.

i-tin-er-ar-y *n.* A scheduled route of a trip.

it'll *contr.* It will.

i-vo-ry *n.* The white tusks an an elephant and walrus.

i-vy *n.* A climbing plant having glossy evergreen leaves.

J

J, j The tenth letter of the English alphabet .

jab *v.* To poke.

jab-ber *v.* To chatter. **-er** *n.*

jacks *n.* A childs game.

jack-al *n.* A dog-like mammal.

jack-et *n.* A short coat. **-ed** *adj.*

jack-ham-mer *n.* A tool used to break pavement or rock.

jack--in--the--box *n.* A toy where a clown pops out of a box.

jack-knife *n.* A pocket knife.

jack-pot *n.* A large money winnings.

jack rab-bit *n.* Type of large rabbit.

jac-quard *n.* Type of material with a print in the weave.

jag *v.* To cut and form teeth.

jag-ged *adj.* To be sharp notches; serrated.

jag-uar *n.* Type of large feline mammal.

jai alai *n.* A game like handball.

jail *n.* A place of confinement. **-er** *n.*

jail-bird *n.* A prisoner of a jail.

jail-break *n.* An escape performed at the jail.

ja-lou-sie *n.* A window having adjustable slats.

jam *v.* To wedge in a tight position. **-mer** *n.*

jamb *n.* A vertical sidepiece of a door.

jam-bo-ree *n.* A festive gathering.

jam ses-sion *n.* An informal group of musicians.

jan-gle *v.* To make a harsh noise. **-ly** *adj.*, **-er** *n.*

jan-i-tor *n.* One who cleans; building caretaker. **-rial** *adj.*

Jan-u-ar-y *n.* The first month of the year.

Jap-a-nese bee-tle *n.* A destructive type of beetle.

jar *n.* A wide mouthed vessel. **-ful** *n.*

jar-di-niere *n.* Decorative pot for plants.

jar-gon *n.* A confused language.

jas-mine *n.* A shrub with fragrant flowers.

jaun-dice *n., Pathol.* A liver disease. **-ed** *adj.*

jaunt *n.* A short journey.

jaun-ty *adj.* Stylish; sprightly. **-tiness** *n.*, **-tily** *adv.*

Ja-va *n.* Type of coffee.

jave-lin *n.* A light spear.

jaw *n.* The bony structures forming the mouth.

jaw-bone *n.* Mandible.

jaw-break-er *n.* A hard piece of candy.

jay *n.* A type of bird.

jay-walk *v., Slang* To cross street carelessly. **-er** *n.*

jazz *n.* A kind of music. **-ist** *n.*, **-y** *adj.*

jeal-ous *adj.* Suspicious; envious **-y** *n.*

jean *n.* A strong cotton cloth. **jeans** Pants made of denim.

jeep *n.* A military vehicle.

jeer *v.* To mock; sarcastic comment. **-er** *n.*

jell *v.* To become like jelly in consistency.

jel-ly *n.* A fruit cooked with sugar. **-like, -lied** *adj.*

jel-ly-fish *n.* A jelly-like sea animal.

jeop-ard-y *n.* Exposure to danger. **-dize** *v.*

jerk *v.* To give a sharp twist. **-y** *adj.*, **-iness** *n.*, **-ily** *adv.*

jer-kin *n.* A close-fitting jacket.

jer-ry-built *adj.* Built poorly. **-er** *n.*, **-build** *v.*

jer-sey *n.* A clinging knitted cloth.

jest *n.* Prank; joke. **-er** *n.*

Jesus *n.* The Messiah.

jet *n.* A sudden spurt of liquid.

jet en-gine *n.* The engine of an airplane.

jet-lag *n.* The physical fatigue from travel.

jet-sam *n.* Things dropped overboard as on a ship.

jet set *n.* A group of people having a lot of money.

jet stream *n.* The high-velocity wind near the troposphere.

jet-ti-son *v.* To discard.

jet-ty *n.* Landing pier.

Jew *n.* A believer in Judaism.

jew-el *n.* A very rare gem. **-ly** *adj.*

jew-eler *n.* A person who makes jewelry.

jib *n.* A triangular sail.

jif-fy *n.* A very short time.

jig *n.* A fast lively dance. **-ger** *n.*

jig-gle *v.* To move or jerk up and down. **-gly** *adj.*

jig-saw *n.* A thin bladed saw for cutting curved lines.

jig-saw puz-zle *n.* A type of puzzle.

jilt *v.* To discard a lover. **-er** *n.*

jim-my *n.* A short crowbar.

jin-gle *v.* To make a clinking sound.

jin-go-ism *n.* Extreme nationalism.

jinx *n.* Bad luck.

jit-ney *n.* A vehicle for carrying passengers.

jit-ters *n.* Nervousness. **-tery** *adj.*

jit-ter bug *n.* A type of quick moving dance.

jive *n.* Jazz; tease.

job *n.* Work; occupation. **-less** *adj.*

job-ber *n.* One who distributes goods.

job-hold-er *n.* One who has a job.

jock *n. Slang* A male athlete.

jock-ey *n.* A horse rider.

joc-u-lar *adj.* To be playful. **-ity** *n.*

joc-und *adj.* To be cheerful **-ity** *n.*

jog *n.* A slight movement; form of exercise. **-ger** *n.*

jog-gle *v.* To move or shake slightly.

john *n., Slang* Toilet.

john-ny-cake *n.* A type of thin bread.

join *v.* To bring or put together. **-able** *adj.*

joint *n.* A place where two or more things meet. **-er** *n.*

joist *n.* The parallel beams to support a floor.

joke *n.* A brief story with a punch line. **-ingly** *adv.*

joker *n.* A playing card.

jolt *v.* To knock about. **-y** *adj.*, **-ingly** *adv.*, **-er** *n.*

jon-quil *n.* A daffodil.

josh *v., Slang* To make good-humored fun of.

jos-tle *v.* Pushing; shoving. **-er** *n.*

jot *v.* To make a brief note.

jounce *v.* To bump; to shake.

jour-nal *n.* A diary; a record of happenings.

jour-nal-ism *n.* The writing and publishing of newspapers.

jour-nal-ist *n.* One who writes news stories. **-tic** *adj.*

jour-ney *n.* A trip.

jour-ney-man *n.* A skilled worker.

joust *n.* A formal combat on horseback.

jo-vi-al *adj.* To be good-natured. **-ity** *n.*

jowl *n.* The lower jaw. **-y**, **-ed** *adj.*

joy *n.* Happiness. **-less**, **-ful** *adj.*

joy ride *n., Slang* A car ride for pleasure only.

ju-bi-lant *adj.* To be exultantly joyful. **-cy** *n.*

ju-bi-lee *n.* A special anniversary.

Ju-da-ism *n.* The religious practices or beliefs of the Jewish people. **-ical** *adj.*

judge *n.* The public officer in the court.

judg-ment or judge-ment *n.* The ability to make a wise decision. **-tal** *adj.*

ju-di-cial *adj.* Administering of justice.

ju-di-ci-ar-y *adj.* Pertaining to judges, courts, etc.

ju-di-cious *adj.* · Referring to the use of judgement.

ju-do *n.* A form of self-defense.

jug *n.* A small pitcher for holding liquids. **-ful** *adj.*

jug-ger-naut *n.* A destructive force.

jug-gle *v.* To keep several objects moving continuously in the air. **-er** *n.*

jug-u-lar *adj.* Referring to the neck.

jug-u-lar vein *n., Anat.* The large veins in the neck.

juice *n.* The liquid part of fruits. *Slang* An electric current. **-less** *adj.*

juic-er *n.* A device for extracting juice from fruit.

juic-y *adj.* Abounding with juice; full of interest. **-iness** *n.*, **-ily** *adv.*

ju-jit-su *or* **ju-jut-su** *n.* Japanese system of self defense.

juke box *n.* An automatic coin-operated record player.

ju-lep *n.* A mint julep.

ju-li-enne *adj.* Thin strips, way of serving food.

Ju-ly *n.* The seventh month of the year.

jum-ble *v.* To mix; confuse.

jum-bo *n.* A large thing.

jump *v.* To leap. **-ing** *adj.*

jump-er *n.* A sleeveless dress.

jump-y *adj.* To be nervous; jittery. **-iness** *n.*

junc-tion *n.* A meeting place.

junc-ture *n.* A point where two things join; crisis.

June *n.* The sixth month of the year.

June bug *n.* The beetle of summer.

jun-gle *n.* A densely covered forest.

jun-ior *adj.* Younger in years; third year student.

jun-ior col-lege *n.* A two year college.

jun-ior high school *n.* A

school between elememtary and high school.
ju-ni-per *n.* An evergreen shrub.
junk *n.* Discarded material. **-y** *adj.*, **-man** *n.*
jun-ket *n.* A party, banquet, or trip. **-teer** *n.*
junk food *n.* The food containing very little nutritional value.
junk-ie *n., Slang* A drug addict that uses various drugs.
jun-ta *n.* A body of persons who controls a government.
ju-ris-dic-tion *n.* The power; the control. **-al** *adj.*
ju-ris-pru-dence *n.* Relating to law. **-tial** *adj.*
ju-rist *n.* A judge.
ju-ror *n.* A person who serves on a jury.
ju-ry *n.* A group of persons summoned to set in judgment in court.
just *adj.* To be fair and impartial. **-ness** *n.*, **-ly** *adv.*
jus-tice *n.* An ideal defined; a judge. **-less** *adj.*
jus-tice of the peace *n.* The magistrate having power to perform marriages.
jus-ti-fi-ca-tion *n.* Being justified.
jus-ti-fy *v.* To declare guiltless. **-iable** *adj.*

jut *v.* To project.
jute *n.* A fiber material for making rope.
ju-ve-nile *adj.* Not yet an adult.
ju-ve-nile court *n.* In law, court for a juvenile.
ju-ve-nile de-lin-quent *n.* A young person whose behavior is out of control. **-ency** *n.*
jux-ta-pose *v.* To put side by side. **-ition** *n.*

K

K, k The eleventh letter of the English alphabet.
ka-bu-ki *n.* A traditional Japanese drama.
Kad-dish *n.* A type of Jewish prayer.
kale *n.* A green cabbage-like vegetable.
ka-lie-do-scope *n.* A tubular instrument rotated to make symmetrical designs of changing colors by using mirrors.
ka-mi-ka-ze *n.* A Japanese pilot used in a suicide attack.
kan-ga-roo *n.* The leaping animal of Australia.
kan-ga-roo court *n.* Self-appointed illegal court.
ka-o-lin *or* **ka-o-line** *n.* A fine clay used in ceramics.
ka-pok *n.* Stuffing for cushions and life preser-

vers.

ka-put *adj., Slang* To be out of order.

kar-at *n.* Unit of measure for gold and precious stones.

ka-ra-te *n.* The art of self-defense.

kar-ma *n.* An over-all effect of one's behavior.

ka-ty-did *n.* An insect related to grasshoppers.

kay-ak *n.* Type of watertight Eskimo boat.

ka-zoo *n.* A child's musical toy.

kedge *n.* A type of small anchor.

keel *n.* The main stem on a ship.

keel-haul *v.* To drag a person under water as a form of punishment.

keen *adj.* Having a fine cutting edge; sharp.

keep *v.* To have, and hold; maintain, as business records.

keep-sake *n.* A type of souvenir.

keg *n.* A small barrel.

keg-ler *n.* A bowler.

kelp *n.* Brown seaweed.

kel-pie *n.* A sheep dog.

ken-nel *n.* A shelter for dogs and cats.

ke-no *n.* A game of chance.

kep-i *n.* A French military cap.

ker-chief *n.* A cloth worn around the neck.

ker-nel *n.* A grain, as of corn.

ker-o-sene *n.* The oil from petroleum used for fuel.

ketch *n.* A small sailing vessel.

ketch-up *n.* A thick, smooth sauce made from tomatoes.

ket-tle *n.* A pot for boiling food.

ket-tle-drum *n.* A large musical drum.

key *n.* A device to unlock doors.

key-board *n.* The keys on a piano or typewriter.

key club *n.* A type of private club.

key-note *n., Mus.* The first tone of a scale.

key-note ad-dress *n.* An opening speech that outlines issues.

key-stone *n.* A wedge-shaped stone at the center of an arch.

khak-i *n.* An olive-drab color. **khakis** Uniform of khaki cloth.

khan *n.* The title of respect.

kib-itz *v.* **Slang** To offer meddlesome advice to others.

kick *v.* To strike or hit with the foot.

kick back *n.* Money returned illegally.

kick off *n.* The opening

kick of a football game.

kid *n.* A young goat; a tease.

kid-nap *v.* To seize a person, unlawfully, often for ransom.

kid-ney *n., pl.* **-neys** A type of body organ.

kid-ney bean *n.* A bean grown for its edible seeds.

kiel-ba-sa *n.* Type of Polish sausage.

kill *n.* To put to death; slaughter for food.

kill-er whale *n.* A carnivorous whale, black and white in color.

kill-joy *n.* One who spoils the fun of others.

kiln *n.* An oven for firing ceramics.

kil-o-bit *n.* One thousand binary digits.

kil-o-gram *n.* Metric system unit of weight less than one third of a pound.

kil-o-watt *n.* The unit of power equal to one thousand watts.

kilt *n.* The knee-length wool skirt worn by men in Scotland.

ki-mo-no *n.* A loose robe with a wide sash.

kin *n.* The relatives by blood.

kind *adj.* Gentle; sort.

kin-der-gar-ten *n.* The school for pre-school children.

kin-dle *v.* To ignite; to catch fire.

kin-dling *n.* A material used to start a fire.

kin-dred *n.* Relatives.

kin-e-mat-ics *n.* The branch of dynamics dealing with motion.

kin-e-scope *n.* A cathode-ray tube in a television set.

king *n.* The ruler of a country.

king-bolt *n.* The front axle bolt.

king crab *n.* A large crablike crustacean.

king-pin *n.* The foremost pin in bowling or tenpins; esssential person.

kink *n.* A tight twist or curl; a muscle cramp.

kink-a-jou *n.* A tropical American mammal.

kink-y *adj.* To be sexually uninhibited.

ki-osk *n.* A refreshment booth.

kip *n.* The untanned skin of a calf.

kip-per *n.* A smoked herring or salmon.

kir-tle *n.* A woman's long skirt.

kitch-en *n.* The room used to cook and prepare food.

kite *n.* A framework of wood and paper used to fly in a steady breeze.

kitsch *n.* Anything in

poor taste.

kit-ten *n.* A young cat.

ki-wi *n.* A flightless bird; a fuzzy-skinned edible fruit.

knack *n.* A natural talent for something.

knack-wurst *or* **knock-wurst** *n.* Type of seasoned sauage.

knap-sack *n.* A bag worn on the shoulders.

knave *n.* A dishonest person. **-ish** *adj.*

knead *v.* To shape and mold dough.

knee *n.* The joint between the calf and thigh.

knee cap *n.* Protective covering for knee bone.

knell *v.* To sound a bell.

knick-ers *pl. n.* Short loose-fitting pants.

knife *n.* A tool for cutting.

knight *n.* A medieval soldier. **-hood** *n.*

knish *n.* Fried dough with filling.

knit *v.* To form by intertwining yarn. **-ter** *n.*

knit-ting nee-dle *n.* A pointed rod for knitting.

knob *n.* The rounded handle to open a door.

knock *v.* To strike with a hard blow. **Slang knock out** To make unconscious.

knock-er *n.* A metal ring on a docr.

knock-knee *n.* Knees turn inward while walking.

knoll *n.* A type of small round hill.

knot *n.* The fastening made by tying together string, etc.

knot-hole *n.* A hole in lumber.

knout *n.* A whip for flogging criminals.

know *v.* To be certain of; to be familiar with.

ko-a-la *n.* A bear-type animal from Australia.

kohl-ra-bi *n.* A variety of cabbage.

kook *n., Slang* A type of crazy person.

Ko-ran *n.* The sacred book of Islam.

ko-sher *adj.* Eatting according to Jewish dietary laws. *Slang* Proper.

kow-tow *v.* To show servile deference.

kraal *n.* A village of southern African natives; enclosure for animals in Africa.

Krem-lin *n.* The citadel of Moscow which houses the Soviet government offices.

kryp-ton *n.* A white, inert gaseous chemical used mainly in fluorescent lamps.

ku-dos *n.* The prestige resulting from notable achievement.

kum-quat *n.* A small, round orange fruit.

kung fu *n.* The Japanese art of self-defense.

kwash-i-or-kor *n.* The severe malnutrition in children, caused by protein deficiency.

L

L, l The twelfth letter of the English alphabet.

la *n.* A sixth tone in a scale of music.

la-bel *n.* Something that identifies. **-er** *n.*

la-bi-al *n.* Relating to the lips. **-ly** *adv.*

la-bi-um *n.* Any of the four folds of the vulva.

la-bor *n.* Physical work; pains of childbirth. **-er** *n.*, **-iously** *adv.*

lab-o-ra-to-ry *n.* A place equipped for conducting scientific testing.

lab-y-rinth *n.* A system of winding, intricate passages. **-ian** *adj.*

lace *n.* A delicate openwork fabric. **-ed** *adj.*, **-er** *n.*

lac-er-ate *v.* To open with a jagged tear. **-tion** *n.*

lach-ry-mal *adj.* Relating to or producing tears.

lack *n.* An absence of something. **-ing** *adj.*

lack-a-dai-si-cal *adj.* Lacking life, or spirit. **-ly** *adv.*

lack-ey *n.* A male servant of very low status.

lack-lus-ter *adj.* Lacking sheen.

la-crosse *n.* A game of American Indian origin.

lac-tate *v.* To secrete. **-tion** *n.*

lac-te-al *adj.* Resembling milk.

lac-tic acid *n.* A syrupy acid that is present in sour milk.

lac-tose *n.* A white odorless crystalline sugar.

la-cu-na *n.* A space from which something is missing.

lad *n.* A boy or young man.

lad-der *n.* An implement used for climbing.

lad-en *adj.* Heavily burdened.

lad-ing *n.* A cargo; freight.

la-dle *n.* A vessel with a deep bowl and a long handle.

la-dy *n.* A mature woman.

la-dy-fin-ger *n.* A small spongy cake.

lag *v.* To stray or fall behind.

la-ger *n.* Beer.

la-goon *n.* A body of water separated from the ocean.

laid *v.* Past tense of lay.

laid back *adj., Slang* Casual or relaxed in character.

lain v. Past tense of lie.

lais-sez--faire n. A policy of government affairs.

la-i-ty n. A laymen, non-cleric people.

lake n. A large inland body of water.

lake trout n. A type of trout in the lakes of the U.S.

lamb n. A young sheep.

lam-baste v., Slang To scold severely.

lam-bent adj. Move over a surface carefully.
-**ly** adv., -**cy** n.

lame adj. Disabled or crippled. -**ly** adv.,
-**ness** n.

la-mel-la n. In bone, a scale. -**lar** adj.

la-ment v. Expressing sorrow; mourn for.
-**able** adj., -**bly** adv.

lam-i-nate v. To press into thin sheets.
-**tion** n., -**ed** adj.

lamp n. A device for generating heat or light.

lam-poon n. A satirical attack in verse.

lam-prey n. An eel-like fish.

lance n. A spear-like implement. -**like** adj.

land n. A solid, exposed surface of the earth.

land-er n. A space vehicle for landing on a celestial body.

land grant n. A grant of land made by a govern-ment.

land-ing n. The act of coming, going, or placing ashore from any kind of vessel or craft.

land-lord n. A person who owns property and rents to another.

land-mark n. A mark to indicate a boundary.

land-own-er n. A person who owns land.
-**ship**, -**ing** n.

land-scape n. A view of natural scenery. -**er** n.

land-slide n. The fall of rock or stone from top of hillside.

lane n. A small or narrow path.

lan-guage n. The contents of speech; expression of ideas by words or written symbols.

lan-guid adj. Lacking in energy. -**ly** adv.

lan-guish v. To become weak; lose strength.
-**ingly** adv., -**ing** adj.

lank adj. Tall and thin.
-**ness** n., -**y** adj.

lan-o-lin n. The grease obtained from sheep's wool.

lan-tern n. A portable light.

lan-yard n. A rope used to secure objects on ships.

lap v. To eat food with the use of the tongue, like a dog. -**per** n.

lap·is laz·u·li *n.* A semiprecious stone that is azure blue in color.

lapse *n.* A fall to a less desirable state.

lar·ce·ny *n.* An unlawful taking of another person's property. **-nous** *adj.*

lar·der *n.* A place, where food is stored.

large *adj.* Greater than usual in amount or size. **-ness** *n.*, **-ly** *adv.*

lar·gess *n.* An excessive giving to an inferior; donation.

lar·i·at *n.* A light rope with a noose at the end to catch livestock.

lark *n.* A bird having melodious ability to sing.

lar·va *n.* A worm-like form of a newly hatched insect. **-al** *adj.*

lar·yn·gi·tis *n.* An inflammation of the larynx.

lar·ynx *n.* An upper portion of the trachea.

lash *v.* To move violently or suddenly. **-ing** *n.*

lass *n.* A young girl or woman.

las·si·tude *n.* A condition of weariness.

las·so *n.* A long rope with a noose used to catch animals. **-er** *n.*

last *adj.* Following all the rest; endure wear. **-ing** *adj.*, **-ingly** *adv.*

latch *n.* A device used to secure a gate or door. **-ed** *adj.*

latch·key *n.* A key for opening an outside door.

late *adj.* Happening after the usual time. **-ness** *n.*

lat·er·al *adj.* Relating to the side. **-ly** *adv.*

la·tex *n.* A fluid from certain plants.

lath *n.* A narrow strip of wood. **-er** *n.*

lathe *n.* A machine for holding and shaping material.

lath·er *n.* The foam formed by soap and water. **-y** *adj.*, **-er** *n.*

lat·i·tude *n.* The distance of the earth's surface from the equator. **-dinal** *adj.*

la·trine *n.* A toilet.

lat·ter *adj.* Being the second of two things.

lat·tice *n.* Criss-crossed wooden pieces. **-ed** *adj.*

laud *v.* To praise; to extol. **-ably** *adv.*, **-able** *adj.*

laugh *v.* To express amusement, satisfaction. **-ingly** *adv.*, **-er** *n.*

launch *v.* To send a vessel into the water or air. **-er** *n.*

launch *n.* A large boat carried by a ship.

launch pad *n.* An area from which space missiles are launched.

laun-der v. To wash clothes in soap and water. **-er** n.

laun-dry n. A place where laundering is done.

lau-re-ate n. A person honored for his accomplishments.

la-va n. The molten rock which erupts from a volcano.

lav-a-to-ry n. A room with washing and toilet facilities.

lav-en-der n. A plant with pale violet flowers.

lav-ish adj. Generous in spending. **-ness** n., **-ly** adv.

law n. A rule of conduct or action which everyone must obey.

law--a-bid-ing adj. Obeying the laws.

law-break-er n. A person that does not follow the law. **-ing** n.

law-ful adj. Legal. **-ness** n., **-ly** adv.

law-giv-er n. A person who makes the laws. **-ing** n.

law-less adj. Not following the law. **-ness** n., **-ly** adv.

law-mak-er n. A person who writes laws. **-ing** n.

lawn n. A stretch of ground covered with grass.

lawn mow-er n. A pushed machine for cutting yards.

law-ren-ci-um n. A short-lived radioactive element.

law-suit n. A case brought before a court of law for settlement.

law-yer n. A person trained in the legal profession.

lax adj. Lacking disciplinary control. **-ly** adv., **-ness** n.

lax-a-tive n. A medicine taken to empty the bowels.

lay v. To place on a surface.

lay-er n. A single thickness, coating, that lies over.

lay-ette n. A clothing, and bedding, for a newborn child.

lay-man n. Not belonging to a particular profession.

lay-out n. A planned arrangement of something.

la-zy adj. Unwilling to work. **-iness** n., **-ily** adv.

lea n. A grassy field or meadow.

leach v. To cause liquid to pass through a filter.

lead v. To go ahead so as to show the way.

lead-en adj. To be dull. **-ness** n., **-ly** adv.

lead-er *n.* A person who guides others. **-ship** *n.*, **-less** *adj.*

leaf *n.* A flat outgrowth from a plant or tree. **.-less** *adj.*

leaf-y *adj.* To have leaves. **-iness** *n.*

league *n.* An organization of people with the same interests.

leak *n.* A small crack, permitting an escape of fluid. **-y** *adj.*, **-iness** *n.*

lean *v.* To incline the weight of the body for support. **-ness** *n.*, **-ly** *adv.*

leap *v.* Sudden thrust from the ground with a spring. **-er** *n.*

learn *n.* A process of acquiring knowledge. **-er** *n.*, **-ed** *adj.*, **-edly** *adv.*

lease *n.* A contract for temporary use in exchange for payments.

leash *n.* A cord for restraining a dog.

leath-er *n.* An animal skin or hide with the hair removed. **-y** *adj.*

leave *v.* To go or depart from. **-er** *n.*

lech-er-y *n.* Unrestrained indulgence in sexual activity. **-ous** *adj.*

lec-tern *n.* A tall desk, usually with a slanted top.

lec-ture **n.** A speech on a specific subject. **-er** *n.*

led *v.* Past tense of lead.

ledge *n.* A narrow, shelf-like projection forming a shelf.

ledg-er *n.* A book in which money is recorded.

lee *n.* A side of a ship sheltered from the wind.

leech *n.* Any of various bloodsucking worms.

leek *n.* A culinary herb of the lily family.

leer *n.* A glance. **-ingly** *adv.*

lee-way *n.* A lateral drift of a plane away from the correct course.

left *adj.* Opposite of right; past tense of leave. **-ist** *n.*

left--hand-ed *adj.* The left hand is the dominant hand. **-ness** *n.*, **-ly** *adv.*

leg *n.* An appendage serving as a means of support.

leg-a-cy *n.* Personal property, that is bequeathed by a will.

le-gal *adj.* Pertaining to the law or lawyers. **-ization** *n.*, **-ly** *adv.*

le-gal-ism *n.* A strict conformity to the law. **-ist** *n.*

le-ga-tion *n.* An official diplomatic mission.

le-ga-to *adv.* Flowing with successive notes connected.

leg-end *n.* A story handed down from the past.

leg-en-dar-y *adj.* Based on, or of the nature of a legend.

leg-horn *n.* A hat made from plaited wheat straw.

leg-i-ble *adj.* Capable of being read. **-bly** *adv.*

le-gion *n.* Any various honorary or military organizations.

leg-is-late *v.* To pass or make laws. **-tor** *n.*, **-tive** *adj.*

leg-is-la-tion *n.* An act or procedures of passing laws.

leg-is-la-ture *n.* A body of persons who make and change laws.

lei *n.* A wreath of flowers worn around the neck.

lei-sure *n.* A time of freedom from work or duty. **-liness** *n.*, **-ly** *adj.*

lem-on *n.* A citrus fruit grown on a tree.

le-mur *n.* A small monkey-like animal.

lend *v.* Temporary use or possession of something. **-er** *n.*

length *n.* A linear extent of something from end to end. **-y** *adj.*, **-iness** *n.*

length-en *v.* To make or become longer.

le-ni-ent *adj.* Gentle, forgiving, and mild.

-ly *adv.*, **-cy** *n.*

len-i-tive *adj.* The ability to ease pain.

lens *n.* The curved piece of glass in eyeglasses.

lent *v.* Past tense of lend.

len-til *n.* A leguminous plant having edible seeds.

leop-ard *n.* A large member of the cat family.

le-o-tard *n.* A tight fitting garment worn by dancers.

lep-er *n.* The one who suffers from leprosy.

lep-ro-sy *n.* A chronic communicable disease.

les-bi-an *n.* A homosexual woman.

le-sion *n.* An injury; a wound.

less *adj.* Smaller in size or importance; not as much as.

les-see *n.* The one who leases a property.

les-son *n.* An instance from which something is to be learned.

les-sor *n.* One who grants a lease to another.

let *v.* To give permission; to allow.

le-thal *adj.* Pertaining to or being able to cause death. **-ly** *adv.*

leth-ar-gy *n.* A state of excessive drowsiness. **-ical** *adj.*

let's *contr.* Let us.

let-ter *n.* A standard

character used in writing or printing. **-er** *n.*

let-tuce *n.* A plant having green edible leaves.

leu-ke-mi-a *n.* Generally fatal disease of the blood.

le-vee *n.* An embankment along the shore of a body of water.

lev-el *v.* To make or become flat.

lev-er *n.* A handle used to operate a mechanism.

lev-er-age *n.* Use of a lever.

lev-i-tate *v.* Apparent defiance of gravity. **-tion** *n.*

lev-i-ty *n.* A lack of seriousness.

lev-y *v.* To collect by authority or force.

lewd *adj.* Preoccupied with sex; indecent. **-ly** *adv.*

lex-i-cog-ra-phy *n.* A profession of compiling dictionaries. **-ical** *adj.*, **-pher** *n.*

li-a-bil-i-ty *n.* A condition or state of being liable; obligation.

li-a-ble *adj.* Legally or rightly responsible.

li-ai-son *n.* A close connection or relationship.

li-ar *n.* A person who tells falsehoods.

li-bel *n.* A written statement that damages one's reputation. **-er** *n.*

lib-er-al *adj.* Characterized by generosity. **-ness** *n.*, **-ly** *adv.*

lib-er-ate *v.* To set free, as from bondage. **-tor** *n.*

lib-er-ty *n.* A state of being free from oppression.

li-bi-do *n.* One's sexual desire or impulse.

li-brar-i-an *n.* A person in charge of a library.

li-brar-y *n.* A collection of reference books used for studying.

li-cense *n.* A document that gives permission in a specified activity. **-er** *n.*

li-cen-ti-ate *n.* Licensed to practice a profession.

li-cen-tious *adj.* Lacking in moral restraint; immoral. **-ly** *adv.*, **-ness** *n.*

li-chen *n.* Flowerless plants consisting of fungi.

lic-it *adj.* Lawful; allowed. **-ly** *adv.*

lick *v.* To pass the tongue over the surface. **-ing, -er** *n.*

lick-e-ty--split *adv.* Full speed.

lic-o-rice *n.* A perennial herb of Europe, used in making candy.

lid *n.* A removable cover for a container. **-ded** *adj.*

lie *n.* A false or untrue statement.

liege *n.* A feudal lord or sovereign.

lien *n.* A legal claim on property for satisfaction of a debt.

lieu *n.* A place stead.

lieu-ten-ant *n.* The ranks below a captain.

life *n.* A form of existence that distinguishes living organisms from dead organisms. **-like** *adj.*

life-guard *n.* An expert swimmer to protect people in and around water.

life-raft *n.* An inflatable material used by people forced in water.

life-work *n.* The main work of a person's lifetime.

lift *v.* To raise from a lower to a higher position. **-er** *n.*

lift off *n.* a takeoff of an aircraft or spacecraft.

lig-a-ment *n.* A tough band of tissue joining organs.

li-gate *v.* To tie with a bandage.

lig-a-ture *n.* A cord, that is used to bind.

light *n.* An electromagnetic radiation. **-ness** *n.*

light house *n.* A tower on the seacoast with a beacon light to warn ships of danger.

light-ning *n.* A flash of light produced by natural electric in a storm.

light-ning rod *n.* A metal rod used to protect from lightning.

light-ship *n.* A ship, having a powerful light or horn.

light show *n.* A display of colored lights.

light-weight *n.* A boxer who weighs between 127 and 135 pounds.

lig-ne-ous *adj.* Resembling wood.

lig-ni-fy *v.* To make or become woody or woodlike.

lig-nite *n.* A brownish-black soft coal.

lig-ro-in *n.* A volatile, flammable fraction of petroleum.

lik-a-ble *adj.* Friendly, affectionate. **-ness** *n.*

like--mind-ed *adj.* Same way of thinking.

lik-en *v.* To describe as being liked.

like-ness *n.* A resemblance; similar.

like-wise *adv.* In a similar way.

lilt *n.* Rhythmical way of speaking. **-ing** *adj.*

lil-y *n.* Any of various plants bearing trumpet-shaped flowers.

lil-y--liv-ered *adj.* Timid.

li-ma bean *n.* An edible vegetable.

limb *n.* A large bough of

a tree. **-ed** *adj.*

lim-ber *adj.* Bending easily. **-ness** *n.*

lime *n.* A tropical citrus tree. **-like** *adj.*

lime-light *n.* A focus of public attention. **-er** *n.*

lim-er-ick *n.* A humorous verse of five lines.

lim-it *n.* The maximum or a minimum number or amount. **-less** *adj.*, **-er** *n.*

limn *v.* To describe; to depict by drawing.

li-mo-nite *n.* An iron oxide used as an ore of iron.

lim-ou-sine *n.* A luxurious large vehicle.

limp *v.* To walk lamely. **-ingly** *adv.*, **-er** *n.*

lim-pet *n.* A marine gastropod mollusks.

lim-pid *adj.* Transparently clear. **-ness** *n.*, **-ly** *adv.*

linch-pin *n.* A locking pin to keep a wheel from slipping off.

lin-den *n.* Various shade trees having heart-shaped leaves.

lin-e-age *n.* A direct line of descent from an ancestor.

lin-e-a-ment *n.* A feature of the body and especially the face.

lin-e-ar *adj.* Pertaining to, or resembling a line. **-ly** *adv.*

line-back-er *n.* One of the defensive players on a football team.

line-man *n.* One who works on electric power lines.

lin-en *n.* A thread, yarn, or fabric made of flax.

lin-er *n.* A large passenger ship.

lines-man *n.* An official in a court game, as in tennis.

lin-ger *v.* Slow in leaving; remain behind. **-ingly** *adv.*, **-er** *n.*

lin-ge-rie *n.* A women's undergarments.

lingo *n., pl.* **-goes** A language that is unfamiliar.

lin-guist *n.* One who is fluent in more than one language.

lin-i-ment *n.* A liquid medicine applied to the skin.

lin-ing *n.* A material used to cover an inside surface.

link *n.* One of the rings forming a chain.

links *pl., n.* A golf course.

lin-net *n.* A small Old World finch.

li-no-le-um *n.* A floor covering.

lin-seed *n.* The seed of flax, used in paints.

lint *n.* Fuzz. **-y** *adj.*

lin-tel *n.* A beam which supports weight.

li-on *n.* A large carnivorous mammal of the cat family. **-like** *adj.*

li-on--heart-ed *adj.* Very courageous.

li-on-ize *v.* To treat someone as a celebrity. **-zation** *n.*

lip-stick *n.* A coloring for the lips.

liq-ue-fy *v.* To make liquid. **-ier** *n.*, **-iable** *adj.*

li-queur *n.* An alcoholic beverage.

liq-ui-date *v.* To settle a debt by payment. **-tion** *n.*

liq-uor *n.* A distilled alcoholic beverage.

li-ra *n.* The monetary unit of Italy.

lisp *n.* A speech defect. **-ingly** *adv.*

lis-some *adj.* Nimble. **-ness** *n.*, **-ly** *adv.*

list *n.* A series of numbers or words. **-er** *n.*, **-ed** *adj.*

lis-ten *v.* To attend closely; heed advice. **-er** *n.*

list-less *adj.* Lacking energy. **-ness** *n.*, **-ly** *adv.*

li-tchi *n.* Chinese tree bearing edible fruit.

lit-er-al *adj.* Conforming to the exact meaning of a word. **-ly** *adv.*, **-ness** *n.*

lit-er-ar-y *adj.* Pertaining to literature. **-iness** *n.*, **-ily** *adv.*

lit-er-ate *adj.* Having the ability to read and write. **-ly** *adv.*

lit-er-a-ti *pl., n.* An educated class.

lit-er-a-ture *n.* Printed material, as leaflets for a political campaign.

lithe *adj.* Bending easily; supple. **-ly** *adv.*, **-ness** *n.*

lith-i-um *n.* A silver-white, soft metallic element.

li-thog-ra-phy *n.* A printing process.

li-thol-o-gy *n.* A microscopic study of rocks.

lit-i-gate *v.* To conduct a legal contest by judicial process. **-tor** *n.*

lit-mus *n.* A blue powder obtained from lichens.

lit-ter *n.* A stretcher; birth of a animal; accumulation of waste material.

lit-ter-bug *n.* One who litters in a public area.

lit-to-ral *adj.* Existing on a shore.

lit-ur-gy *n.* Body of rites for public worship. **-ical** *adj.*

live-li-hood *n.* A means of support; sustenance.

live-ly *adj.* Vigorous; spirited. **-iness** *n.*

liv-er *n.* A vascular body organ that secretes bile.

liv-er-wurst *n.* A kind of sausage made of liver.

liv-er-y *n.* The uniform

worn by servants.
-man *n.*, **-ied** *adj.*

liv-er-y-man *n.* A keeper or employee of a livery stable.

live-stock *n.* A farm animals raised for human use.

liv-id *adj.* To be discolored from a bruise.
-ness *n.*

liz-ard *n.* One of various reptiles.

lla-ma *n.* South American ruminant, related to the camel family.

load *n.* A weight that is lifted or supported.
-er *n.*, **-ed** *adj.*

loaf *n.* Food, especially bread.

loam *n.* Rich, fertile soil.
-y *adj.*

loan *n.* The money lent with interest to be repaid.

loan shark *n.* One who lends money.

loath *adj.* Not willing; averse. **-ness** *n.*

loathe *v.* To dislike intensely; hate strongly.

loath-some *adj.* Arousing disgust. **-ness** *n.*, **-ly** *adv.*

lob *v.* To throw or hit in a high arc.

lob-by *n.* A foyer, as in a hotel or theatre.

lobe *n.* A curved or rounded projection or division. **-ed** *adj.*

lob-lol-ly *n.* A mudhole; mire.

lo-bo *n.* Those who reside in the western U.S.

lob-ster *n.* A large, edible marine crustacean.

lob-ule *n.* A subdivision of a lobe.

lo-cal *adj.* Being in, or serving a particular area.
-ly *adv.*

lo-cale *n.* A setting or scene of a movie or novel.

lo-cal-i-ty *n.* A specific neighborhood, or place.

lo-cate *v.* To determine the place, or position.

lo-ca-tion *n.* A place where something is.

loch *n.* A lake.

lock *n.* A device used, to secure or fasten.

lock-et *n.* A small case on a chain for a picture.

lock-jaw *n.* A tetanus; disease in which the jaws become locked.

lock-smith *n.* One who repairs locks.

lo-co *adj.* Insane; crazy.

lo-co-mo-tion *n.* An act of moving. **-tor** *n.*

lo-co-mo-tive *n.* A self-propelled vehicle used for moving railroad cars.

lo-cust *n.* Grasshoppers which damage vegetation.

lode-star *n.* The North Star, used as a

reference.

lodge *n.* A cabin used as temporary shelter. **-er** *n.*

lodg-ment *n.* A place for lodging.

loft *n.* An attic.

loft-y *adj.* Exceedingly high. **-iness** *n.*

log *n.* Unhewn piece of timber; record of a ship's voyage.

lo-gan-ber-ry *n.* A prickly plant with edible fruit.

loge *n.* A theatre box; compartment.

log-ger-head *n.* A large marine turtle.

log-gi-a *n.* An open balcony in a theatre.

log-ic *n.* A science dealing with the principles of reasoning. **-cian** *n.*

log-i-cal *adj.* Consistency of reasoning. **-ly** *adv.*, **-ity** *n.*

lo-gis-tics *pl., n.* A military transportation of material and troops.

lo-go-type *n.* An identifying symbol for a publication.

lo-gy *adj.* Something marked by sluggishness.

loin *n.* A cut of meat from an animal.

loins The thighs and groin.

loi-ter *v.* To stay for no apparent reason. **-er** *n.*

loll *v.* To move in a lazy manner.

lol-li-pop *n.* A candy on a stick.

lol-ly-gag *v., Slang* To fool around.

lone *adj.* Single; isolated; sole.

lone-ly *adj.* Being without companions; dejected. **-iness** *n.*, **-ily** *adv.*

lon-er *n.* A person who avoids the company of others.

lone-some *adj.* Dejected because of the lack of companionship. **-ness** *n.*, **-ly** *adv.*

lon-gev-i-ty *n.* Long life.

long-hair *n.* Lover of the arts.

long-hand *n.* A cursive handwriting.

lon-gi-tude *n.* A distance that is east and west across the earth.

lon-gi-tu-di-nal *adj.* Relating to the length. **-ly** *adv.*

long-shore-man *n.* A dock hand who loads and unloads cargo.

long--wind-ed *adj.* Excessive talking; able to run a long distance with ease.

look *v.* To examine with the eyes.

look-out *n.* A person positioned to keep watch.

loom *v.* To come into view as a image;

machine for weaving cloth.

loon *n.* A large fish-eating bird.

loo-ny *n.* Crazy person. **-iness** *n.*

loop *n.* A circular length of line.

loop-hole *n.* A means of escape.

loose *adj.* Not tightly fastened. **-ness** *n.*, **-ly** *adv.*

loot *n.* The goods, usually of significant value. **-er** *n.*

lop *v.* To remove branches.

lope *v.* To run with a steady gait. **-er** *n.*

lop-sid-ed *adj.* Heavier on one side than on the other.

lo-qua-cious *adj.* Overly talkative. **-ness** *n.*, **-ly** *adv.*

Lord *n.* God; having power over other people.

lore *n.* A traditional fact; knowledge.

lor-gnette *n.* A pair of opera glasses.

lorn *n.* A forlorn; desolate.

lose *v.* To mislay; to fail to keep.

loss *n.* A suffering or damage used by losing.

lost *adj.* Unable to find one's way.

lot *n.* A parcel of land having boundaries.

lo-tion *n.* A liquid for moisturizing the body.

lot-ter-y *n.* A contest in which players win money.

lo-tus *n.* An aquatic plant.

loud *adj.* Intense sound and high volume. **-ness** *n.*

lounge *v.* To move in a lazy manner; room in which people may relax. **-ing** *adj.*, **-er** *n.*

louse *n.* A small, wingless biting or sucking insect.

lous-y *adj.* Infested with lice. **-iness** *n.*, **-ily** *adv.*

lout *n.* An awkward, stupid person.

lou-ver *n.* An opening in a wall fitted with movable slats.

love *n.* An intense affection for another.

love-bird *n.* Various Old World parrots.

love-ly *adj.* Beautiful. **-iness** *n.*

lov-er *n.* A sexual partner.

love seat *n.* A small couch which seats two.

love--sick *adj.* Languishing with love.

lov-ing cup *n.* A large, ornamental cup.

low *adj.* Not high; being below or under normal height.

low beam *n.* A low-intensity headlight.

low-brow *n.* An uncultured person.

low-down *n.* The whole truth.

low-er class *n.* A group in society that ranks below the middle class.

low-est com-mon mul-ti-ple *n.* The least common multiple.

low fre-quen-cy *n.* A radiowave frequency between 30 and 300 kilohertz.

low-ly *adj.* Low in position or rank.

low pro-file *n.* An inconspicuous life style or posture.

low--ten-sion *adj.* Having a low voltage.

lox *n.* A smoked salmon; liquid oxygen.

loy-al *adj.* Faithful to a person, cause, or ideal.

loy-al-ist *n.* One who remains loyal to political cause.

loz-enge *n.* A small medicated candy.

lu-au *n.* A traditional Hawaiian feast.

lub-ber *n.* An awkward, clumsy or stupid person.

lu-bri-cant *n.* A material, as grease or oil. **-tion** *n.*

lu-bri-cous *adj.* Smooth, unstable.

lu-cid *adj.* Easily understood. **-ness** *n.*

lu-cite *n.* A transparent thermoplastic acrylic resin.

luck *n.* Good fortune.

lu-cra-tive *adj.* Producing profits or great wealth.

lu-cre *n.* Money; profit.

lu-cu-brate *v.* To study or work laboriously. **-tion** *n.*

lu-di-crous *adj.* Amusing or laughable through obvious absurdity. **-ly** *adv.*

luff *v.* To turn a sailing vessel toward the wind.

lug *n.* An ear-like handle or projection used as a hold.

luge *n.* A small sled similar to a toboggan.

lug-gage *n.* A suitcases or a traveler's baggage.

lu-gu-bri-ous *adj.* Mournful; dejected. **-ly** *adv.*

luke-warm *adj.* Mildly warm; tepid; unenthusiastic.

lull *v.* To cause to rest or sleep.

lul-la-by *n.* A song to lull a child to sleep.

lum-ba-go *n.* Painful rheumatic pain of the muscles.

lum-bar *adj.* Part of the back between the ribs and the pelvis.

lum-ber *n.* A timber, sawed or split into boards.

lum-ber-jack *n.* One who cuts and prepares timber for the sawmill.

lum-ber-yard *n.* A business place where lumber is sold.

lu-mi-nar-y *n.* A celestial body, as the sun.

lu-mi-nes-cence *n.* An emission of light without heat.

lu-mi-nous *adj.* Emitting or reflecting light.

lum-mox *n.* A clumsy oaf.

lump *n.* A projection; a protuberance.

lu-na-cy *n.* Insanity. **-tic** *n.*

lu-nar *adj.* Relating to, caused by the moon.

lu-nar e-clipse *n.* An eclipse where the moon passes partially through the umbra of the earth's shadow.

lu-na-tic *n.* Crazy person.

lunch-eon *n.* A lunch.

lunch-eon-ette *n.* A modest restaurant at which light meals are served.

lung *n.* A organs that constitute the basic respiratory system.

lunge *n.* A sudden forward movement.

lu-pus *n.* A bacterial disease of the skin.

lurch *n.* A sudden roll of a ship to one side.

lure *n.* A decoy; something appealing.

lu-rid *adj.* Startling; ghastly pale.

lurk *v.* To lie in concealment, as in an ambush. **-ingly** *adv.*

lus-cious *adj.* Very pleasant to smell or taste.

lush *adj.* Producing luxuriant growth.

lust *n.* An intense sexual desire.

lus-ter *n.* A glow of reflected light.

lust-y *adj.* Vigorous; healthy.

lute *n.* A medieval musical stringed instrument.

lu-te-ti-um *n.* A silvery, rare earth metallic element.

lux-u-ri-ant *adj.* Growing or producing abundantly.

lux-u-ri-ate *v.* To enjoy luxury or abundance; to grow abundantly.

lux-u-ry *n.* Something which adds pleasure but is not necessary.

ly-ce-um *n.* A hall where public programs are presented.

lye *n.* A powerful caustic solution yielded by leaching wood ashes.

ly-ing--in *n.* A confinement in childbirth.

lymph node *n.* A roundish body of lymphoid tissue.

lynch v. To execute without authority or the due process of law.

lynx adj. Having acute eyesight; wild cat.

lyre n. An ancient Greek stringed instrument related to the harp.

lyr-ic adj. Concerned with thoughts and feelings.

M

M, m The thirteenth letter of the English alphabet.

ma-ca-bre adj. Suggesting death and decay. -ly adv.

mac-a-ro-ni n. Tube-shaped pasta.

mac-a-roon n. A small cookie.

ma-caw n. A tropical American parrot.

mace n. An aromatic spice.

mac-er-ate v. To make a solid substance soft. -tion n.

ma-chet-e n. A large, heavy knife.

ma-chine n. A device built to use energy to do work. -ry n., -able adj.

ma-chin-ist n. One who operates or repairs machines.

mack-er-el n. A fish.

mac-ra-me n. The craft of tying knots.

mad adj. Angry; insane -ness n., -ly adv.

mad-ri-gal n., Music Unaccompanied song. -ist n.

maes-tro n. A person mastering any art.

Ma-fi-a n. A secret criminal organization in Sicily.

mag-a-zine n. A publication; explosives storehouse.

mag-got n. A legless larva insects. -y adj.

mag-ic n. The art of illusions. -ically adv., -ical adj.

mag-is-trate n. A civil officer of law. -ically adv.

mag-nan-i-mous adj. Forgiving; generous. -ness n., -ly adv.

mag-nate n. A business tycoon.

mag-net n. A body attracting other magnetic material. -ically adv., -ize v.

mag-nif-i-cent adj. Beautiful; grand. -cence n., -cently adv.

mag-ni-fy v. To increase in size. -fication n., -fiable adj.

mag-ni-tude n. A greatness in size.

mag-no-lia n. A flowering tree.

mag-num n. A wine bottle holding two quarts.

mag-pie n. A large, noisy bird.

ma-hog-a-ny n., pl. -ies

Trees with hard wood.

maid-en *n.* A young girl.
-**hood** *n.*

mail *n.* Printed matter.
-**box** *n.,* -**ed** *adj.*

maim *v.* To cripple, disfigure. -**er** *n.*

main *adj.* The most important part. -**ly** *adv.*

main-tain *v.* To keep in existence. -**er** *n.*
-**able** *adj.*

maize *n.* Corn.

ma-jor *adj.* Greater in importance.

ma-jor med-i-cal *n.* Type of insurance policy.

ma-jor-i-ty *n.* A greater number.

make *v.* To create; to cause to happen. -**er** *n.,*
-**able** *adj.*

make--be-lieve *n.* Imagined; pretended.

make--up *n.* Composition.

mal-a-droit *adj.* Lacking in skill. -**ness** *n.,* -**ly** *adv.*

mal-a-dy *n., pl.* -**ies** A chronic disease or sickness.

ma-lar-i-a *n., Pathol.* A disease caused by the bite of mosquitos.
-**ious** *adj.*

mal-con-tent *adj.* Unhappy your with surroundings.

male *adj.* A male person.
-**ness** *n.*

mal-for-ma-tion *n.* A defective form.

mal-func-tion *n.* A failure to work.

mal-ice *n.* The desire to harm others.
-**ciously** *adv.,* -**cious** *adj.,* -**ciousness** *n.*

ma-lign *v.* To speak evil of. -**ly** *adv.,* -**er** *n.*

ma-lig-nant *adj., Pathol.* Relating to tumors and abnormal growth.
-**ly** *adv.,* -**cy** *n.*

ma-lin-ger *v.* To pretend sickness to avoid work.
-**er** *n.*

mal-lard *n.* A wild duck.

mal-let *n.* A hammer with a short handle.

mal-nour-ished *adj.* Underfed; lacking food.

mal-oc-clu-sion *n.* Improper alignment of the teeth.

mal-prac-tice *n.* Mistreatment by a doctor.
-**er** *n.*

malt *n.* A grain. -**y** *adj.*

mal-treat *v.* To treat unkindly. -**ment** *n.*

mam-mal *n.* Animals who suckle their young.
-**ian** *adj.*

mam-mog-ra-phy *n.* X-ray of the breast for detection of cancer.

mam-moth *n.* An extinct form of an elephant.

man *n.* The adult male; human race.

man-a-cle *n.* Handcuffs.

man-age *v.* To direct or control. -**able** *adj.,*

-ability n.

man-ag-er n. One in charge. -ship n.

man-a-tee n. An aquatic mammal.

man-date n. An order or command.

man-da-to-ry adj. Required; needed. -ily adv.

man-do-lin n. A musical instrument. -ist n.

mane n. The long hair on an animals neck. -ed adj.

mange n. A skin disease of dogs.

man-ger n. A box for animal feed.

man-gle v. To disfigure or mutilate.

man-grove n. A tropical tree.

man-han-dle v. To handle roughly. -ed adj.

man-hole n. A sewer drain.

ma-ni-a n. The desire for something.

man-i-cot-ti n. A form of pasta.

man-i-cure n. The care of the fingernails. -ist n.

man-i-fest n. A list of cargo. -ation n.

man-i-fold adj. Having many parts, or types. -ly adv., -ness n.

ma-nip-u-late v. To manage shrewdly. -tion n.

man-kind n. The human race.

man-ner n. The way in which things are done. -less adj.

man-ner-ly adj. Being well-behaved. -iness n.

ma-nom-e-ter n. An instrument to measure pressure.

man-or n. An estate. -ial adj.

man-slaugh-ter n., Law Unlawful killing without malice.

man-tel n. The shelf over a fireplace. -piece n.

man-til-la n. A light scarf.

man-u-al adj. Operated by the hand. -ly adv.

man-u-fac-ture v. To make a product. -er n., -able adj.

ma-nure n. Animal dung used for fertilizer.

man-u-script n. A typed copy of an article, or book.

man-y adj. An indefinite number.

map n. A plane surface of a region. -per n.

ma-ple syr-up n. The sap of the sugar maple.

mar v. To deface. -rer n.

mar-a-thon n. A foot race of 26 miles.

mar-ble n. Limestone. -ize v., -ing n.

march v. To walk with measured steps. -ing n.

mare n. The female of the horse.

mar-ga-rine *n.* A butter substitute.

mar-gin *n.* The edge of printed text. **-al** *adj.,* **-ally** *adv.*

mar-i-jua-na *n.* A hallucinogenic drug.

ma-ri-na *n.* A harbor for boats.

mar-i-nade *n.* A brine for soaking meat.

ma-rine *adj.* Pertaining to the sea. **-er** *n.*

mar-i-o-nette *n.* A puppet operated by strings.

mark *n.* A visible impression.

mar-ket *n.* A public place to purchase or sell goods. **-er** *n.*,

marks-man *n.* The skill in firing a gun.

mar-lin *n.* A large marine game fish.

ma-roon *v.* To abandon on shore.

mar-riage *n.* A legal union of wedlock. **-ability** *n.,* **-able** *adj.*

mar-row *n.* The tissue in bone cavities. **-y** *adj.*

marsh *n.* Low, wet land; swamp. **-y** *adj.,* **-iness** *n.*

mar-shal *n.* A military officer.

marsh-mal-low *n.* A soft confection.

mar-su-pi-al *n.* Animals with external pouchs.

mar-tial arts *pl., n.* The art of self-defense, such as karate.

mar-ti-ni *n.* A cocktail of gin and vermouth.

mar-tyr *n.* A person who would die for a cause. **-dom** *n.*

mar-zi-pan *n.* A paste of almonds, sugar and egg whites made into candy.

mar-vel *n.* Be in awe. **-ous** *adj.,* **-ously** *adv.*

mas-car-a *n.* A cosmetic for eyelashes.

mas-cot *n.* An object to bring good luck.

mash *n.* A mixture to distill alcohol.

mask *n.* A covering to conceal the face. **-like** *adj.*

mas-o-chism *n.* Sexual pleasure derived from pain. **-istic** *adj.,* **-ist** *n.*

ma-son *n.* A brick layer.

mas-quer-ade *n.* A costume party.

mass *n.* A body of matter with no form.

mas-sa-cre *n.* The savage killing of human beings. **-er** *n.*

mas-sage *n.* A body rub down. **-er** *n.*

mas-sive *adj.* Having great intensity.

mast *n.* The pole which supports the sails.

mas-ter *n.* A person with control. **-ful** *adj.*

mas-ter-piece *n.* A work of art.

mas-ti-cate *v.* To chew.

-tor, -tion n., -able adj.

mas-to-don n. An extinct mammal.

mas-tur-ba-tion n. Sexual arousement without intercourse.

mat-a-dor n. A bull-fighter.

match n. Identical; piece of wood that ignites. **-er** n.

ma-te-ri-al-ize v. To take form or shape.

ma-te-rial n. Equipment or supplies.

ma-ter-nal adj. Relating to mother. **-ly** adv., **-istic** adj.

math-e-mat-ics n. A study of form, quantity and magnitude of numbers and symbols. **-cally** adv., **-cal** adj.

mat-i-nee n. An afternoon movie.

mat-ri-cide n. One who kills his mother.

ma-tric-u-late v. To enroll into a college. **-tion** n.

mat-ri-mo-ny n. The ceremony of marriage. **-ial** adj.

ma-tron n. A married woman. **-ly** adv.

mat-ter n. The substance of anything.

ma-ture adj. Being completely developed. **-ity** n.

mat-zo n. A flat piece of unleavened bread.

maud-lin adj. Being sentimental.

maul n. A heavy hammer.

maun-der v. To talk incoherent.

mau-so-le-um n. A large tomb.

mav-er-ick n. An unbranded calf.

max-i-mum n. The greatest possible quantity.

may v. To permit or allow.

may-be adv. Perhaps; possibly.

may-on-naise n. A dressing for salads.

may-or n. The chief magistrate of a town. **-alty** n.

maze n. A complicated network. **-y** adj.

mead n. An alcoholic beverage.

mead-ow n. A tract of grassland.

mea-ger adj. Being thin; lean in quantity. **-ness** n., **-ly** adv.

mean v. Having purpose or intent; bad tempered. **-ness** n.

me-an-der v. To wander about. **-ingly** adv.

mea-sles n. A contagious disease.

mea-sly adj. Very small.

meas-ure n. The dimension of anything. **-er** n.

meat n. The flesh of an animal used as food.

me-chan-ic *n.* A person skilled with tools.
  -cal *adj.*
mech-a-nism *n.* The parts of a machine.
med-al *n.* An award.
  -ist *n.*
med-dle *v.* To interfere in other's affairs.
  -some *adj.,* **-er** *n.*
me-di-al *adj.* Situated in the middle.
me-di-ate *v.* To help settle a dispute.
med-ic *n.* An intern; a corpsman.
med-i-cal *adj.* The study of medicine. **-ly** *adv.*
Med-i-care *n.* Medical care for elderly people.
med-i-cine *n.* The treatment of diseases.
me-di-o-cre *adj.* Common; plain. **-rity** *n.*
med-i-tate *v.* To be in contemplative thought.
  -tor *n.,* **-tive** *adj.*
me-di-um *n.* In the middle; intermediary professing to give messages from the dead.
med-ley *n.* A jumble; musical composition.
meek *adj.* Lacking spirit.
  -ness *n.*
meet *v.* To come upon.
  -er *n.*
meg-a-ton *n.* One million tons.
mel-an-chol-y *adj.* Being gloomy or sad.
  -iness *n.,* **-ically** *adv.*

mel-a-no-ma *n.* A malignant mole.
mel-io-rate *v.* To improve. **-tor** *n.,* **-able** *adj.*
mel-lif-er-ous *adj.* Producing honey.
mel-o-dra-ma *n.* A dramatic presentation.
  -tic *adj.,* **-tics** *n.*
mel-on *n.* The fruit of the gourd family.
melt *v.* To change from solid to liquid. **-er** *n.,*
  -able *adj.*
melt-down *n.* The melting of a nuclear-reactor core.
mem-ber *n.* A person belonging to a club.
  -ship *n.,* **-less** *adj.*
mem-brane *n.* The thin layer of skin. **-nous** *adj.*
me-men-to *n.* A keepsake.
mem-oir *n.* An autobiography.
mem-o-ra-ble *adj.* Worth remembering. **-bly** *adv.*
mem-o-rize *v.* To commit to memory.
  -zation *n.,* **-zable** *adj.*
men-ace *n.* A threatening person.
  -ly *adv.*
me-nar-che *n.* The beginning of menstruation.
me-ni-al *adj.* Requiring little skill. **-ly** *adv.*
men-o-pause *n., Physiol.* The time of final menstruation. **-sal** *adj.*

men-tal *adj.* Of the mind. **-ly** *adv.*

men-tal re-tar-da-tion *n.* A mental deficiency.

men-tion *v.* To refer to briefly. **-er** *n.*, **-able** *adj.*

men-u *n.* A list of food at a restaurant.

mer-can-tile *adj.* Relating to commerce.

mer-ce-nar-y *n.* A greedy person. **-ily** *adv.*

mer-cer-ize *v.* To treat cotton yarn.

mer-chan-dise *n.* Goods bought and sold. **-er** *n.*

mer-chant *n.* A person who operates a retail business.

mer-cu-ry *n.* The silvery liquid in thermometers.

mer-cy *n., pl.* **-ies** Kind treatment of others. **-iless** *adj.*, **-ifully** *adv.*

mere *adj.* No more than is stated. **-ly** *adv.*

merge *v.* To unite as one. **-gence** *n.*

mer-it *n.* An act worthy of praise. **-edly** *adv.*, **-less** *adj.*

mer-maid *n.* An imaginary sea creature.

mer-ry-go-round *n.* A carousel.

me-sa *n.* A flat-topped hill.

mesh *n.* The open spaces in wire.

mes-mer-ize *v.* To put into a trance. **-er** *n.*

mess *n., pl.* **messes** A disorderly confused heap. **-ily** *adv.*

mes-sage *n.* Information sent from one person to another.

mes-sen-ger *n.* One who does errands for another.

mess-y *adj.* Untidy; dirty.

me-tab-o-lism *n.* The chemical changes in living cells.

met-a-gal-ax-y *n.* The universe.

met-a-mor-pho-sis *n.* The change in the structure and formation of animals.

me-te-or *n.* The moving particle in the solar system.

me-te-or-ol-o-gy *n.* The science of weather forecasting. **-ical** *adj.*

meth-a-done *n.* The man-made narcotic used to treat heroin addiction.

meth-od *n.* The manner of doing something.

me-tic-u-lous *adj.* Being very precise. **-ly** *adv.*

met-ro *n.* A subway system.

met-ro-nome *n.* An instrument designed to mark musical time. **-nomic** *adj.*

me-trop-o-lis *n.* A large capital city.

mew *n.* A hideaway.

mez-za-nine *n.* The lowest balcony.

mi-crobe *n.* A minute living organism. **-bial** *adj.*

mi-cro-com-put-er *n.* A computer using a microprocessor.

mi-cro-film *n.* A film used to record reduced size printed material.

mi-cro-phone *n.* An instrument which amplifies sound. **-nic** *adj.*

mi-cro-proc-es-sor *n.* A semiconductor processing unit.

mi-cro-scope *n.* A device to magnify small objects.

mi-cro-scop-ic *adj.* Very small; minute. **-ically** *adv.*

mi-cro-wave *n.* An electromagnetic wave.

mi-cro-wave o-ven *n.* An oven using microwaves to heat food.

mid-day *n.* Noon.

mid-dle *adj.* The center.

midg-et *n.* A very small person.

mid-night *n.* 12 o'clock p.m.

mid-point *n.* Near the middle.

mid-riff *n.* The mid-section of the human torso.

mid-ship-man *n.* Person in training at the U.S. Naval Academy.

mid-term *n.* The middle of academic term.

miff *n.* Displeasure.

might *n.* Force. **-y** *adj.*, **-ily** *adv.*

mi-graine *n.* Very severe headaches.

mi-grant *n.* A person moving from place to place to find work.

mi-grate *v.* To move from place to place. **-tory** *adj.*, **-tion** *n.*

mild *adj.* Being gentle in manner. **-ness** *n.*, **-ly** *adv.*

mile *n.* 5,280 feet.

mil-i-ta-rize *v.* To train for war.

mi-li-tia *n.* Armed forces used in an emergency.

Milk-y Way *n.* The luminous galaxy in the solar system.

mil-li-ner *n.* A person who sells women's hats.

mil-lion *n.* The number equal to 1,000 x 1,000.

mim-e-o-graph *n.* A duplicating machine.

mim-ic *v.* To imitate another person. **-ical** *adj.*

mince *v.* To chop into small pieces. **-ing** *adj.*, **-er** *n.*, **-ingly** *adv.*

mind *n.* The organ for thought. **-ful** *adj.*, **-fulness** *n.*

mine *n.* An underground excavation; belonging to me. **-er** *n.*

min-er-al *n.* An inorganic substance.

min-e-stro-ne *n.* A thick vegetable soup.

min-gle *v.* To mix

together.

min-i-a-ture *n.* A copy greatly reduced in size.

mini-disk *n.* 5.25 inch floppy disk used for storing data.

min-i-mum *n.* The least amount.

min-is-ter *n.* The pastor of a church. **-rial** *adj.*

mink *n.* An animal with valuable fur.

min-now *n.* A small, fresh water fish.

mi-nor *adj.* Under the legal age.

mi-nor-i-ty *n., pl.* **-ies** Smaller in number.

min-u-et *n.* A slow, stately dance.

mi-nus *prep., Math.* Reduced, by subtraction.

min-ute *n.* 60 seconds in time; small in size.

mir-a-cle *n.* A supernatural event.

mi-rage *n.* An optical illusion.

mir-ror *n.* A glass which reflects images.

mirth *n.* Merriment or joyousness. **-fulness** *n.,* **-ful** *adj.*

mis-an-thrope *n.* Hatred of mankind.

mis-ap-pro-pri-ate *v.* To embezzle money. **-tion** *n.*

mis-car-riage *n.* The premature birth of a fetus.

mis-cel-la-ne-ous *adj.* A mixed variety of parts.

mis-chief *n.* Behavior causing harm or damage.

mis-con-ceive *v.* To misunderstand the meaning.

mis-de-mean-or *n., Law* A crime less serious than a felony.

mis-er *n.* A person who hoards money. **-ly** *adj.,* **-liness** *n.*

mis-er-a-ble *adj.* Being very unhappy. **-bly** *adv.,* **-ness** *n.*

mis-er-ly *n.* A state of great unhappiness.

mis-fire *v.* To fail to explode.

mis-fit *n.* One not adjusted to his environment.

mis-for-tune *n.* Bad luck.

mis-giv-ing *n.* A feeling of doubt.

mis-han-dle *v.* To manage inefficiently.

mis-hap *n.* An unfortunate accident.

mish-mash *n.* A jumble or hodgepodge.

mis-in-ter-pret *v.* To understand incorrectly. **-er** *n.*

mis-judge *v.* To make a mistake in judgment. **-ment** *n.*

mis-lay *v.* To lose something.

mis-lead *v.* To deceive. **-er** *n.,* **-ing** *adj.*

mis-no-mer *n.* An

inappropriate name.

mis-pro-nounce v. To pronounce incorrectly.

mi-sog-a-my n. The hatred of marriage.

mi-sog-y-ny n. The hatred of women.

Miss n. The title for an unmarried girl.

mis-sile n. An object that shot at a target.

mis-sion n. A task to be carried out.

mis-take n. A wrong decision. **-able** adj.

mis-tle-toe n. A parasitic plant.

mis-tress n. A woman in authority.

mis-trust v. To have doubts. **-ingly** adv., **-ful** adj.

mite n. A very small insect.

mit-i-gate v. To make less painful. **-tor** n., **-tive** adj.

mitt n. A women's hand warmer; a baseball glove.

mix v. To blend; to combine; to unite. **-able** adj., **-ability** n.

mix-up n. A state of confusion.

moan n. A dull sound of pain.

moat n. A trench around a castle.

mob n. An unruly crowd. **-bish** adj.

mo-bi-lize v. To put into motion. **-zation** n.

mock-up n. A model for demonstration.

mode n. A method of doing something.

mod-el n. A clothing displayer. **-er** n.

mod-er-ate adj. Not excessive. **-ness** n., **-ly** adv.

mod-ern adj. Up-to-date.

mod-ern-ize v. To improve. **-zation** n.

mod-est adj. Shy and reserved. **-ly** adv.

mod-i-fy v. To make different in form. **-fier** n., **-fiable** adj.

mod-ule n. A series of standardized components. **-lar** adj.

mod-us op-er-an-di n. A method of operating.

moist adj. Slightly wet; damp. **-en** v., **-ly** adv., **-ener** n.

mois-ture n. Dampness. **-ize** v., **-izer** n.

mo-lar n. The grinding tooth.

mo-las-ses n. The syrup produced from sugar.

mold n. The growth produced on damp organic matter; a pattern. **-y** adj., **-eer** n.

mole n. A spot on the human skin; a small burrowing mammal.

mol-e-cule n. The smallest part retaining its identity.

mo-lest v. To accost

sexually. **-ation** *n.*

mol-li-fy *v.* To make less angry. **-fier** *n.*, **-fiable** *adj.*

molt *v.* To cast off or shed feathers. **-er** *n.*

mol-ten *adj.* Transform to liquid form by heat. **-ly** *adv.*

mo-men-tous *adj.* Of great importance.

mo-men-tum *n.* Increasing force; body in motion.

mon-arch *n.* Person who reigns over an empire.

mon-as-ter-y *n., pl.* **-ies** A place where monks work and live.

mon-e-tar-y *adj.* Relating to money. **-ily** *adv.*

mon-ey *n.* The medium of exchange.

mon-grel *n.* A mixed breed animal.

mo-ni-tion *n.* A caution or warning.

monk *n.* A member of a religious order. **-ishness** *n.*, **-ishly** *adv.*

mon-key *n., pl.* **-keys** A member of the primates, excluding man.

mon-o-cle *n.* An eyeglass for one eye.

mo-nog-a-my *n.* A sexual relationship with only one person.

mon-o-graph *n.* A book on a particular subject. **-ic** *adj.*, **-er** *n.*

mon-o-logue *n.* A

speech by one person. **-guist** *n.*

mon-o-ma-ni-a *n.* A mental disorder. **-cal** *adj.*

mon-o-nu-cle-o-sis *n.* An infectious disease.

mon-o-plane *n.* An airplane with one set of wings.

mo-nop-o-ly *n., pl.* **-ies** An exclusive ownership.

mon-o-rail *n.* A train traveling on a single rail.

mon-o-the-ism *n.* A belief that there is just one God. **-tic** *adj.*, **-ist** *n.*

mon-o-tone *n.* Sounds uttered in a single unvarying tone. **-ic** *adj.*

mo-not-o-nous *adj.* Dull, lacking variety. **-ness** *n.*, **-ly** *adv.*

mon-ox-ide *n.* An oxide containing one oxygen atom per molecule.

mon-soon *n.* A periodic wind.

mon-ster *n.* An animal having abnormal form.

mon-tage *n.* A composite picture.

month-ly *adj.* Payable each month.

mon-u-ment *n.* An object in the memory of a person. **-al** *adj.*, **-ally** *adv.*

mooch *v. Slang* To acquire by begging. **-er** *n.*

mood *n.* A temporary state of mind.

mood-y *adj.* Gloomy; depression. **-iness** *n.*, **-ily** *adv.*

moon *n.* The earth's only satellite. **-y** *adj.*, **-iness** *n.*

moon-lit *adj.* Lit by the moon.

moor *v.* To fasten with anchors.

moose *n.* A very large deer.

moot *v.* To debate; to argue.

mope *v.* To be dejected; quietly unhappy. **-ingly** *adv.*, **-er** *n.*, **-ish** *adj.*

mo-ped *n.* A motorbike.

mor-al *adj.* Pertaining to conduct of right or wrong. **-ly** *adv.*

mo-rale *n.* An individual's state of mind.

mor-a-to-ri-um *n.* A temporary pause.

mor-bid *adj.* Gruesome; gloomy. **-ness** *n.*, **-ly** *adv.*

more *adj.* Of greater number or degree.

more-o-ver *adv.* Furthermore.

mo-res *n.*, *pl.* The moral customs of a social group.

morgue *n.* A place to keep dead bodies.

morn-ing *n.* The early part of the day.

mo-roc-co *n.* A soft leather made of goatskin.

mo-ron *n.* An adult with low intelligence.

-ism *n.*, **-ic** *adj.*

mor-ose *adj.* Marked by gloom. **-ity** *n.*, **-ly** *adv.*

mor-phine *n.* A highly addictive narcotic, derived from opium.

mor-sel *n.* A small quantity of food.

mor-tal *adj.* Having caused death; about to cause death.

mort-gage *n.* The conveyance as security for the repayment of a debt.

mor-ti-cian *n.* An undertaker.

mo-sa-ic *n.* The decorative inlaid design of tile.

mos-qui-to *n.*, *pl.* **-toes** *or* **-tos** Insects which suck the blood of animals or humans.

moss *n.* Small green plants.

most *adj.* The majority of; greatest in quantity.

mo-tel *n.* A roadside dwellings for travelers.

moth *n.* A nocturnal insect.

moth-er *n.* A female parent.

mother--in--law *n.* The mother of one's spouse.

mo-tif *n.* The main element or theme.

mo-tile *adj.* Capable of moving alone.

mo-tion *n.* The act of changing position.

mo-tive *n.* The need or desire to act.

mo-tor *n.* A device which develops energy for motion.

mo-tor-boat *n.* A boat with an internal combustion engine.

mo-tor-cy-cle *n.* A two-wheeled vehicle. **-ist** *n.*

mot-tle *v.* To be marked with spots or streaks of colors.

mot-to *n.* A phrase, or word expressing purpose.

mound *n.* A small hill of earth.

moun-tain *n.* A land mass rising above its surroundings.

mourn *v.* To express grief or sorrow.

mouse *n., pl.* **mice** A small rodent.

mouth *n., pl.* **mouths** A bodily opening used to eat or talk.

mouth--to--mouth *adj.* A method of artificial resuscitation.

move *v.* To change one's location.

mov-ie *n.* A motion picture.

mow *v.* To cut down.

moz-za-rel-la *n.* A white cheese with a mild flavor.

muck *n.* A moist, sticky soil.

mu-cus *n.* A liquid secreted by glands.

mud *n.* A mixture of water and earth.

mud-dle *v.* To mix up or confuse.

muf-fin *n.* A small cup-shaped bread.

muf-fle *v.* To suppress; to deaden sound.

muf-fler *n.* A scarf worn around the neck.

mug *n.* A large drinking cup.

mug-gy *adj.* Humid and sultry.

mul-ber-ry *n.* Trees having an edible fruit.

mulch *n.* A protective covering of compost or wood chips.

mule *n.* A hybrid offspring of a female horse.

mull *v.* To ponder; to think over.

mul-let *n.* An edible freshwater fish.

mul-li-gan stew *n.* A stew of meats and vegetables.

multi- *prefix* Multiple; two or more.

mul-ti-far-i-ous *adj.* Having great variety.

mul-ti-ple *adj.* Consisting of more than one individual or part.

mul-ti-ply *v.* To increase in amount or number.

mul-ti-tude *n.* A large amount or number.

mum *adj.* Not speaking.

mum-ble *v.* To speak in

a confused manner.

mum-bo jum-bo *n.* A complicated ritual.

mum-my *n., pl.* **-ies** A body embalmed for burial. **-ify** *v.*

mumps *pl. n.* A contagious viral disease.

munch *v.* To chew noisily.

mun-dane *adj.* Relating to the world. **-ly** *adv.*

mu-nic-i-pal *adj.* Relating to local affairs.

mu-ral *n.* A painting created on a wall.

mur-der *n.* The crime of killing a person.

mur-mur *n.* A low muttered sound.

mus-cle *n.* The bodily tissue which produces strength.

mus-cu-lar *adj.* Having large powerful muscles.

mus-cu-lar dys-tro-phy *n.* A hereditary disease of the muscles.

mush *n.* A porridge of cornmeal.

mush-room *n.* An edible fungus plant.

mu-sic *n.* Organized tones in sequences.

mu-si-cian *n.* A performer of music.

mus-ket *n.* A heavy shoulder gun.

musk-mel-on *n.* A sweet fruit in the melon family.

mus-lin *n.* A sheer, or coarse fabric.

muss *v.* To mess up.

mus-sel *n.* A freshwater bivalve mollusk.

must *v.* To be forced to; to be obligated.

mus-tache *n.* The hair growing on the human upper lip.

mus-tang *n.* A wild horse.

mus-tard *n.* A condiment made from the seeds of the mustard plant.

mus-ter *v.* To come or bring together.

mustn't *contr.* Must not.

mute *adj.* Unable to speak.

mu-ti-late *v.* To maim or cripple.

mu-ti-ny *n., pl.* **-ies** A revolt against lawful authority.

mutt *n., Slang* A mixed breed of dog.

mut-ter *v.* To speak or utter in a low voice.

mut-ton *n.* The flesh of a fully grown sheep.

mu-tu-al *adj.* Having the same relationship. **-ity** *n.*

mu-tu-al fund *n.* An investment company.

muu-muu *n.* A dress which hangs loosely; Hawaiian dress.

muz-zle *n.* Projecting jaws and mouth of certain animals; the barrel of a gun.

my *adj.* Of myself *interj.* to express surprise,

dismay, or pleasure.

my-ce-li-um *n., pl.* **-lia** A mass of filaments which form the main structure of a fungus.

my-col-o-gy *n.* The scientific study of fungi. **-gist** *n.*

my-e-li-tis *n.* The inflammation of the spinal cord or bone marrow.

my-elo-ma *n.* A tumor of the bone marrow.

my-na *or* **my-nah** *n.* A dark brown, slightly crested bird.

myo-car-dio-graph *n.* A recording tool which traces the action of the heart muscles.

myo-car-di-um *n.* A muscular layer of the heart, located in the middle of the heart wall.

my-o-pia *n.* A visual defect; near-sightedness.

myr-i-ad *adj.* Having large, indefinite aspects or elements.

myr-mi-don *n.* A loyal follower.

myrrh *n.* An aromatic gum resin yielded from shrubs and trees, used in incense and perfumes.

myr-tle *n.* An evergreen shrub.

my-self *pron.* One identical with me.

mys-te-ri-ous *adj.* Being a mystery; impossible or difficult to comprehend.

mys-ter-y *n., pl.* **-ies** Something that is not understood; a problem or puzzle; an enigma; a Christian sacrament.

mys-tic *n.* A person practicing or believing in mysticism. **-al** *adj.*, **-ally** *adv.*

mys-ti-cism *n.* A spiritual discipline of communion with God.

mys-ti-fy *v.* To perplex.

mys-tique *n.* A body of beliefs connected with a group or person.

myth *n.* A story dealing with supernatural ancestors; a person having an imaginary existence.

my-thol-o-gy *n., pl.* **-ies** A body of myths dealing with gods.

my word *interj.* An expression of surprise.

N

N, n Fourteenth letter of the English alphabet.

nab *v.* To grab onto something.

na-cho *n.* A tortilla.

nag *v.* To bother by scolding.

nail *n.* A piece of metal to hold wood.

na-ked *adj.* To be without clothes. **-ness** *n.*

name *n.* A title by which someone is known. **-er** *n.*

name-less *adj.* Having no name. **-ness** *n.*

nap *n.* A short rest or sleep. **-per** *n.*, **-less** *adj.*

nape *n.* The back of the neck.

nap-kin *n.* A cloth for wiping the lips.

nar-co-sis *n.* A drug-induced state of uncon-sciousness.

nar-cot-ic *n.* A habit-forming drug. **-ally** *adv.*

nar-rate *v.* To tell a story. **-tor** *n.*, **-tional** *adj.*

nar-row *adj.* To be small in width. **-ness** *n.*

na-sal *adj.* Of the nose. **-ly** *adv.*, **-ity** *n.*

na-stur-tium *n.* A five-petaled garden plant.

nas-ty *adj.* Dirty, or filthy.

na-tal *adj.* Pertaining to birth. **-ity** *n.*

na-tion *n.* A group of people under one government.

na-tion-al-i-ty *n.* Be-longing to a nation.

na-tive *n.* A person born in a country. **-ness** *n.*, **-ly** *adv.*

na-tiv-i-ty *n.* The birth of Christ.

nat-u-ral *adj.* Not artifi-cial. **-ness** *n.*, **-ly** *adv.*

nat-u-ral-ize *v.* To confer full citizenship.

na-ture *n.* Kind, sort, or type.

naught *n.* Nothing.

nau-se-a *n.* An upset stomach. **-ate** *v.*

nau-ti-cal *adj.* Pertaining to ships. **-ly** *adv.*

na-vel *n.* Depression in the abdomen.

nav-i-ga-ble *adj.* Deep and wide enough for ships.

nav-i-gate *v.* To steer a course. **-tion** *n.*

na-vy *n.* The nation's fleet of ships.

near *adv.* Within a short distance. **-ness** *n.*

neat *adj.* Tidy. **-ness** *n.*, **-ly** *adv.*

neb-u-lous *adj.* To be confused or vague.

nec-es-sar-y *adj.* To be required. **-iness** *n.*, **-ily** *adv.*

ne-ces-si-tate *v.* Make necessary. **-tive** *adj.*

neck *n.* Connects the head and body. **-less** *adj.*

nec-tar *n.* A good-tasting beverage. **-ous** *adj.*

nee *n.* Born.

need *n.* Something necessary. **-fully** *adv.*

nee-dle *n.* A sharp sewing device.

need-n't *contr.* Need not.

ne-far-i-ous *adj.* To be extremely wicked. **-ness** *n.*, **-ly** *adv.*

ne-gate *v.* To nullify; to deny. **-tor** *n.*

neg-a-tive *adj.* To be not positive. **-ness** *n.*

ne-glect *v.* To ignore; to disregard. **-fully** *adv.*,

-ful *adj.*

neg-li-gee *n.* A woman's dressing gown.

neg-li-gent *adj.* Neglect what needs to be done. **-ly** *adv.*

ne-go-ti-ate *v.* To reach an agreement.

Ne-gro *n.* A member of the Black race.

neigh-bor *n.* The person who lives near another person.

nei-ther *adj.* Not one or the other.

ne-o-plasm *n.* A tumor tissue.

neph-ew *n.* A sister or brother's son.

ne-phrit-ic *adj.* Relating to the kidneys.

nep-o-tism *n.* Undue favoritism. **-tical** *adj.*, **-tist** *n.*

nerve *n.* The bundles of fibers which convey sensations throughout the body.

nerv-ous *adj.* Affecting the nerves. **-ness** *n.*, **-ly** *adv.*

nest *n.* A home built by a bird.

nes-tle *v.* To settle snugly. **-er** *n.*

net *n.* A meshed fabric; a profit. **-able** *adj.*

neth-er *adj.* To be situated below. **-most** *adj.*

neu-ral *adj.* To be relating to nervous system.

-ly *adv.*

neu-ri-tis *n.* An inflammation of a nerve. **-tic** *adj.*

neu-tral *adj.* Not supporting either side of a debate. **-ly** *adv.*, **-ity** *n.*

neu-tron *n.* The neutral electrical particle.

new *adj.* Never used before. **-ness** *n.*

news *n., pl.* Current information.

news-pa-per *n.* The daily publication of information.

next *adj.* To be immediately following or proceeding.

nib-ble *v.* To bite a little at a time. **-er** *n.*

nice *adj.* State of being pleasing. **-ness** *n.*

niche *n.* A recess or alcove.

nick *n.* A small chip or cut. **-er** *n.*

nick-el *n.* The coin worth five cents. **-ous** *adj.*

nic-o-tine *n.* The poison which is found in tobacco.

niece *n.* A sister or brother's daughter.

nigh *adv.* To be near in time.

night *n.* The hours of darkness.

night-mare *n.* A frightening dream. **-ish** *adj.*

nim-ble *adj.* State of quick agility. **-bly** *adv.*

nine *n.* The cardinal number which is equal to 8 + 1.

nip *v.* To pinch, to bite, or to grab at something or someone.

nip-ple *n.* The small gland through which milk passes.

ni-tro-gen *n.* The gaseous element, essential to life. **-ous** *adj.*

ni-tro-glyc-er-in *n.* The powerful oily liquid explosive.

no-bil-i-ty *n.* The state of being noble.

no-bod-y *pron.* Not anybody.

noc-tur-nal *adj.* To be pertaining to the night.

node *n.* A swollen enlargement. **-al** *adj.*

noise *n.* A disagreeable sound. **-less** *adj.*

nom-i-nal *adj.* In name or form only. **-ly** *adv.*

nom-i-nate *v.* To select a candidate for office.

non-cha-lant *adj.* Unconcern. **-ly** *adv.*

non-sense *n.* Senseless. **-sically** *adv.*

nook *n.* A corner.

noon *n.* 12:00 o'clock.

noose *n.* A loop of rope.

nor-mal *adj.* State of being ordinary; to be average. **-ly** *adv.*, **-lty** *n.*

north *n.* The direction to a person's left while facing east.

nose *n.* The organ of the body used for detecting smells. **-less** *adj.*

nos-tal-gia *n.* A yearning for the past. **-cally** *adv.*

nos-tril *n.* The openings of the nose.

not *adv.* In no manner.

no-ta-rize *v.* To acknowledge. **-zation** *n.*

no-ta-tion *n.* The system symbols used in specialized fields. **-al** *adj.*

notch *n.* A v-shaped indentation. **-ed** *adj.*

note *n.* A short message or memo. **-er** *n.*

noth-ing *n.* Not anything.

no-tice *n.* An announcement.

no-tice-a-ble *adj.* To be worth noticing; to be easily seen. **-bly** *adv.*

no-ti-fy *v.* To give notice. **-fier** *n.*

no-tion *n.* An idea.

no-to-ri-ous *adj.* State of having a bad reputation.

noun *n.* A person, a place, or a thing.

nour-ish *v.* To furnish nutriments for growth. **-ing** *adj.*, **-er** *n.*

nov-el *n.* A book.

nov-el-ty *n.* Something unusual.

nov-ice *n.* The person who is new in business.

now *adv.* At the present time.

no-where *adv.* Not at any place.

nox-ious *adj.* State of being harmful.

noz-zle *n.* A projecting spout.

nu-ance *n.* A slight variation.

nu-bile *adj.* To be ready for marriage.

nu-cle-ar *adj.* Resembling a nucleus.

nu-cle-us *n.* The central element around which other are grouped.

nudge *v.* To poke or to push gently.

nui-sance *n.* An annoyance.

numb *adj.* To be paralyzed or stunned.

num-ber *n.* The symbol for counting.

nu-mer-ous *adj.* To be made up of many units.

nun *n.* A woman in convent.

nup-tial *adj.* Referring to a wedding.

nurse *n.* The person trained to care for sick people.

nur-ture *n.* The care of a child.

nutrient *n.* The substance which nourishes.

nu-tri-tion *n.* The process of using food for good health.

ny-lon *n.* A strong, elastic material.

nymph *n.* The nature goddesses.

O

O, o The fifteenth letter of the English alphabet.

O *n.* A word used before a name when talking to that person; an interjection.

oaf *n.* A stupid or clumsy person. **-ish** *adj.*, **-ishly** *adv.*

oak *n.* A large tree of durable wood bearing acorns. **-en** *adj.*

oar *n.* A long pole, flat at one end, used in rowing a boat.

oasis *n., pl.* **oases** A fertile section in the desert which contains water.

oat *n.* A cultivated cereal grass whose grain or seed is used as food.

oath *n.* A solemn promise in the name of God or on a Bible.

oat-meal *n.* A cooked cereal food made from rolled oats.

ob-du-rate *adj.* Stubborn. **-racy** *n.*

o-be-di-ent *adj.* Obeying or willing to do what one is told. **-ence** *n.*

ob-e-lisk *n.* A tall, four-sided stone pillar which slopes from a pointed top.

o-bese *adj.* Very fat. **-ity** *n.*

o-bey *v.* To carry out instructions. **-er** *n.*

o-bit *n. Slang* An obituary.

o-bit-u-ar-y *n., pl.* **-ies** A published announcement that a person has died.

ob-ject *v.* To voice disapproval. *Grammar* A word in a sentence which explains who or what is acted upon.

ob-jec-tive *adj.* Pertaining to or dealing with material objects rather than mental concepts.

ob-la-tion *n.* A religious offering or the act of sacrifice.

ob-li-ga-tion *n.* A promise or feeling of duty; something one must do because one's conscience or the law demands it.

o-blige *v.* To constrain; to put in one's debt by a service or favor. **-er** *n.*, **-ingly** *adv.*

o-blique *adj.* Inclined; not level or straight up and down. **-ness, -ity** *n.*

o-blit-er-ate *v.* To blot out or eliminate completely; to wipe out. **-tion, -tor** *n.*, **-tive** *adj.*

o-bliv-i-on *n.* The condition of being utterly forgotten.

ob-liv-i-ous *adj.* Not aware or conscious of what is happening; unmindful. **-ly** *adv.*, **-ness** *n.*

ob-long *adj.* Rec-tangular; longer in one direction than the other.

ob-nox-ious *adj.* Very unpleasant; repugnant. **-ness** *n.*

o-boe *n.* A double-reed, tube-shaped woodwind instrument. **-ist** *n.*

ob-scene *adj.* Indecent.

ob-scure *adj.* Remote; not clear; faint. *v.* To make dim; to conceal by covering. **-ly** *adv.*, **-ity** *n.*

ob-serve *v.* To pay attention; to watch. **-able, -ant** *adj.*, **-ably** *adv.*, **-er** *n.*

ob-ser-va-tion *n.* The act of observing something; that which is observed; a judgment or opinion. **-al** *adj.*, **-ally** *adv.*

ob-ser-va-to-ry *n., pl.* **-ies** A building or station furnished with instruments for studying the natural phenomenon.

ob-sess *v.* To preoccupy the mind with an idea or emotion. **-sion** *n.*

ob-so-lete *adj.* No longer in use; out-of-date. **-scence** *n.*, **-scent** *adj.*

ob-sta-cle *n.* An obstruction; anything which opposes or stands in the way of.

ob-ste-tri-cian *n.* A physician who specializes in the care of a woman during pregnancy and childbirth.

ob-stet-rics *pl.*, *n.* The branch of medicine which deals with pregnancy and childbirth.

ob-sti-nate *adj.* Stubbornly set to an opinion or course of action. **-acy** *n.*, **-ately** *adv.*

ob-strep-er-ous *adj.* Noisy, unruly, or boisterous in resistance to advice or control.

ob-struct *v.* To block, hinder or impede. **-tor**, **-tion** *n.*, **-tive** *adj.*

ob-tain *v.* To acquire or gain possession of. **-able** *adj.*, **-er** *n.*

ob-trude *v.* To thrust forward without request or warrant; to call attention to oneself.

ob-tuse *adj.* Lacking acuteness of feeling; insensitive; not distinct or clear to the senses, as pain or sound.

ob-vi-ate *v.* To counter or prevent by effective measures.

ob-vi-ous *adj.* Easily seen, discovered, or understood.

oc-ca-sion *n.* The time an event occurs; the event itself; a celebration. *v.* To bring about.

oc-ca-sion-al *adj.* Appearing or occurring irregularly or now and then.

oc-ci-den-tal *adj.* Western.

oc-cip-i-tal bone *n.* *Anat.* The bone which forms the back of the skull.

oc-cult *adj.* Concealed. *n.* The action or influence of supernatural agencies or secret knowledge of them. **-ist**, **-ism** *n.*

oc-cu-pan-cy *n.* The state or act of being occupied; the act of holding in possession.

oc-cu-pa-tion *n.* A job, profession, or vocation; a foreign military force which controls an area.

oc-cu-py *v.* To take and retain possession of; to live in. **-pier** *n.*

oc-cur *v.* To suggest; to have something come to mind; to happen. **-rence** *n.*, **-rent** *adj.*

o-cean *n.* An immense body of salt water which covers 3/4 of the earth's surface. **-ic** *adj.*

o-ce-an-og-ra-phy *n.* The science of oceanic phenomena dealing with underwater research.

o'clock *adv.* Of, or according to the clock.

oc-ta-gon *n.* A polygon with eight angles and eight sides. **-al** *adj.*, **-ally** *adv.*

oc-tane *n.* Any of several hydrocarbon compounds

which occur in petroleum.

oc-tave *n., Music* A tone on the eighth degree above or below another tone.

Oc-to-ber *n.* The 10th month of the calendar year, having 31 days.

oc-to-ge-nar-i-an *n.* A person between the ages of 80 and 90.

oc-to-pus *n., pl.* -es *or* -pi A cephalopod with a sac-like body and eight tentacles containing double rows of suckers.

oc-u-lar *adj.* Of or relating to the eye.

OD *n. Slang* An overdose of a drug.

odd *adj.* Unusual; strange; singular; left over; not even. **-ly** *adv.*, **-ness** *n.*

odds *pl, n.* An equalizing advantage given to a weaker opponent.

ode *n.* A lyric poem usually honoring a person or event.

o-dom-e-ter *n.* A device in a vehicle used to measure distance traveled. **-try** *n.*

o-dor *n.* A smell; a sensation which occurs when the sense of smell is stimulated.

od-ys-sey *n.* A long voyage marked by many changes of fortune.

of *prep.* Proceeding; composed of; relating to.

off *adv.* From a position or place; no longer connected or on. *adj.* Canceled. *prep.* Away from.

of-fend *v.* To make angry; to arouse resentment. **-er** *n.*

of-fense *n.* A violation of a duty, rule, or a propriety; the act of causing displeasure; the act of assaulting or attacking.

of-fen-sive *adj.* Disagreeable or unpleasant; causing resentment; insulting.

of-fer *v.* To present for acceptance or rejection; to present as an act of worship; to make available.

of-fer-ing *n.* The act of one who offers; a contribution, as money, given to the support of a church.

off-hand *adv. or adj.* Without preparation or premeditation.

of-fice *n.* A place where business or professional duties are conducted.

of-fi-cer *n.* A person who holds a title, or position of authority.

of-fi-cial *adj.* Something derived from proper authority. **-ism** *n.*, **-ly** *adv.*

of-fi-ci-ate *v.* To carry out the duties and functions of a position or office.

of-fi-cious *adj.* Offering one's services or advice in an unduly forward manner. **-ly** *adv.,* **-ness** *n.*

off-spring *n.* The descendants of a person, plant, or animal.

of-ten *adv.* Frequently.

oh *interj.* Used to express surprise, fear, or pain.

O-hi-o *n.* A state located in the midwestern part of the United States.

oil *n.* Any of various substances, usually thick, which can be burned or easily melted; a lubricant.

oil field *n.* An area rich in petroleum.

oint-ment *n.* An oily substance used on the skin as an aid to healing or to soften the skin.

Ok-la-ho-ma *n.* A state located in the south central part of the United States.

o-kra *n.* A tall tropical and semitropical plant with green pods that can be either fried or cooked in soups.

old *adj.* Having lived or existed for a long time; of a certain age.

old-en *adj.* Of or relating to times long past; ancient.

old--fash-ioned *adj.* Pertaining to or characteristic of former times or old customs; not modern or up-to-date.

Old Glory *n.* The flag of the United States of America.

Old Testament *n.* The first of two parts of the Christian Bible, containing the history of the Hebrews, the laws of Moses, the writings of the prophets, the Holy Scriptures of Judaism, and other material.

Old World *n.* The eastern hemisphere, including Asia, Europe, and Africa.

ol-fac-tory *adj.* Pertaining to the sense of smell.

oli-gar-chy *pl., n.* **-ies** A government controlled by a small group for corrupt and selfish purposes; the group exercising such control.

ol-ive *n.* A small oval fruit from an evergreen tree with leathery leaves and yellow flowers, valuable as a source of oil.

O-lym-pic Games *pl., n.* International athletic competition held every four years, based on an ancient Greek festival.

om-buds-man *n.* A

government official appointed to report and receive grievances against the government.

om·e·let *or* **om·e·lette** *n.* A dish made from eggs and other items, such as bacon, cheese, and ham, and cooked until set.

o·men *n.* A phenomenon which is thought of as a sign of something to come, whether good or bad.

om·i·nous *adj.* Foreshadowed by an omen or by a presentiment of evil; threatening.

o·mis·sion *n.* The state or act of being omitted; anything neglected or left out.

o·mit *v.* To neglect; to leave out.

om·ni·bus *n.* A public vehicle designed to carry a large number of people; a bus. *adj.* Covering a complete collection of objects or cases.

om·nip·o·tent *adj.* Having unlimited or infinite power or authority.

om·nis·cient *adj.* Knowing all things; having universal or complete knowledge.

om·niv·or·ous *adj.* Feeding on both vegetable and animal substances; absorbing everything. **-ly** *adv.*

on *prep.* Positioned upon; indicating proximity; indicating direction toward; with respect to. *adv.* In a position of covering; forward.

once *adv.* A single time; at any one time. *conj.* As soon as.

once-o·ver *n., Slang* A swift but comprehensive glance.

on·col·o·gy *n.* The study of tumors. **-ical, -ic** *adj.,* **-ist** *n.*

one *adj.* Single; undivided. *n.* A single person; a unit; the first cardinal number (1).

one·self *pron.* One's own self.

one--sid·ed *adj.* Partial to one side; unjust. **-ness** *n.*

on·ion *n.* An edible bulb plant having a pungent taste and odor.

on--line *adj. Computer Science* Controlled directly by a computer.

on·ly *adj.* Sole; for one purpose alone. *adv.* Without anyone or anything else. *conj.* Except; but.

on·o·mat·o·poe·ia *n.* The use of a word, as buzz or hiss, which vocally imitates the sound it denotes. **-ic** *adj.*

on-shore *adj.* Moving or coming near or onto the shore.

on-slaught *n.* A fierce attack.

on-to *prep.* To a position or place; aware of.

o-nus *n.* A burden; a responsibility or duty which is difficult or unpleasant; the blame.

on-ward *adv.* Moving forward in time or space.

on-yx *n.* A gemstone; a chalcedony in layers of different colors.

oo-dles *pl., n., Slang* A great or large quantity.

ooze *n.* A soft deposit of slimy mud on the bottom of a body of water; muddy or marshy ground; a bog. *v.* To flow or leak slowly; to disappear little by little.

o-pal *n.* A translucent mineral composed of silicon, often marked with an iridescent play of colors. **-ine** *adj.*

o-paque *adj.* Not transparent; dull; obscure. **-city, -ness** *n.*

OPEC *abbr.* Organization of Petroleum Exporting Countries.

o-pen *adj.* Having no barrier; not covered, sealed, locked, or fastened. *n.* A contest for both amateurs and professionals. *v.* To begin or start. **-ness** *n.*, **-ly** *adv.*

o-pen--and--shut *adj.* Easily settled; simple to decide.

op-era *n.* A drama having music as a dominant factor, an orchestral accompaniment, acting, and scenery.

op-er-ate *v.* To function, act, or work effectively; to perform an operation, as surgery. **-tive** *adj.*

op-er-a-tion *n.* The process of operating; a procedure performed with surgical instruments to restore health.

op-er-a-tor *n.* A person who operates a machine; the owner or person in charge of a business.

oph-thal-mol-o-gy *n.* A branch of medical science dealing with diseases of the eye, its structure, and functions.

o-pin-ion *n.* A judgment held with confidence; a conclusion held without positive knowledge.

o-pi-um *n.* A bitter, highly addictive drug; a narcotic.

o-pos-sum *n., pl.* **-sum** *or* **-sums** A nocturnal animal which hangs by its tail and carries its young in a pouch.

op-po-nent *n.* An adversary; one who opposes another.

op-por-tune *adj.* Occurring at the right or appropriate time. **-ist** *n.*, **-ly** *adv.*

op-por-tu-ni-ty *n., pl.* **-ies** A favorable position; a chance for advancement.

op-pose *v.* To be in direct contention with; to resist; to be against. **-able** *adj.*, **-sition** *n.*

op-po-site *adj.* Situated or placed on opposing sides. **-ness** *n.*

op-press *v.* To worry or trouble the mind; to weigh down; to burden as if to enslave. **-ion**, **-or** *n.*

op-tic *adj.* Pertaining or referring to sight or the eye.

op-ti-cal *adj.* Pertaining to sight; constructed or designed to assist vision. **-ly** *adv.*

op-ti-cian *n.* A person who makes eyeglasses and other optical articles.

op-ti-mism *n.* A doctrine which emphasizes that everything is for the best.

op-ti-mum *n., pl.* **-ma** The degree or condition producing the most favorable result. *adj.* Conducive to the best result.

op-tion *n.* The act of choosing or the power of choice; a choice. **-ally** *adv.*

op-tion-al *adj.* Left to one's decision; elective; not required.

op-tom-e-try *n.* The occupation or profession of examining the eyes and prescribing corrective lenses.

op-u-lence *n.* Wealth in abundance; affluence.

or *conj.* A word used to connect the second of two choices or possibilities, indicating uncertainty. *suffix* Indicating a person or thing which does something.

or-a-cle *n.* A seat of worship where ancient Romans and Greeks consulted the gods for answers; a person of unquestioned wisdom. **-lar** *adj.*

o-ral *adj.* Spoken or uttered through the mouth; taken or administered through the mouth. **-ly** *adv.*

or-ange *n.* A citrus fruit which is round and orange in color. *adj.* Yellowish-red.

o-rang-u-tan *n., pl.* **-tans** A large, anthropoid ape, having brownish-red hair and very long arms.

o-rate *v.* To speak in an elevated manner.

orb *n.* A globe or sphere.

or-bit *n.* The path of a celestial body or a man-made object. *v.* To revolve or move in an orbit; to circle. **-al** *adj.*

or-chard *n.* Land that is devoted to the growing of fruit trees.

or-ches-tra *n.* A group of musicians performing together on various instruments. **-al** *adj.*

or-ches-tra pit *n.* In theatres, the space reserved for musicians.

or-chid *n.* A plant found the world over having three petals in various colors.

or-dain *v.* To appoint as a minister, priest, or rabbi by a special ceremony; to decree.

or-deal *n.* A painful or severe test of character or endurance.

or-der *n.* A condition where there is a logical arrangement or disposition of things; sequence or succession; method; an instruction for a person to follow; a request for certain objects. *v.* To command; to demand.

or-der-ly *adj.* Neat, tidy.

or-di-nance *n.* A command, rule, or order; a law issued by a municipal body.

or-di-nar-y *adj.* Normal; average; plain.

ore *n.* A natural underground substance, as a mineral or rock, from which valuable matter is extracted.

o-reg-a-no *n.* A bushy perennial herb of the mint family, used as a seasoning for food.

Or-e-gon *n.* A state located in the northwestern part of the United States.

or-gan *n.* A musical instrument of pipes, reeds, and keyboards which produces sound by means of compressed air; a part of an animal, human, or plant that performs a definite function, as the heart, a kidney, or a stamen.

or-gan-dy *or* **or-gan-die** *n., pl.* **-ies** A translucent, stiff fabric of cotton or silk.

or-gan-ic *adj.* Effecting or pertaining to the organs of an animal or plant; of or relating to the process of growing plants with natural fertilizers with no chemical additives. **-ally** *adv.*

or-gan-i-za-tion *n.* The state of being organized or the act of organizing; a group of people united for a particular purpose. **-al** *adj.*

or-gan-ize *v.* To assemble or arrange with

an orderly manner; to arrange by planning.
-zation n.

or-gasm n. Physiol. Intensive emotional excitement; the culmination of a sexual act.

o-ri-ent v. To determine the bearings or right direction with respect to another source.

Orient n. The countries located east of Europe. -al adj.

or-i-fice n. An opening through which something may pass; a mouth.

or-i-gin n. The cause or beginning of something; the source; a beginning place.

o-rig-i-nal adj. Belonging to the first or beginning. n. A new idea produced by one's own imagination; the first of a kind. -ity n., -ly adv.

or-i-ole n. A songbird having brightly colored yellow and black plumage in the males.

or-na-ment n. A decoration. v. To adorn or beautify. -al adj., -ally adv., -ation n.

or-nate adj. Excessively ornamental; elaborate; showy, as a style of writing.

or-phan n. A child whose parents are deceased.

or-ris n. Any of several

species having a fragrant root and used in medicine, perfumes, and cosmetics.

or-tho-don-tics n. The branch of dentistry dealing with the correction and prevention of irregularities of the teeth.

or-tho-dox adj. Following established traditions and beliefs, especially in religion.

Orthodox Judaism n. The branch of Jewish faith which accepts the Mosaic Laws as interpreted in the Talmud.

or-tho-pe-dics n. The branch of surgery or manipulative treatment concerned with the disorders of the bones, joints, and muscles. -ist n.

os-cil-late v. To swing back and forth with regular motion, as a pendulum. -tion, -tor n., -tory adj.

os-mi-um n. A hard, but brittle metallic element symbolized as OS.

os-mo-sis n. The tendency of fluids separated by a semipermeable membrane to pass through it and become mixed and equal in strength. -ic adj.

os-ten-ta-tion n. The act of displaying pretentiously in order to excite.

os-teo *n. comb. form* Bone; pertaining to the bones.

os-te-op-a-thy *n.* A medical practice based on the theory that diseases are due chiefly to abnormalities of the body, which can be restored by manipulation of the parts by therapeutic measures.

os-teo-po-ro-sis *n.* A disorder causing gradual deterioration of bone tissue, usually occurring in older women.

os-tra-cize *v.* To exile or exclude from a group; to shut out.

oth-er *adj.* Additional; alternate; different from what is implied or specified. *pron.* A different person or thing.

oth-er-wise *adv.* Under different conditions of circumstances.

ot-ter *n., pl.* **-ter** *or* **-ters** Web-footed aquatic mammals, related to the weasel.

ouch *n. interj.* An exclamation to express sudden pain.

ought *v.* Used to show or express a moral duty or obligation; to be advisable or correct.

ounce *n.* A unit of weight which equals 1/16 of a pound.

our *adj.* Of or relating to us ourselves. *pron.* The possessive case of the pronoun we. **ourselves** Our own selves.

oust *v.* To eject; to remove with force.

out *adv.* Away from the center or inside. *adj.* Away. *n.* A means of escape. *prep.* Through; forward from.

out-age *n.* A loss of electricity.

out-break *n.* A sudden outburst; an occurrence.

out-cast *n.* A person who is excluded; a homeless person.

out-come *n.* A consequence or result.

out-dated *adj.* Old-fashioned and obsolete.

out-do *v.* To excel in achievement.

out-fit *n.* The equipment or tools required for a specialized purpose; the clothes a person is dressed in. *v.* To supply.

out-land-ish *adj.* Extremely ridiculous, unusual, or strange.

out-law *n.* A person who habitually defies or breaks the law; a criminal. *v.* To ban; prohibit; to deprive of legal protection.

out-let *n.* An exit.

out-line *n.* A rough draft

showing the main features of something.

out-look n. A person's point of view; an area offering a view of something.

out-num-ber v. To go over or exceed in number.

out-pa-tient n. A patient who visits a clinic or hospital for treatment but does not spend the night.

out-post n. Troops stationed at a distance away from the main group as a guard against attack; a frontier or outlying settlement.

out-put n. Production or yield during a given time.

out-rage n. An extremely violent act of violence or cruelty; the violent emotion such an act engenders. **-eous** adj.

out-right adj. Free from reservations or complications; complete; entire.

out-side n. The area beyond the boundary lines or surface; extreme. adv. Outdoors.

out-spo-ken adj. Spoken without reserve; candid. **-ly** adv.

out-stand-ing adj. Excellent; prominent; unsettled, as a bill owed; projecting.

out-ward adj. Pertaining to the outside or exterior; superficial. **-wards** adv.

out-wit v. To trick, baffle, or outsmart with ingenuity.

o-val adj. Having the shape of an egg; an ellipse.

o-va-ry n., pl. **-ies** One of the pair of female reproductive glands. **-ian** adj.

o-va-tion n. An enthusiastic display of approval for a person or a performance; applause.

ov-en n. An enclosed chamber used for baking, drying, or heating.

o-ver prep. Above; across; upon. adv. Covering completely; thoroughly; again; repetition. adj. Higher; upper. prefix Excessive, as overstuffed or overcrowded.

o-ver-act v. To act in an exaggerated way.

o-ver-all adj. Including or covering everything; from one side or end to another; generally. n. Pants with a bib and shoulder straps.

o-ver-arm adj. Thrown or executed with the arms raised above the shoulders.

o-ver-bear v. To crush

or bear down by superior force or weight. **-ing** *adj.*

o-ver-board *adv.* Over the side of a boat or ship into the water.

o-ver-cast *adj.* Gloomy; obscured. *Meteor.* Clouds covering more than 9/10 of the sky.

o-ver-coat *n.* A coat worn over a suit for extra warmth.

o-ver-come *v.* To prevail; to conquer or defeat. **-er** *n.*

o-ver-con-fi-dence *n.* Extreme or excessive confidence.

o-ver-do *v.* To do anything excessively; to overcook.

o-ver-dose *n.* To take an excessive dose of medication, especially narcotics.

o-ver-draw *v.* To withdraw money over the limits of one's credit.

o-ver-drive *n.* A gearing device in a vehicle that turns a drive shaft at a greater speed than that of the engine, therefore decreasing power output.

o-ver-due *adj.* Past the time of return or payment.

o-ver-flow *v.* To flow beyond the limits of capacity; to overfill.

o-ver-hand *v.* To execute something with the hand above the level of the elbow or shoulder. **-ed** *adv.*

o-ver-haul *v.* To make all needed repairs.

o-ver-head *n.* The operating expenses of a company, including utilities, rent, and upkeep. *adj.* Situated above the level of one's head.

o-ver-look *v.* To disregard or fail to notice something purposely; to ignore.

o-ver-night *adj.* Lasting the whole night; from dusk to dawn.

o-ver-pass *n.* A raised section of highway which crosses other lines of traffic. *v.* To cross, pass over, or go through something; to overlook.

o-ver-ride *v.* To disregard; to take precedence over; to declare null and void.

o-ver-rule *v.* To put aside by virtue of higher authority.

o-ver-run *v.* To spread out; to extend or run beyond.

o-ver-seas *adv.* Abroad, across the seas.

o-ver-see *v.* To supervise; to direct. **-er** *n.*

o-ver-sexed *adj.* Having an overactive interest in sex.

o-ver-shoe *n.* A galosh worn over a shoe for protection from snow or water.

o-ver-sight *n.* A mistake made inadvertently.

o-ver-size or oversized *adj.* Larger than the average size of something.

o-ver-step *v.* To go beyond a limit or restriction.

o-vert *adj.* Open to view.

o-ver--the--coun-ter *adj.* Not traded on an organized security exchange; of or relating to drugs or medicine which can be purchased without a prescription.

o-ver-throw *v.* To remove from power by force; to bring about destruction.

o-ver-time *n.* The time worked beyond or before the specified hours.

o-ver-whelm *v.* To overcome completely; to make helpless.

o-void *adj.* Having the shape of an egg.

ovu-late *n.* To discharge or produce eggs from an ovary.

o-vum *n., pl.* **ova** The female reproductive cell.

owe *v.* To be in debt for a certain amount; to have a moral obligation.

owl *n.* A predatory nocturnal bird, having large eyes, a short hooked bill, and long powerful claws. **-ish** *adj.*

own *adj.* Belonging to oneself. *v.* To possess; to confess; to admit. **-er** *n.*

ox *n., pl.* **oxen** A bovine animal used domestically in much the same way as a horse; an adult castrated bull.

ox-ford *n.* A shoe which is laced and tied over the instep.

ox-ide *n.* A compound of oxygen and another element.

ox-y-gen *n.* A colorless, odorless, tasteless gaseous element essential to life, symbolized by O.

ox-y-gen mask *n.* A device worn over the mouth and nose through which a person can receive oxygen as an aid to breathing.

oys-ter *n.* An edible marine mollusk.

o-zone *n.* A pale-blue gas formed of oxygen with an odor like chlorine, formed by an electrical discharge in the air. *Slang* Fresh air.

P

P, p The sixteenth letter of the English alphabet.

pace *n.* A length of a person's step. **-d** *adj.*

pac-i-fy *v.* To quiet or soothe anger. **-fistic** *adj.*

pack *n.* A bundle; band of animals. **-ing** *n.*

pack-age *n.* Something tied or bound together. **-er** *n.*

pact *n.* An agreement between nations.

pad *n.* A cushion; writing tablet. **-ding** *n.*

pad-dle *n.* An implement used to propel a boat.

pa-dre *n.* A title for a priest.

pa-gan *n.* A heathen. **-ism** *n.*, **-ish** *adj.*

page *n.* A person who runs errands; leaf of a book.

pag-eant *n.* A spectacular parade. **-try** *n.*

paid *v.* Past tense of pay.

pail *n.* A cylindrical container. **-ful** *adj.*

pain *n.* An unpleasant feeling from an injury. **-fully** *adv.*, **-lessness** *n.*

paint *n.* Coloring pigments. **-er** *n.*

pair *n.*, *pl.* **pairs** *or* **pair** Two things that are similar.

pa-ja-mas *pl.*, *n.* A garment used for sleeping.

pal-ace *n.* A royal residence.

pal-at-a-ble *adj.* Pleasant tasting. **-bly** *adv.*

pal-ette *n.* An artist's board for mixing colors.

pall *n.* A cloth used to cover a coffin.

pall-bear-er *n.* A person who carrys a coffin.

palm *n.* The inner area of the hand. **-ceous** *adj.*

pal-sy *n.*, *pl.* **-ies** The loss of control of one's movements.

pam-phlet *n.* A brief publication.

pan-a-ce-a *n.* A remedy for all diseases.

pan-cre-as *n.*, *Anat.* A gland that produces insulin.

pan-da *n.* A large black and white bear.

pan-el *n.* A wooden surface; a jury.

pan-ic *n.* An unreasonable fear. **-y** *adj.*

pan-o-ram-a *n.* An unlimited view. **-ically** *adv.*, **-ic** *adj.*

pan-sy *n.* A garden plant.

pant *v.* To breathe in short gasps. **-ing** *n.*

pan-ther *n.* A black leopard.

pan-to-mime *n.* A gesture without speaking.

pants *pl, n.* Trousers.

pa-per *n.* A substance made from wood and rags. **-back** *n.*

pa-pri-ka *n.* A red seasoning powder.

par-a-ble *n.* A short story with a moral. **-bolist** *n.*

par-a-chute *n.* A folded fabric to assure safe landing from an airplane.

par-a-dise *n.* A place of beauty; heaven.

par-a-dox *n.* A statement which contradicts itself. **-ical** *adj.*

par-a-gon *n.* A model of perfection.

par-a-graph *n.* A composition dealing with a single idea. **-ical** *adj.*, **-er** *n.*

par-a-keet *n.* A small parrot.

par-al-lel *adj.* Moving in the same direction.

pa-ral-y-sis *n., pl.* **-ses** Lose the ability to feel or to move.

par-a-mount *adj.* Above all others. **-ly** *adv.*, **-ship** *n.*

par-a-noi-a *n.* A mental delusions of grandeur.

par-a-pher-na-lia *n.* Personal effects.

par-a-phrase *v.* To express in other words.

par-a-site *n.* One that lives off another. **-ically** *adv.*, **-ical** *adj.*

par-a-sol *n.* A small umbrella.

par-boil *v.* To precook something.

par-cel *n.* A package.

parch *v.* To become very dry. **-ed** *adj.*

parch-ment *n.* A sheepskin for writing.

par-don *v.* To forgive; excuse. **-able** *adj.*

pare *v.* To remove the outer surface.

par-ent *n.* A mother or father. **-hood** *n.*, **-al** *adj.*

pa-ren-the-sis *n.* Curved lines to enclose qualifying remark.

par-ish *n.* A district under a priest. **-ioner** *n.*

park *n.* A recreation area. **-er** *n.*

par-ka *n.* A hooded coat.

par-lia-ment *n.* A lawmaking body of various countries. **-arian** *n.*

pa-ro-chi-al *adj.* Belonging to a parish.

pa-role *n.* An early release of a prisoner.

par-rot *n.* A semitropical bird which can be taught to talk. **-y** *adj.*

pars-ley *n.* An herb for seasoning.

par-son *n.* A clergyman. **-age** *n.*, **-ical** *adj.*

part *n.* A division of a whole.

par-tial *adj.* Incomplete. **-ly** *adv.*

par-tic-i-pate *v.* To join in. **-tion** *n.*

par-ti-cle *n.* Very small piece.

par-tic-u-lar *adj.* Having to do with a specific person. **-ist** *n.*

part-ing *n.* Separation.

part-ner *n.* An associate in business. **-ship** *n.*

par-tridge *n.* A game bird.

par-ty *n., pl.* **-ies** People who gather for pleasure.

pass *v.* To proceed; move. **-er** *n.*

pas-sen-ger *n.* One who travels in a vehicle.

pas-sion *n.* Powerful feeling; sexual desire. **-less** *adj.*

pas-sive *adj.* Inactive. **-ness** *n.,* **-ly** *adv.*

pass-port *n.* An official permission to travel to foreign countries.

pass-word *n.* A secret word to enter.

paste *n.* A mixture for holding things together.

pas-tor *n.* A clergyman of a church. **-ship** *n.*

pas-try *n.* A dessert made of dough.

pas-ture *n.* An area for grazing. **-er** *n.*

pat *v.* To tap lightly.

patch *n.* Used to repair a torn garment.

pat-ent *n.* Inventors copyright to invention.

pa-ter-nal *adj.* Inherited from a father. **-nally** *adv.,* **-ism** *n.*

path *n.* A track or route.

pa-thet-ic *adj.* Arousing pity. **-ally** *adv.*

pa-thol-o-gy *n.* A science dealing with diseases. **-gically** *adv.,* **-gical** *adj.*

pa-tience *n.* An ability to be calm.

pa-tient *adj.* A person under medical care.

pa-ti-o *n.* An area attached to a house.

pa-tri-arch *n.* A leader of a family; a revered man.

pa-tri-ot *n.* The one who defends his country. **-tism** *n.,* **-ically** *adv.*

pa-trol *n.* A guard to keep an area secure. **-ler** *n.*

pa-tron *n.* A person who supports a cause; a customer. **-al** *adj.*

pat-tern *n.* A guide; a sample. **-ed** *adj.*

pau-per *n.* A very poor person.

pause *v.* To linger, or hesitate. **-er** *n.*

pave *v.* To surface a road with asphalt or other material. **-er** *n.*

pa-vil-ion *n.* A sheltered area.

paw *n.* A foot of an animal. **-er** *n.*

pawn *n.* A security for a loan; chess piece. **-er** *n.,* **-able** *adj.*

pay-roll *n.* The money paid to employees.

peace *n.* A state of mental serenity.
 -able *adj.*
peach *n.* A sweet, juicy fruit. **-y** *adj.*
peak *n.* A summit of a mountain. **-ed** *adj.*
peal *n.* The ringing of bells.
pear *n.* An edible fruit.
pearl *n.* A white gem from the oyster. **-ly** *adj.*, **-er** *n.*
peas-ant *n.* A person of low class. **-ry** *n.*
peat moss *n.* A plant food and mulch.
peb-ble *n.* A small, smooth stone. **-ly** *adj.*
peck *v.* To strike with the beak. **-er** *n.*
pe-cu-liar *adj.* Strange. **-ly** *adv.*
ped-al *n.* A lever worked by the foot.
ped-dle *v.* To sell merchandise. **-er** *n.*
ped-es-tal *n.* A base for a statue.
pe-des-tri-an *n.* A person on foot. **-ism** *n.*
pe-di-at-rics *n.* A branch of medicine dealing with children and infants. **-ic** *adj.*
ped-i-gree *n.* A line of ancestors. **-ed** *adj.*
peek *v.* To look shyly or quickly.
peel *n.* The skin of a fruit. **-ing** *n.*
peer *v.* To look searchingly.
peg *n.* A small pin.
pei-gnoir *n.* A woman's dressing gown.
pelt *n.* The hide of an animal. **-ry** *n.*
pen *n.* An instrument for writing.
pe-nal *adj.* Pertaining to punishment. **-ization** *n.*
pen-al-ty *n.* The legal punishment for crime.
pen-ance *n.* Repentance for sin.
pend-ing *adj.* Not yet decided.
pen-e-trate *v.* To force a way into. **-ingly** *adv.*, **-ing** *adj.*
pen-i-cil-lin *n.* An antibiotic derived from mold to treat infections.
pen-in-su-la *n.* A piece of land projecting into water. **-lar** *adj.*
pe-nis *n.* The male sex organ.
pen-i-tent *adj.* Being sorry. **-ly** *adv.*
pen-ny *n., pl.* **-ies** U.S. coin worth one cent ($.01).
pen-sion *n.* Money received after retirement.
pen-sive *adj.* Quiet, serious thought. **-ness** *n.*, **-ly** *adv.*
pen-ta-gon *n.* An object having five sides.
pe-on *n.* A servant.
peo-ple *n.* Human beings.

pep-per *n.* A strong aromatic condiment. -**ish** *adj.*, -**er** *n.*

per an-num *adv.* In each year.

per-cale *n.* Cotton fabric.

per-ceive *v.* Become aware of. -**er** *n.*, -**able** *adj.*

per-cent-age *n.* The rate per hundred.

per-cept *n.* A mental impression. -**ible** *n.*

perch *n.* A place on which birds sit.

per-en-ni-al *adj.* From year to year. -**ly** *adv.*

per-fect *adj.* Flawless; accurate. -**ness** *n.*, -**ly** *adv.*

per-form *v.* To carry out an action. -**er** *n.*, -**able** *adj.*

per-fume *n.* A sweet fragrance. -**er** *n.*

per-haps *adv.* Maybe.

per-il *n.* A source of danger. -**ous** *adj.*, -**ously** *adv.*

pe-ri-od *n.* An interval of time. -**ic** *adj.*

per-ish *v.* To ruin or spoil; untimely death. -**able** *adj.*, -**ableness** *n.*

per-jure *v.* To lie under oath. -**er** *n.*

per-me-ate *v.* To spread through. -**tive** *adj.*, -**tion** *n.*

per-mit *v.* To consent to; to allow. -**er** *n.*

per-ni-cious *adj.* Harmful. -**ness** *n.*, -**ly** *adv.*

per-pen-dic-u-lar *adj.* At right angles to the horizon. -**ly** *adv.*, -**ity** *n.*

per-pe-trate *v.* To commit a crime. -**tor** *n.*

per-pet-u-al *adj.* Lasting forever. -**ly** *adv.*

per-plex *v.* To confuse. -**ingly** *adv.*, -**ing** *adj.*

per-se-cute *v.* To harass or annoy. -**tor** *n.*

per-se-vere *v.* To persist in any purpose or idea. -**ingly** *adv.*, -**ing** *adj.*

per-sist *v.* To continue despite obstacles. -**ence** *n.*

per-son *n.* A human being.

per-son-i-fy *v.* To represent; be a symbol of. -**fier** *n.*

per-son-nel *n.* People working for a business.

per-spec-tive *n.* A drawing technique which seems to give depth. -**ly** *adv.*

per-spi-ra-tion *n.* Fluid excreted from the glands.

per-suade *v.* To convince by means of reasoning. -**er** *n.*, -**able** *adj.*

per-tain *v.* To relate to; refer to.

per-ti-na-cious *adj.* Stubbornly persistent. -**ness** *n.*, -**ly** *adv.*

per-ti-nent *adj.* Relating

to the matter being discussed. **-ly** *adv.*

per-turb *v.* To disturb; to make uneasy. **-able** *adj.*

per-vade *v.* To spread through every part. **-er** *n.*

per-ver-sion *n.* A deviant form of sexual behavior.

pes-si-mism *n.* A gloomy view of a situation. **-stic** *adj.*

pest *n.* An annoying person; an insect.

pes-ter *v.* To harass; bother.

pes-ti-cide *n.* A chemical used to destroy insects.

pes-ti-lence *n.* A widespread often fatal infectious disease.

pe-tite *adj.* Being small in size. **-ness** *n.*

pet-it four *n.* Small cakes.

pe-ti-tion *n.* A solemn request. **-er** *n.*

pet-ri-fy *v.* To convert into a stony mass.

pet-ti-coat *n.* An undergarment for women.

pet-ty *adj.* Having little importance. **-iness** *n.*

pet-ty cash *n.* Cash on hand.

pew *n.* A row of seats in church.

phan-tasm *n.* A fantasy; phantom. **-al** *adj.*

phar-ma-ceu-ti-cal *adj.* Relating to a pharmacy.

phar-ma-cy *n.* A drugstore.

phase *n.* A stage in development. **-ic** *adj.*

phe-nom-e-non *n.* A rare occurrence.

phi-lat-e-ly *n.* A collection of postage stamps. **-ically** *adv.*, **-ic** *adj.*

phi-los-o-phy *n., pl.* **-ies** The study of human knowledge or human values.

pho-bi-a *n.* The compulsive fear of a situation.

phon-ic *adj.* Pertaining to sounds in speech.

pho-no-graph *n.* A record player.

phos-phate *n., Chem.* An acid which contains phosphorus and oxygen.

pho-to-cop-y *v.* To reproduce printed material.

pho-to-graph *n.* An image recorded by a camera.

phrase *n., Gram.* The words forming part of a sentence.

phy-si-cian *n.* One licensed to practice medicine.

phys-ics *n.* The scientific study of energy.

pi-an-o *n.* A musical instrument with a keyboard.

pi-ca *n.* A printer's type

size.

pic-co-lo *n.* A small flute.

pick-pock-et *n.* A person who steals from another.

pic-nic *n.* An outdoor social gathering.

piece *n.* A part of a whole.

piece-meal *adv.* In small amounts; gradually.

pier *n.* A dock to provide access to vessels.

pierce *v.* To penetrate.

pi-geon *n.* A bird.

pig-ment *n.* A coloring matter.

pig-skin *n.* A football.

pile *n.* Anything thrown in a heap.

pil-fer *v.* To steal.

pil-grim *n.* A traveler to a holy place.

pill *n.* A small tablet; oral contraceptive.

pil-lar *n.* A column.

pil-low *n.* A case filled with feathers.

pi-lot *n.* A person licensed to operate a plane.

pi-men-to *n.* A sweet pepper.

pim-ple *n.* A small eruption of the skin.

pin-a-fore *n.* A sleeveless garment.

pinch *v.* To squeeze between a finger and thumb.

pine *n., Bot.* An evergreen tree.

pine-ap-ple *n.* A tropical fruit.

pin-na-cle *n.* A peak.

pi-noch-le *n.* A card game.

pint *n.* A half of a quart or two cups.

pi-o-neer *n.* The first settlers.

pi-ous *adj.* Devout. **-ness** *n.*

pique *n.* A feeling of resentment.

pi-rate *n.* A robber on the high seas.

pis-ta-chi-o *n.* A nut.

pis-til *n.* The seed-producing organ of a flower.

pit *n.* A manmade hole in the ground.

pitch *n.* The residue of coal tar.

pitch-er *n.* A baseball player; container for liquids.

pit-fall *n.* A trap.

pith *n., Bot.* The center part of stem.

pit-y *n., pl.* **-ies.** A feeling of sorrow.

piz-za *n.* Italian food covered with tomato sauce, and toppings.

pla-cate *v.* To appease satisfy.

place *n.* A region; an area.

pla-cen-ta *n.* An organ which supplies a fetu

with nourishment.

plac-id *adj.* Peaceful; calm.

plaid *n.* A checkered design.

plain *adj.* Flat; open, as in view.

plain-tiff *n.* A person who brings suit.

plan *n.* An arrangement; a scheme.

plane *n.* A tool for smoothing wood.

plan-et *n., astron.* A celestial body.

plank *n.* A broad piece of wood.

plant *n.* A living organism.

plaque *n.* An engraved tablet for mounting.

plas-ter-board *n.* A building material.

plas-tic *n.* A synthetically made material.

plas-tic sur-ger-y *n.* Restoration of destroyed body parts.

plate *n.* A dish used for serving food.

pla-teau *n.* A level expanse of elevated land.

plat-form *n.* An elevated stage.

pla-toon *n.* A military unit.

plat-ter *n.* A large serving dish.

plau-si-ble *adj.* Probable; seeming to be true.

play *v.* To amuse oneself.

pla-za *n.* An open-air marketplace.

plea *n.* An urgent request.

plea bar-gain-ing *v.* Making a pretrial agreement.

pleas-ant *adj.* Giving pleasure.

please *v.* To make happy.

pleas-ure *n.* Satisfaction; enjoyment.

pleat *n.* A fold in a cloth.

plebe *n.* A freshman at the U.S. Naval Academy.

pledge *n.* A solemn promise.

plen-ty *n.* An ample amount.

pli-a-ble *adj.* Flexible; easy to bend.

pli-ers *pl. n.* An implement used for holding.

plight *n.* A distressing situation.

plot *n.* A small piece of ground.

plow *n.* An implement for turning soil.

plug *n.* A hole stopper.

plum-age *n.* The feathers of a bird.

plumb *n.* A lead weight to test the perpendicular line of something.

plumb-er *n.* A person who repairs or installs plumbing.

plume *n.* A feather.

plu-ral *adj.* Containing more than one.

plus *prep.* The symbol (+) indicates addition.

ply *v.* To mold or bend; thickness of yarn, etc.

ply-wood *n.* A building material.

pneu-mo-nia *n.* Inflammation of the lungs.

poach *v.* To cook in a liquid; steal wild game. **-er** *n.*

pock-et *n.* A small pouch in a garment.

po-di-um *n.* A small raised platform.

po-em *n.* A composition in verse.

po-et *n.* A person who writes poetry. **-ic** *adj.*, **-ically** *adv.*

point *n.* The tapered end of something. **-ed** *adj.*

poise *v.* To hold one's balance; self-confidence.

poi-son *n.* A substance which kills. **-ous** *adj.*

poke *v.* To push or prod.

pok-er *n.* A card game.

pole *n.* The two ends of the earth axis.

pol-i-o-my-e-li-tis *n.* Inflammation of the spinal cord; also known as polio.

po-lice-man *n.* A law officer.

pol-i-cy *n., pl.* **-ies** A plan which guides decision making.

po-lite *adj.* Mannerly.

-ness *n.*, **-ly** *adv.*

poll *n.* Votes in an election; a survey.

pol-lute *v.* To contaminate. **-tion** *n.*

po-lo *n.* A game played on horseback.

pol-ter-geist *n.* A mischievous ghost.

pol-y-es-ter *n.* A synthetic material.

pol-y-graph *n.* A lie detector machine.

pomp-ous *adj.* An appearance of importance. **-ness** *n.*, **-ly** *adv.*

pond *n.* A body of still water.

pon-der *v.* To weigh or think about. **-er** *n.*, **-able** *adj.*

pon-der-ous *adj.* Massive. **-ness** *n.*, **-ly** *adv.*

pon-tiff *n.* The pope.

po-ny *n., pl.* **-ies** A small horse.

pool *n.* A small body of water.

poor *adj.* Lacking money; satisfactory. **-ness** *n.*, **-ish** *adj.*, **-ly** *adv.*

pop *v.* To cause to burst. *Slang* Soda.

pope *n.* The head of the Catholic Church.

pop-u-lar *adj.* Widely liked. **-ly** *adv.*, **-ity** *n.*

pop-u-la-tion *n.* Total people in a given area.

porch *n.* A covered entrance.

pore *v.* To ponder. *n.* A skin opening.

por-nog-ra-phy *n.* Pictures which arouse sexual excitement.

po-rous *adj.* Full of tiny holes. **-ness** *n.*, **-ly** *adv.*

port *n.* A city with a harbor; a wine.

port-a-ble *adj.* Move-able. **-bly** *adv.*, **-bility** *n.*

por-ter *n.* A person who carries baggage.

port-fo-li-o *n.* A carrying case.

por-tion *n.* A part of a whole; a share.

por-tray *v.* To represent by drawing.

pose *v.* To place, as for a picture; assume a specific position. **-er** *n.*

po-si-tion *n.* A spot where something is placed; a job. **-er** *n.*, **-al** *adj.*

pos-i-tive *adj.* Absolutely certain. **-ness** *n.*, **-ly** *adv.*

pos-se *n.* A deputized group to assist the sheriff.

pos-ses-sive *adj.* Not wanting to share. **-ness** *n.*, **-ly** *adv.*

pos-si-ble *adj.* Capable of happening. **-bility** *n.*

post *n.* An upright piece of wood.

post-age *n.* A fee for mailing something.

pos-te-ri-or *adj.* In the back.

post-mor-tem *adj.* An autopsy.

post-pone *v.* To put off; defer. **-er**, **-ment** *n.*, **-able** *adj.*

pos-ture *n.* The carriage of the body.

pot *n.* A deep container for cooking; marijuana.

po-ta-to *n.*, *pl.* **-toes** An edible, tuber vegetable.

po-tent *adj.* Having strength. **-ly** *adv.*

po-ten-tial *adj.* Possible. **-ly** *adv.*

pot-pour-ri *n.* A dried sweet-smelling flower petals.

pouch *n.* A small bag.

poul-try *n.* A fowl grown for its meat and eggs.

pound *n.* A weight equal to sixteen ounces.

pov-er-ty *n.* A state of being poor.

pow-der *n.* A finely ground substance.

pow-er-ful *adj.* Possessing great force. **-ness** *n.*, **-ly** *adv.*

prac-ti-cal *adj.* Serving a purpose. **-ness** *n.*, **-ly** *adv.*

prai-rie *n.* A wide area of rolling land devoid of trees.

praise *v.* To express approval. **-er** *n.*

prank *n.* A mischievous

trick.

pray *v.* To address prayers to God.

prayer *n.* A devout request.

pre- *pref* Prior to something.

preach *v.* To deliver a sermon. **-er** *n.*

pre-cau-tion *n.* Care taken in advance. **-ary** *adj.*

pre-cede *v.* To go before in time.

pre-cept *n.* A rule to guide one's conduct.

pre-cinct *n.* An electoral district.

pre-cious *adj.* Having great value. **-ness** *n.*, **-ly** *adv.*

pre-cip-i-ta-tion *n.* Snow, rain, sleet, etc.

pre-cip-i-tous *adj.* Being very steep. **-ness** *n.*, **-ly** *adv.*

pre-cise *adj.* Exact; strictly following rules. **-ness** *n.*, **-ly** *adv.*

pre-clude *v.* To shut out; prevent.

pre-co-cious *adj.* Developing skills early in life. **-ness** *n.*, **-ly** *adv.*

pre-con-ceive *v.* To form a notion beforehand.

pred-a-tor *n.* A person who lives by stealing.

pre-des-ti-na-tion *n.* Destiny; fate.

pred-i-cate *n. gram.* A word which says something about the subject.

pre-dict *v.* To tell beforehand. **-able** *adj.*, **-ability** *n.*, **-ably** *adv.*

pree-mie *n. Slang* A baby born before the due date.

pre-empt *v.* To take hold of before someone else. **-tor** *n.*

pre-fab-ri-cate *v.* To built in sections. **-cation** *n.*

pref-ace *n.* An introduction in the front of a book.

pre-fer *v.* Being the favorite. **-ability** *n.*

pre-fix *v.* To put at the beginning.

preg-nant *adj.* Carrying a baby.

prej-u-dice *n.* A biased opinion.

prel-ude *n.* An introductory action.

pre-ma-ture *adj.* Being born before the natural time. **-turity** *n.*

pre-med-i-tate *v.* To plan in advance.

pre-mi-um *n.* An object offered free.

pre-na-tal *adj.* Prior to birth.

pre-pare *v* To make ready.

pre-pay *v.* To pay for in advance.

prep-o-si-tion *n.* A part of speech.

pre-pos-ter-ous *adj.*

Ridiculous; impossible.

pres-age *n.* An omen; feeling of danger.

pre-scribe *v.* To impose as a guide.

pres-ent *adj.* Going on; not past.

pres-en-ta-tion *n.* A formal introduction.

pre-serve *v.* To keep or save.

pre-side *v.* To be in charge.

pres-i-dent *n.* The chief executive.

press *v.* To exert steady pressure; to squeeze.

pres-sure *n.* A constraining moral force; burden.

pres-tige *n.* An importance based on achievements.

pre-sume *v.* To take for granted. **-sumably** *adv.*

pre-tend *v.* To make believe.

pre-text *n.* A hidden purpose.

pret-ty *adj.* Attractive.

pre-vail *v.* To win control over.

pre-vent *v.* To keep from happening.

pre-vi-ous *adj.* Occurring earlier. **-ly** *adv.*

price *n.* A set amount of money.

prick *n.* A puncture.

pride *n.* A sense of personal dignity.

priest *n.* A clergyman.

pri-ma-ry *adj.* First in origin.

prim-i-tive *adj.* Of the earliest time.

prince *n.* A son of a king.

prin-cess *n.* The daughter of a king.

prin-ci-pal *adj.* Most important; headmaster of a school.

prin-ci-ple *n.* A moral standard.

print *n.* An impression made with ink. **-able** *adv.*

print-out *n.* An output of a computer.

pri-or *adj.* Previous in time.

pris-on *n.* A place of confinement; jail.

pri-vate *adj.* Secluded; secret. **-vacy** *n.*

priv-i-lege *n.* A special right.

prize *n.* An award given to winner.

pro *n.* In favor of something.

prob-a-ble *adj.* Likely to take place. **-bility** *n.*

pro-ba-tion *n.* A period to test qualifications. **-ary** *n.*

prob-lem *n.* A perplexing situation.

pro-ce-dure *n.* A method of doing something.

pro-ceed *v.* To carry on.

proc-ess *n.* A course toward a result.

pro-ces-sion *n.* A group moving in a formal manner.

pro-ces-sor *n.* A central unit of a computer.

pro-claim *v.* To announce publicly.

pro-cras-ti-nate *v.* To put of; deter: **-nation** *n.*

pro-cure *v.* To acquire.

prod *v.* To poke.

prod-i-gal *adj.* Wasteful of money.

pro-duce *v.* To bring forth; to manufacture.

pro-fane *adj.* Vulgar.

pro-fess *v.* To admit openly.

pro-fes-sor *n.* A faculty member of a college.

pro-fi-cient *adj.* Highly skilled.

pro-file *n.* An outline of a person's face or figure.

prof-it *n.* A financial return after expenses.

pro-found *adj.* Deeply felt.

pro-fuse *adj.* Overflowing.

prog-e-ny *n., pl.* **-ies** An offspring.

pro-gram *n.* A pre-arranged plan.

prog-ress *n.* An advancement to a higher goal.

pro-hib-it *v.* To forbid.

pro-ject *n.* A plan of action. **-ivity** *n.*

pro-jec-tile *n.* Anything hurled through the air.

pro-lif-er-ate *v.* To grow with great speed.

pro-logue *n.* An introductory statement of a song or play.

pro-long *v.* To extend in time.

prom-e-nade *n.* An unhurried walk.

prom-i-nent *adj.* Widely known. **-nence** *n.*

pro-mis-cu-ous *adj.* Lacking discrimination. **-ity** *n.*

prom-ise *n.* An agreement; a pledge. **-issory** *adj.*

pro-mote *v.* To raise to a higher rank. **-motion** *n.*

prompt *adj.* On time; punctual. **-ly** *n.*

pro-noun *n., gram.* A word used in the place of a noun.

proof *n.* A fact established by evidence.

proof-read *v.* To read in order to detect errors in printer's proof.

prop *n.* A support.

prop-a-gate *v.* To reproduce. **-tion** *n.*

prop-er *adj.* Appropriate.

prop-er-ty *n., pl.* **-ies** A piece of land.

proph-et *n.* A person who foretells the future.

pro-pi-ti-ate *v.* To win the goodwill of.

pro-por-tion *n.* The relation of one thing to another.

pro-pose v. To make an offer.

prop-o-si-tion n. A scheme or plan offered for consideration.

pro-rate v. To divide proportionately.

pro-scribe v. To outlaw.

pros-e-cute v. To bring suit against.

pros-pect n. Something that has the possibility of future success.

pros-per v. To be successful.

pros-ti-tute n. A harlot.

pros-trate adj. Lying face down.

pro-tect v. To guard against injury.

pro-test v. To make a strong objection.

pro-to-col n. The rules of state etiquette.

pro-trude v. To thrust outward.

proud adj. Have a feeling of satisfaction; self-respect.

prove v. To show evidence.

prov-erb n. An old saying which illustrates a truth.

pro-vide v. To furnish what is needed. **-r** n.

pro-voke v. To incite to anger.

prox-i-mate adj. Near.

prox-y n. An authority to act for another.

pru-dent adj. Being cautious.

prune n. The dried fruit of a plum. **-er** n.

psalm n. A sacred hymn.

psy-chi-a-try n. The treatment of mental disorders.

psy-chic n. A person who communicates with the spirit world.

psy-cho-path n. A mental disorder with antisocial behavior.

pu-ber-ty n. The beginning of sexual development.

pub-lic adj. For everyone's use. **-ness** n.

pub-lish v. To print and distribute printed matter. **-er** n.

puck n. A hard disk used in the game of hockey.

pull v. To apply force. **-er** n.

pul-sate v. To beat rhythmically.

pulse n., physiol. The beating of the heart, felt in the arteries.

pul-ver-ize v. To reduced to dust. **-zation** n., **-zable** adj.

pump n. A mechanical device for moving liquid.

pump-kin n. An edible yellow-orange fruit.

punch n. A tool for piercing; hit with the fist. **-er** n.

punc-tu-al adj. Arriving on time. **-ly** adv., **-ity** n.

punc-tu-ate *v.* To give or show emphasis. **-ation** *n.*

punc-túre *v.* To prick or pierce. **-able** *adj.*

pun-gent *adj.* Sharp in smell or taste. **-gency** *n.*

pun-ish-ment *n.* A penalty for a crime.

punk *n., Slang* A bizarre style of clothing.

punt *n.* A flatbottomed boat; kick a football.

pup *n.* A young dog.

pupil *n.* A person attending school.

pup-pet *n.* A figure which is manipulated by strings. **-eer** *n.*

pur-chase *v.* To obtain by money; buy. **-er** *n.*

pure *adj.* To free from contaminates. **-ness** *n.*

purge *v.* To make clean; free from guilt or sin.

pur-port *v.* To imply, with the intent to deceive. **-ed** *adj.*

pur-pose *n.* A desired goal. **-ly** *adv.*

purse *n.* A handbag.

pur-sue *v.* To chase; follow.

pur-vey *v.* To supply provisions. **-ance** *n.*

pus *n.* A secretion from infected tissue.

push *v.* To exert force; sell illegal drugs. **-er** *n.*

put *v.* To place in a location.

pu-tre-fy *v.* To decay.

putt *n.* A light stroke in golf. **-er** *n.*

puz-zle *v.* To confuse. **-zling** *adj.*

py-or-rhe-a *n., pathol.* Inflammation of the gums.

pyr-a-mid *n.* A structure with square base and triangular sides which meet at a point. **-ic** *adj.*

pyre *n.* A material for burning a dead body.

py-ro-ma-ni-a *n.* A compulsion to set fires. **-cal** *adj.*

py-thon *n.* A large nonvenomous snake.

Q

Q, q The seventeenth letter of the English alphabet.

qat *n.* A small plant found in Africa, the fresh leaf is chewed for a stimulating effect.

Q fev-er *n.* A mild disease with high fever, muscular pains, and chills and transmitted by ticks or raw milk.

Qa-tar *n.* A country located on the western coast of the Persian Gulf.

qi-vi-ut *n.* Yarn spun from the fine, soft hair of the musk ox.

quack *n.* A harsh, croaking cry of a duck. **-ery** *n.*

quad-ran-gle *n.* Plane figure with four sides and

four angles. **-gular** *n.*

quad-rant *n.* A quarter section of a circle, subtending or enclosing a central angle of 90 degrees.

quad-ru-ped *n.* Any animal having four feet.

quad-ru-ple *adj.* Consisting of four parts; multiplied by four. **-plication** *n.*

quad-ru-plet *n.* A group of four of a kind.

quaff *v.* To drink with abundance.

quag-mire *n.* An area of soft muddy land that gives away underfoot; a marsh.

quail *n., pl.* A small game bird.

quaint *adj.* Pleasing in an old-fashioned, unusual way. **-ly** *adv.,* **-ness** *n.*

quake *v.* To shake or tremble violently.

Quak-er *n.* A religious sect called the Society of Friends.

qual-i-fi-ca-tion *n.* Act of qualifying; the ability, skill, or quality which makes something suitable for a given position.

qual-i-fy *v.* To prove something able; restrict; limit; modify. **-fied** *adj.,* **-fier** *n.*

qual-i-ta-tive *adj.* Having to do with the quality of anything.

qual-i-ty *n.* A distinguishing character which makes something such as it is.

qualm *n.* A sudden feeling of sickness; uneasiness. **-ish** *adj.*

quan-da-ry *n.* A state of perplexity.

quan-ti-ty *n.* A number; amount.

quan-tum *n.* An amount or quantity.

quar-an-tine *n.* A period of enforced isolation to prevent the spread of disease.

quar-rel *n.* An unfriendly or angry disagreement. **-er** *n.,* **-some** *adj.*

quar-ry *n.* An animal hunted for food; an open pit or excavation from which limestone or other material is being extracted. **-ing** *n.*

quart *n.* Unit of measurement equaling four cups.

quar-ter *n.* One of four equal parts into which anything may be divided; a place of lodging; coin worth 25 cents.

quar-ter--deck *n.* The upper deck of a vessel.

quar-ter-mas-ter *n.* An officer in charge of supplies for army troops.

quar-ter-ly *adj.* Four times a year.

quar-tet *n.* A musical

composition for four voices or instruments.

quartz *n.* A hard, transparent crystallized mineral.

qua-sar *n.* One of the most distant and brightest bodies in the universe.

quea-sy *adj.* Nauseated; sick. **-siness** *n.*

queen *n.* The wife of a king; a woman sovereign or monarch; in chess, the most powerful piece on the board. **-ly** *adj.*

queer *adj.* Strange; unusual; different from the normal.

quell *v.* To put down with force **-er** *n.*

quench *v.* To extinguish or put out; to cool metal by thrusting into water. **-able** *adj.*

quer-u-lous *adj.* Complaining or fretting; expressing complaints. **-ness** *n.*, **-ly** *adv.*

que-ry *n.* An injury; a question.

quest *n.* A search; pursuit.

ques-tion *n.* An expression of inquiry which requires an answer. **-able** *adj.*, **-er** *n.*

ques-tion mark *n.* A mark of punctuation, (?), used in writing to indicate a question.

ques-tion-naire *n.* Writ-

ten series of questions.

queue *n.*, *Computer Science* A sequence of stored programs or data on hold for processing.

quib-ble *v.* To raise trivial objection; argue over minor things. **-bler** *n.*

quiche *n.* An unsweetened custard baked in a pastry shell.

quick *adj.* Moving swiftly; occurring in a short time. **-ness** *n.*

quick-freeze *v.* To preserve food.

quick-sand *n.* A bog of very fine, wet sand of considerable depth.

quid *n.* A small portion of tobacco; a cow's cud.

qui-es-cent *adj.* Being in a state of quiet repose.

qui-et *adj.* Silent; making very little sound; still; tranquil; calm. **-ly** *adv.*

quill *n.* A strong bird feather; a spine from a porcupine.

quilt *n.* A bed coverlet made of two layers of cloth with a soft substance between and held in place by lines of stitching. **-ing** *n.*

qui-nine *n.* A very bitter, colorless, crystalline powder used in the treatment of malaria.

quin-sy *n.*, *Pathol.* Severe inflammation of the tonsils.

quin·tes·sence *n.* A most essential and purest form of anything.

quin-tet *n.* A musical composition written for five people.

quin-tu-ple *adj.* Increased five times.

quirk *n.* A sudden, sharp bend or twist; a personal mannerism.

quis-ling *n.* A person who is a traitor, working against his own country from within.

quit *v.* To cease; to give up; to depart; to abandon.

quite *adv.* The fullest degree; really; actually. **-ness** *n.*

quiz *v.* To question, as with an informal oral or written examination. **-zed** *v.*, **-zer** *n.*

quoin *n.* An external corner or angle of a building.

quoit *n.* A game in which a metal ring connected to a rope is thrown in an attempt to encircle a stake.

quo-rum *n.* Number of members needed in order to validate a meeting.

quo-ta *n.* Allotment or proportional share.

quo-ta-tion *n.* An exact quoting of words as a passage.

quo-ta-tion mark *n.*
Marks of punctuation (" ") showing a direct quote.

quote *v.* To repeat exactly what someone else has stated. **-ed** *v.*

quo-tid-i-an *adj.* Occurring or recurring daily.

quo-tient *n.* Amount or number which results when one number is divided by another.

R

R, r The eighteenth letter of the English alphabet.

rab-bet *n.* The recess or groove on the edge of a piece of wood.

rab-bi *n.* An ordained leader of Jews.

rab-bit *n.* A burrowing mammal related to the hare.

rab-ble *n.* A disorderly crowd.

rab-id *adj.* Being affected with rabies; mad; furious. **-ness** *n.*

ra-bies *n.* A disease of the nervous system.

rac-coon *n., pl.* **-coons**, **-coon** A nocturnal mammal with a black, mask-like face.

race *n.* The division of the human population having common origin and traits; a contest.

ra-cial *adj.* Characteristic of a race.

rac-ism *n.* The belief that a particular race is superior.

rack *n.* The framework for displaying or holding something.

rack-et *n.* A lightweight bat-like object used in tennis.

rac-y *adj.* Having a spirited or strongly marked quality. **-iness** *n.*

ra-dar *n.* A device for detection of aircraft or other objects.

ra-di-al *adj.* Pertaining to a ray or radius.

ra-di-ant *adj.* Emitting rays of heat or light.

ra-di-a-tion *n.* An energy radiated from nuclear particles.

rad-i-cal *adj.* Making extreme changes in views, or habits.

ra-di-o *n.* The technique of communicating by radio waves.

ra-di-o-ac-tiv-i-ty *n., Physics* A spontaneous emission of electromagnetic radiation.

rad-ish *n.* The edible root of the radish plant.

ra-di-um *n.* A radioactive metallic element symbolized by Ra.

ra-di-us *n.* A line from the center of a circle to its surface.

ra-don *n.* A radioactive gaseous element symbolized by Rn.

raf-fi-a *n.* A fiber from an African palm tree for making baskets, hats, etc.

raf-fle *n.* A game of chance; lottery.

raft *n.* A structure made from logs or planks and used for water transportation.

raf-ter *n.* A beam that supports a roof.

rag *n.* A waste piece of clothing.

rag-ged *adj.* Unkempt; having an irregular edge.

rage *n.* A violent anger.

raid *n.* A sudden invasion.

rail *n.* A horizontal bar of metal forming a track on a railroad.

rain *n.* Water from atmospheric vapor.

rain-bow *n.* Rays of light appearing in the sky after a rain.

rain-check *n.* A stub for merchandise which is out of stock.

raise *v.* To cause to move upward; to rear as children.

rai-sin *n.* Grapes that are dried and then eaten.

rake *n.* A tool with a long handle and teeth used to gather leaves.

ral-ly *v.* To call together for a purpose.

ram *n.* A male sheep; an implement used to crush on impact.

RAM *abbr.* Random access memory.

ram-ble *v.* To stroll or walk aimlessly; to talk in a long winded fashion. **-blingly** *adv.*

ram-bunc-tious *adj.* Overly rough or boisterous.

ramp *n.* An incline which connects two different levels.

ram-page *n.* A course of destruction or violent behavior.

ram-pant *adj.* Out of control; wild in actions.

ram-rod *n.* A metal rod used for cleaning barrels of a rifle or other firearm.

ram-shack-le *adj.* Falling apart due to poor construction or maintenance.

ranch *n.* A large establishment for raising livestock or crops.

ran-cid *adj.* Having a sour smell and taste from spoilage.

ran-cor *n.* Malice; deep resentment.

ran-dom *adj.* Done without a purpose or direction.

r and r *abbr.* Rest and relaxation.

rang *v.* Past tense of ring.

range *n.* A cooking stove; a tract of land on which animals graze; a row especially of moun-

tains.

rank *n.* A degree of official position or status.

rank *adj.* Having a strong and disagreeable odor, smell, or taste.

ran-sack *v.* To plunder through every part of something.

ran-som *n.* Money demanded or paid to free a kidnaped person.

rant *v.* To talk in a wild, loud way.

rap *v.* To strike with a blow; knock. *slang* to converse; talk.

ra-pa-cious *adj.* Living on prey seized alive; plundering. **-ly** *adv.*, **-ness** *n.*

rape *n.* The crime of forcible sexual intercourse.

rap-id *adj.* Having great speed. **-ness** *n.*

ra-pi-er *n.* A long, slender straight sword with two edges.

rap-ine *n.* The forceable taking of another's property.

rap-port *n.* A harmonious relationship.

rapt *adj.* Deeply absorbed or engrossed with something.

rap-ture *n.* A state of extreme ecstasy.

rare *adj.* Scarce; infrequent or far apart; not fully cooked.

rare-bit *n.* A dish made

with cheese.

rare-ly *adv.* Seldom.

ras-cal *n.* A person full of mischief; a person who is not honest.

rash *adj.* Acting without consideration or caution. *n.* A skin irritation.

rasp *n.* A coarse file. *v.* To scrape with a course file. **-er** *n.*

rasp-berry *n.* A small edible fruit, red or black in color.

rat *n.* A rodent similar to the mouse, but having a longer tail; one who betrays his friends.

ratch-et *n.* A mechanism consisting of a pawl that allows movement in one direction only.

rate *n.* A fixed ratio or price on something.

rath-er *adv.* More accurate or precise.

rat-i-fy *v.* To approve something in an official way. **-fication** *n.*

ra-tio *n.* The relationship between two things in amount, size, or degree.

ra-tion *n.* A fixed portion or share allowed. **-ing** *n.*

ra-tio-nal *adj.* Having the faculty of reasoning; being of sound mind. **-ity** *n.*

ra-tion-al-ize *v.* To explain or justify in a logical manner.

rat-tan *n.* A palm whose stems are used to make wickerworks.

rat-tle *v.* To make a series of rapid noises in quick succession; to talk rapidly; to chatter.

rat-tler *n., slang* A venomous snake; a rattlesnake.

rau-cous *adj.* Loud and rowdy; having a rough, hoarse sound.

raun-chy *adj.* Lewd; slovenly.

rav-age *v.* To bring on heavy destruction; to devastate.

rave *v.* To speak incoherently; to speak with enthusiasm.

rav-el *v.* To separate fibers or threads; to unravel.

ra-ven *n.* A large bird, with shiny black feathers.

rav-en-ous *adj.* Starved. **-ly** *adv.*

ra-vine *n.* A long narrow valley.

ra-vi-o-li *n.* A dough enclosing meat or cheese served in sauce.

rav-ish *v.* To seize and carry off with violence.

rav-ish-ing *adj.* Beautiful and entrancing.

raw *adj.* Not fully cooked; sore; lacking refinement.

raw-hide *n.* Untanned skin of cattle.

ray *n.* A thin line of light.

ray-on *n.* A synthetic fiber.

ra-zor *n.* A sharp-edged instrument used for shaving beards, etc.

reach *v.* To extend the outstretched hand so as to touch.

re-ac-tion *n.* A reversed action toward a previous condition.

re-ac-ti-vate *v.* To become effective again.

read *v.* To understand the meaning of something written or printed.

read-er *n.* A schoolbook for instruction in reading.

re-ad-just *v.* To put in order again.

read-y *adj.* Prepared for action.

real *adj.* Genuine; true; existing as fact.

re-al-ize *v.* To understand clearly.

realm *n.* A kingdom; a domain or scope.

ream *n.* A measure of paper equaling 500 sheets.

reap *v.* To harvest a crop with a sickle.

re-ap-pear *v.* To appear anew or again.

rear *n.* The opposite side of the front; the background.

rea-son *n.* The motive or explanation.

re-bate *n.* A discount.

re-bel *v.* To refuse allegiance.

re-bel-lion *n.* An organized uprising to change or overthrow an existing authority.

re-birth *n.* A revival or renaissance.

re-bound *v.* To spring back.

re-buff *v.* To refuse sharply.

re-buke *v.* To reprimand.

re-call *v.* To order or summon to return something.

re-cant *v.* To confession publicly.

re-cede *v.* To move back.

re-ceipt *n.* Proof of purchase.

re-ceive *v.* To take or obtain something.

re-cent *adj.* Fresh; newer.

re-cep-ta-cle *n.* An electrical outlet.

re-cep-tion *n.* A formal entertainment for guests.

re-cess *n.* A rest period.

rec-i-pe *n.* The directions and a list of ingredients for preparing food.

re-cip-ro-cate *v.* To give something in return.

re-cite *v.* To repeat from memory; to give an account of something in detail.

reck-on *v.* To calculate.

re-claim *v.* To redeem.

re-cline *v.* To assume a supine position.

rec-og-nize *v.* To experience or identify something or someone. **-nizable** *adj.*

rec-ol-lect *v.* To remember something.

rec-om-mend *v.* To suggest to another as desirable; to advise. **-ation** *n.*

rec-on-cile *v.* To restore a friendship.

re-con-sid-er *v.* To think about again with a view to changing.

re-cord *v.* To preserve sound on a tape or disk for replay.

re-coup *v.* To be reimbursed; to recover.

re-course *n.* A turning to or an appeal for help.

re-cover *v.* To regain something which was lost; be restored to good health.

rec-re-a-tion *n.* A diversion; an amusement.

re-cruit *v.* To enlist for military duty.

rec-tan-gle *n.* A parallelogram with all right angles.

rec-ti-fy *v.* To correct something.

rec-tum *n.* Part of the intestine connecting the colon and anus.

re-cu-per-ate *v.* To regain strength.

re-deem *v.* To buy back; to recover.

re-doubt *n.* A small fortification.

re-duce *v.* To make less; to diminish in quantity or size.

reef *n.* The coral near the surface of water.

reek *v* To emit a strong and unpleasant odor.

re-fer *v.* To direct for help. **-ral** *n.*

ref-er-ee *n.* An official in football; one who settles a dispute.

re-fine *v.* To make pure; to free from impurities.

re-fin-ish *v.* To apply a new surface on wood, etc.

re-flex *n.* An involuntary reaction.

re-for-ma-to-ry *n.* A jail-like institution.

re-frac-to-ry *adj.* Unmanageable; obstinate.

re-frain *v.* To hold back.

re-frig-er-ate *v.* To chill or cool.

ref-uge *n.* A protection from harm.

ref-u-gee *n.* One who flees to find safety.

re-fund *v.* To pay back; to reimburse.

re-fur-bish *v.* To make clean; to renovate.

re-gain *v.* To recover.

re-gale *v.* To entertain or delight.

re-gard v. To look upon with esteem.

re-gat-ta n. A boat race.

re-gen-er-ate v. To reform morally.

re-gent n. One who acts as a ruler.

regiment n. a military unit; a regulated course of exercise, etc.

re-gion n. A geographical area

re-gis-ter n. A book containing names and accounts, etc.

reg-is-trar n. A keeper of records.

re-gress v. To return to a previous state

re-gret v. To feel sorry about.

reg-u-la-tion n. A governing rule.

re-hash v. To rework or go over old material.

re-hears-al n. The act of practicing for a performance.

re-im-burse v. To pay back.

reign n. The time a monarch rules a country.

rein-deer n. A large deer found in northern regions.

re-in-force v. To support something.

re-in-state v. To restore something to its former condition.

re-it-er-ate v. To do something over and over

again.

re-ject v. To refuse; to discard as useless.

re-joice v. To fill with joy.

re-ju-ve-nate v. To restore to youthful appearance or vigor.

re-lapse v. To fall back.

re-lent v. To slacken.

re-late v. To tell the events of; to narrate.

rel-a-tive adj. Considered in comparison or relationship to other n. A member of one's family.

re-lax v. To make loose or lax; to become less formal or less reserved. **-ation** n.

re-lease v. To set free from confinement; to unfasten.

rel-e-vant adj. Relating to matters at hand.

re-lic n. The ancient remains.

re-lig-ion n. A system of worship.

re-luc-tant adj. Unwilling.

re-mains pl., n. The part left after all other parts have been taken away.

re-mark n. A brief expression or comment.

re-mark-able adj. Extraordinary. **-ably** adv.

re-mem-ber v. To bring back or recall to the mind.

re-mind v. To cause or help to remember.

rem-i-nis-cence n. The

practice or process or recalling the past.
 -cent adj.
re-miss adj. Negligent.
re-mit v. To send money as payment.
re-morse n. Regret for past misdeeds.
re-mote adj. Being distant in time.
ren-ais-sance n. A revival or rebirth; revival of classical art, literature, etc. in Europe.
ren-der v. To submit or give.
ren-dez-vous n. A prearranged meeting.
ren-e-gade n. An outlaw; a traitor.
re-nown n. Famous; widely honored.
rent n. Payment made for the use of another's property.
rep-ar-tee n. Quick reply.
re-pay v. To pay back money.
re-peal v. To withdraw officially.
re-peat v. To say or perform again. -able adj.
re-pel v. To drive back or force away.
re-pent v. To change your ways.
re-per-cus-sion n. Unforeseen effect by an action.
rep-er-toire n. A person's artistic

achievements.
rep-e-ti-tion n. An act of repeating; something done a second time.
 -tious adj.
re-plen-ish v. To supply again; restock.
rep-li-ca n. An reproduction of an original.
re-ply v. To answer; to respond.
re-port v. To bring back or relate an account of facts.
re-pose n. At rest.
rep-re-hend v. To disapprove; to censure.
rep-re-sent v. To act on behalf of.
re-press v. To restrain.
re-prieve v. To delay punishment.
rep-ri-mand v. To censure severely.
re-pri-sal n. Inflected injury.
re-proach v. To blame.
re-pu-di-ate v. To reject or disown.
re-pug-nant adj. Distasteful.
re-pulse v. To repel or drive back.
re-pul-sive adj. Distasteful or disgusting.
re-put-a-tion n. Evaluation of one's character.
re-quest v. To express a desire for something to be granted.
re-quire-ment n. Something necessary.

req-ui-site *adj.* Absolutely needed.

re-scind *v.* To repeal; to void.

res-cue *v.* To free from danger or evil.

re-sent *v.* To show ill feeling.

re-serve *v.* To save for use at a later time.

res-er-voir *n.* A large body of water.

re-side *v.* To occupy a residence.

res-i-due *n.* Something which remains.

re-sign *v.* To give up.

re-sil-ient *adj.* Springing back; buoyant. **-iency** *n.*

res-in *n.* A substance from plants used in making plastics.

re-sist *v.* To withstand; to oppose. **-er** *n.*

re-sist-ance *n.* The act of resisting.

re-sis-tor *n.* A conducting body.

res-o-lute *adj.* Coming from determination. **-ness** *n.*

re-solve *v.* To make a firm decision on.

re-sound *v.* To echo loudly.

re-source *n.* An assistance.

res-pi-ra-tion *n.* An act of breathing.

res-pite *n.* A temporary postponement.

re-splend-ent *adj.* Magnificent.

re-spond *v.* To answer; to react.

re-sponse *n.* A reply; a reaction.

re-spon-si-ble *adj.* Trustworthy. **-bility** *n.*

res-tau-rant *n.* A public building serving food and beverages.

res-ti-tu-tion *n.* A compensation for damage, or loss.

res-tive *adj.* Impatient.

re-store *v.* To bring back to a former condition. **-er** *n.*

re-strain *v.* To hold back.

re-strict *v.* To limit confine within bounds.

re-sume *v.* To start again after an interruption.

re-sur-gent *adj.* Rising again. **-gence** *n.*

re-tail *v.* To sell to the public. **-er** *n.*

re-tain *v.* To keep possession of.

re-tain-er *n.* A fee paid to secure services.

re-take *v.* To recapture.

re-tal-i-ate *v.* To repay; return like for like. **-ation** *n.*

re-tard *v.* To delay the progress.

re-ten-tion *n.* The power of memory.

ret-i-cent *adj.* Reserved.

ret-i-na *n.* A part of the eyeball.

re-tire v. To withdraw; retreat from action.

re-tort v. To reply quickly.

re-trace v. To track back; go over again.

re-tract v. To take back something. **-tor** n.

re-trench v. To economize. **-ment** n.

ret-ri-bu-tion n. A punishment for a wrong doing.

re-trieve v. To recover; to rescue or save.

ret-ro-ac-tive adj. Affecting things past. **-ly** adj.

ret-ro-gress v. To move backward; to revert.

ret-ro-spect n. A review of things in the past.

re-turn v. To give back; restore; to repay.

re-un-ion n. A gathering together again.

rev n. Revolution v., Informal Increase the speed of.

re-veal v. To make known; open to view.

rev-eil-le n. A signal at daybreak to awaken soldiers.

rev-el v. To take great pleasure. **-er** n.

rev-e-la-tion n. A disclosure.

re-venge v. To inflict injury on.

rev-e-nue n. Income.

re-ver-ber-ate v. To reflect; return as sound.

re-vere v. To regard with respect; venerate. **-verence** n.

rev-er-end n. A clergyman.

rev-er-ie n. Irregular train of thought.

re-verse v. To turn in an opposite direction.

re-vert v. To return to former belief.

re-view v. To examine again; study critically; critique.

re-vile v. To speak evil of. **-er** n.

re-vise v. To change and amend.

re-vi-sion n. Re-examination for correction.

re-vive v. To refresh; activate again; present again; to gain vigor.

re-voke v. To make void by recalling; cancel.

re-volt n. Fill with disgust.

rev-o-lu-tion n. A sudden change in a system.

re-volve v. To rotate; travel in an orbit; ponder.

re-ward v. To compensate for a good deed.

rhap-so-dy n. A display of enthusiasm; type of musical composition.

rhe-ni-um n. A metallic element, Re.

rhet-o-ric n. The effective use of language.

rhet-o-ric n. A per-

suasive oratory.
  -rical *adj.*
rheum *n.* Watery matter.
rheu-mat-ic *adj.* Affected with rheumatism.
rheu-mat-ic fe-ver *n.* A severe infectious disease.
rheu-ma-tism *n.* A painful inflammation of the muscles and joints.
rhi-noc-er-os *n.* A very large mammal with horns on the snout.
rho-di-um *n.* A silver-white metallic element, Rh.
rho-do-den-dron *n.* An evergreen shrub with showy flowers.
rhu-barb *n.* A garden plant having edible stalks.
rhyme *n.* A word having a sound similar to another; meter.
rhythm *n.* Movement with a beat.
rib *n.* Curved bones around the chest; a cut of meat; something riblike.
rib-ald *adj.* Vulgar in speech; abusive.
rib-bon *n.* Narrow band of silk, etc.
rice *n.* Starchy grain.
rich *adj.* Wealthy; productive; sweet.
rich-es *n., pl.* Wealth.
rick *n.* A stack of corn or hay.

rick-ets *n.* A bone softening disease.
rick-et-y *adj.* Shaky; irregular.
ric-o-chet *n.* A glancing rebound off a flat surface.
rid *v.* To free; deliver.
rid-dle *n.* A large sieve; puzzling question.
ride *v.* To sit on and manage; be borne along.
rid-er *n.* A passenger; clause added to bill.
ridge *n.* A crest of something; chain of hills.
  -ed *v.*
rid-i-cule *v.* To make fun of.
ri-dic-u-lous *adj.* Absurd; laughable.
rife *adj.* Prevalent; abundant.
riff-raff *n.* A rabble.
ri-fle *n.* A gun carried over the shoulder.
rift *n.* A fault; crack; fissure; geological fault.
right *adj.* Correct; sound or normal; most fitting.
right-eous *adj.* Virtuous; acting within the dictates of morality. **-ness** *n.*
right-ful *adj.* Legitimate.
  -ly *adv.*
right-ism *n.* An advocacy of political conservatism.
rig-id *adj.* Inflexible; rigorous; strick in opinion. **-ity** *n.*
rig-or *n.* Austerity; strictness. **-ous** *adj.*

rile *v.* To anger; irritate.

rim *n.* The edge of an object that is circular.

rind *n.* A firm outward covering of fruits.

ring *n.* A circular band of material; circle; sound of a bell. **-ing** *v.*

ring-lead-er *n.* A leader of a circus performance.

ring-let *n.* A curl.

rink *n.* A smooth area for skating.

rinse *v.* To wash lightly.

ri-ot *n.* A public disturbance of a violent nature.

rip *v.* To tear; cut open.

ripe *adj.* Ready for reaping; matured.

rip-ple *v.* To form small waves; agitate lightly.

rise *v.* To get up; become active; appear.

rite *n.* A formal custom.

rit-u-al *n.* A religious act; any solemn ceremony.

ri-val *n.* A competitor.

river *n.* A natural stream of flowing water.

ri-vet *n.* A short metal pin with a head for joining metal, pants, etc.

road *n.* A highway; route.

roam *v.* To wander or rove.

roar *v.* To howl.

roast *v.* To cook by exposure to heat; dry and parch.

rob *v.* To steal someone's possessions.

robe *n.* A woman's long flowing gown.

ro-bot *n.* A mechanical device resembling man.

ro-bust *adj.* Vigorous; to be possessing great strength.

rock *n.* A large mass of stone.

rock-et *n.* A vehicle orbited into space; firecracker.

ro-dent *n.* A mammal, such as a rat.

ro-de-o *n.* A show of cowboy skills, bronco riding, etc.

roe *n.* Eggs of a female fish.

rogue *n.* A dishonest person.

roll *v.* To move by turning; flow; take the shape of a ball.

ro-mance *n.* A tale of chivalric love; love affair.

roof *n.* A cover of a building.

room *n.* A place of lodging; an amount of space.

room-mate *n.* One who shares a room or rooms with another.

room-y *adj.* Spacious.

roos-ter *n.* The male of the domestic chicken.

root *n.* A part of a plant which is below the earth; foundation.

rope *n.* The cord of twisted fibers. **-ed** *v.*

ro-sa-ry- *n.* A series of

prayers; rose garden.

rose *n.* An attractive flower; pinkish color.

ros-ter *n.* A list of names.

ros-trum *n.* A speaker's platform.

ro-tate *v.* To revolve or move around the center.

ro-tis-ser-ie *n.* A container with a rotating spit for roasting food.

rot-ten *adj.* Decaying; corrupt.

ro-tund *adj.* Rounded; plump; resonant.

ro-tun-da *n.* A round building with a dome.

rouge *n.* A cosmetic for the cheeks.

rough *adj.* Not smooth; uneven; unruly; stormy; rebellious; crude.

rou-lette *n.* A game of chance.

round *adj.* Spherical; having a curved form; plump.

rouse *v.* To wake from sleep; excite to action. **-er** *n.*

rout *n.* Disorder and confusion; uproar.

route *n.* A course taken; regular line of travel.

rou-tine *n.* A schedule followed regularly.

rove *v.* To wander over a wide area.

row *n.* A number of things positioned next to each other.

row-boat *n.* A small boat propelled with oars.

row-house *n.* A group of houses joined by a common wall.

roy-al *adj.* Relating to the king or queen.

rub *v.* To move back or forth on a surface.

rub-ber *n.* A resinous elastic material obtained from the sap of tropical plants or produced synthetically.

rub-bish *n.* Debris; trash.

ru-bid-i-um *n.* A silvery element symbolized by Rb.

ru-by *n.* A deep-red precious stone.

ruck-us *n.* An uproar; disturbance.

rud-der *n.* The steering part of a boat.

rude *adj.* Discourteous; impolite. **-ness** *n.*

ru-di-ment *n.* An underdeveloped state. **-ary** *adj.*

rue *v.* To regret; have compassion.

ruff *n.* A stiff, pleated collar.

ruf-fi-an *n.* A rowdy person.

ruf-fle *n.* A pleated strip or frill.

rug *n.* A heavy textile fabric used to cover the floor.

rug-ged *adj.* Having a rough uneven surface.

ru-in *n.* Destruction;

downfall.

rule *n.* Control; custom; point of law. *v.* to govern; to control.

rul-er *n.* A straight edge used for measuring length; one who rules.

rul-ing *a* Predominant. *n.* A decision settle by a court or judge.

ru-mi-nate *v.* To chew a cud.

rum-mage *v.* To ransack.

rum-my *n.* A card game in which each player tries to get rid of his hand in sequences of three cards or more of the same suit.

ru-mor *n.* An uncertain truth which is circulated from one person to another.

ru-mor-mon-ger *n.* One who spreads malicious rumors.

rump *n.* The buttocks.

rum-ple *v.* To wrinkle; crease.

rum-pus *n.* A disturbance; a riot; loud noise.

run *v.* To hurry busily from one place to another.

run-a-around *n.* Evasive action.

run-a-way *n.* Someone or something that runs away.

run-down *adj.* Tired; dilapidated.

rung *n.* A step of a ladder.

run-in *n.* An altercation.

run-ner *n.* A racer; messenger; that on which something runs or sides; narrow piece of cloth.

run-ning *adj.* Moving rapidly; functioning.

run--of--the--mill *adj.* Average.

runt *n.* The smallest animal in a litter.

run--through *n.* A cursory review; a rapid rehearsal.

run-way *n.* A clear pathway used by airplanes for taking off and landing.

rup-ture *n.* The act of bursting or breaking; hernia.

ru-ral *adj.* Pertaining to country life.

rush *v.* To move quickly; to hurry with speed. *n.* grass-like herb.

rust *n.* A coating which forms on iron when exposed to air and moisture.

rus-tic *n.* A simple person.

ruth-less *adj.* Cruel.

Rx. *n.* A prescription for medicine.

rye *n.* A cultivated cereal grass.

S

S, s Nineteenth letter of the English alphabet.

Sab-bath *n.* The seventh day of the week.

sa-ber *n.* A sword.

sa-ble *n.* A carnivorous mammal.

sab-o-tage *n.* A willful destruction.

sac-cha-rin *n.* A non-caloric sugar substitute.

sa-chet *n.* A bag of sweet-smelling powder.

sack *n.* A large bag used to hold and carry items. **-ing** *n.*

sac-ra-ment *n.* A religious ceremony such as baptism. **-ally** *adv.*

sa-cred *adj.* Dedicated to worship.

sac-ri-fice *v.* To give up something of value. **-fical** *adj.*

sad *adj.* Unhappy, sorrowful. **-ly** *adv.*

sad-dle *n.* A seat for a rider on a horse. **-r** *n.*

safe *adj.* Secure from harm. **-ty** *n.*

sa-ga *n.* A long heroic story.

saint *n.* A holy person. **-ly** *adj.*

sake *n.* A motive for doing something.

sa-la-ry *n.* A set compensation for work done.

sa-li-ent *adj.* Conspicuous.

sa-li-va *n.* A fluid secreted in the mouth.

salm-on *n.* A large game fish.

sa-loon *n.* A place where alcohol is sold.

salt *n.* Sodium chloride.

sa-lute *v.* To show honor to a superior officer.

sal-vage *v.* To save from destruction.

salve *n.* A medicated ointment.

sam-ple *n.* An example; try something. **-r** *n.*

san-a-to-ri-um *n.* An institution for insane people.

sanc-tu-ar-y *n.* A holy place.

sand *n.* The fine grains of disintegrated rock.

sane *adj.* Healthy, sound mind.

sane *adj.* To be of sound mind.

san-i-tar-y *adj.* Free from bacteria or filth.

sa-pi-ent *adj.* Wise.

sap-phire *n.* A deep-blue gem.

sar-dine *n.* A small edible fish.

sar-don-ic *adj.* Scornful.

sat-is-fac-tion *n.* A fulfillment of a desire.

sat-u-rate *v.* To make completely wet.

sauce *n.* Liquid topping for food.

sau-sage *n.* A seasoned, chopped meat.

sav-age *adj.* Wild; uncivilized. -ness n.

save v. To rescue from danger.

sa-voir--faire n. A social skill.

saw-horse n. A frame on which wood rests when being sawed.

sax-o-phone n. A brass wind instrument.

say v. To speak aloud. -ing n.

scaf-fold n. A temporary platform for workers.

scald v. To burn with hot liquid.

scale n. A weighing device; covering on a fish.

scalp n. The skin on top of the head.

scamper v. To run hurriedly.

scan v. Look at quickly.

scan-dal n. Public gossip. -ous adj.

scant adj. Not plentiful. -ling n.

scar n. A permanent mark from an injury.

scarce adj. Being rare; difficult to get.

scat-ter v. To spread around.

scav-en-ger n. A wild animal.

scent n. An odor; perfume. -less adj.

sched-ule n. A routine.

scheme n. A plan of action. -er n.

schol-ar n. An intelligent student. -ly adj.

school n. A place for learning.

sci-ence n. The study of natural phenomena.

scis-sors pl., n. A cutting tool.

scold v. To accuse harshly.

scope n. The range of one's actions.

scorch v. To parch with heat.

scorn n. Contempt. -ful adj.

scowl v. To make an angry look.

scrape v. To rub off roughly.

scratch v. To mark with the fingernails.

screech v. To make a harsh noise.

screen n. A surface for showing a movie.

screw n. A nail-shaped piece of metal with winding threads used for fastening together.

scru-ple n. Principle.

scuff v. To drag feet while walking.

scuf-fle v. To struggle in a confused manner.

scur-ry v. To move quickly.

scut-tle n. A small opening in the hull of a ship.

sea n. A large body of salt water.

seal n. A tight closure; aquatic mammal.

sear *v.* To dry up; burn slightly.

sea-son *n.* A spring, summer, fall and winter; flavor enhancer.

se-cede *v.* To withdraw from a group.

se-clude *v.* To isolate.

se-cret *n.* The knowledge kept from others.

sec-re-tary *n.* A head of a government department; executive's assistant. **-tarial** *adj.*

se-crete *v.* To discharge.

sec-tion *n.* A division of something.

sec-u-lar *adj.* Relating to something worldly.

se-cure *adj.* To be sturdy or strong.

see *v.* Power of sight.

seed *n.* A fertilized plant ovule.

seek *v.* To search for.

seem *v.* To appear to be. **-ly** *adj.*

seg-ment *n.* A portion.

seg-re-gate *v.* To isolate from others.

seize *v.* To take possession forcibly.

sel-dom *adv.* Not often.

sell *v.* To exchange a product for money.

se-man-tics *n.* A study of word meanings.

sem-i-an-nu-al *adj.* Twice a year.

sem-i-nar *n.* A convention on a certain subject.

sen-ate *n.* The upper house of a legislature.

se-nile *adj.* Mental deterioration.

sen-ior *adj.* Being the older of two.

sen-sa-tion *n.* Feelings.

sense *n.* Sensation. **-less** *adj.*

sen-si-ble *adj.* Having good judgment.

sen-si-tive *adj.* Intense feelings. **-ly** *adv.*

sen-tence *n.* A written complete thought.

sen-ti-men-tal *adj.* Very special; emotional.

sen-ti-nel *n.* The one who guards.

sep-a-rate *v.* To keep apart. **-tor** *n.*

se-quence *n.* A set arrangement.

se-rene *adj.* Being calm.

se-ries *n.* The one after another.

se-ri-ous *adj.* Important. **-ly** *adv.*

ser-mon *n.* A religious lecture.

ser-vant *n.* The one employed to care for someone.

serv-ice *n.* The help given to others. **-able** *adj.*

ses-sion *n.* A series of meetings.

set-tle *v.* to arrange or put in order.

sev-en *n.* The cardinal number 7, after 6.

sev-en-teen n. The cardinal number 17 after 16.

sev-en-ty n. The cardinal number 70, after 69.

sev-er v. To cut off or separate.

sev-er-al adj. More than one or two.

se-vere adj. Strict; stern.

sew-er n. A drain pipe to carry away waste.

sex n. The divisions, male and female.

shad-ow n. A shaded area.

shake v. To tremble.

shal-low adj. Not deep.

shame n. A feeling of embarrassment.

sham-poo n. A liquid soap to cleanse the hair.

shape n. The configuration of something.

share n. Divide among others.

shark n. A large marine fish.

shat-ter v. To burst into pieces.

shave v. To remove a thin layer.

shear v. To trim, cut, or remove.

sheath n. A cover for a blade.

sheen n. Luster.

sheep n. A wool producing, cud-chewing mammal.

sheer adj. Very thin.

sheet n. Cloth for covering a bed; piece of paper.

shell n. The outer covering of certain organisms.

shel-ter n. A place giving protection.

shelve v. To put aside.

shep-herd n. One who tends to sheep.

sher-iff n. A law enforcement officer.

shield n. A protective device.

shim-mer v. To shine with a sparkle.

shin n. The front part of the leg.

ship n. A vessel for deep-water travel.

shiv-er v. To tremble or shake.

shock n. A sudden violent impact.

shore n. The land bordering a body of water.

shot n. The discharging of a gun.

shoul-der n. The place where arm is attached to the body.

show v. To put within sight.

shrap-nel n. The fragments of an exploded shell.

shriek n. A loud, sharp scream.

shrill adj. High-pitched sound.

shrine n. A place for sacred relics.

shrink v. To make smaller.

shroud n. A cover.

shrug v. To raise the shoulders briefly.

shuck n. The outer husk of corn.

shud-der v. To tremble uncontrollably.

shuf-fle v. To drag the feet.

shun v. To avoid deliberately.

sib-ling n. The children from the same parents.

siege n. A prolonged sickness.

sieve n. A strainer.

sigh v. To exhale a long breath.

sight n. An ability to see with the eyes.

sign n. A symbol used instead of words.

sig-nal n. A sign of warning.

sig-na-ture n. The name of a person, written by that person.

sig-nif-i-cance n. The quality of being important.

silent adj. Making no sound.

sil-hou-ette n. An outline of something seen against light.

sil-ver n. A white metallic element.

sim-i-lar adj. Almost the same.

sim-ple adj. Easy to do.

sim-pli-fy v. Make easy.

sim-u-late v. Have form.

-lator n.

si-mul-ta-ne-ous adj. To be occurring at the same time.

sin n. A breaking of a religious law.

since adv. Time before the present.

sin-cere adj. Honest.

sing v. To use the voice to make musical tones.

sin-gle adj. Individual.

sink v. To go down slowly.

si-nus n. An opening in the skull above the nose.

si-ren n. A loud noise, as a warning or signal.

sit-u-ate v. To give a place to; fix permanently.

six n. The cardinal number 6, after five.

six-teen n. The cardinal number 16, after fifteen.

six-ty n. The cardinal number 60, after fifty-nine.

size n. A measurement of something.

skein n. The quantity of yarn wound in loose loops.

skel-e-ton n. The framework of bones.

skep-tic n. One who doubts. **-ism** n.

sketch n. A rough drawing.

skid v. To slide to the side of the road.

skill n. Expertise; ability **-ful** adj.

skim *v.* To remove the top layer. **-ming** *n.*

skin *n.* An outside covering of man.

skip *v.* To leap or jump lightly from the ground.

skirt *n.* A woman's garment worn below the waist.

skull *n.* The bony part of the head.

sky *n.* The upper atmosphere above the earth.

sky-light *n.* A window in the roof to admit light.

slack *adj.* Not taut or tense. **-en** *v.*

slan-der *n.* A false statement. **-ous** *adj.*

slang *n.* An informal language.

slant *v.* To slope; lean.

slap *n.* A sharp blow with an open hand.

slash *v.* To reduce or limit greatly.

slaugh-ter *v.* To kill livestock for food.

slave *n.* A person made to work for another.

slaw *n.* A chopped cabbage with dressing.

sled *n.* A vehicle mounted on runners for snow.

sleek *adj.* Smooth and shiny.

sleep *n.* Natural state of rest. **-iness** *n.*

sleet *n.* A frozen rain.

sleigh *n.* A vehicle mounted on runners.

slen-der *adj.* Slim; thin or narrow.

slice *n.* A thin cut.

slide *v.* To move smoothly across a surface.

slight *adj.* Minor in degree. **-ly** *adv.*

slim *adj.* Slender. **-ness** *n.*

slip *v.* Loss one's balance.

slith-er *v.* To slide along a surface.

slo-gan *n.* Motto.

slope *v.* To slant upward or downward.

slot *n.* A narrow, thin opening. **-ted** *v.*

slouch *n.* A sagging in posture. **-er** *n.*

slug-gish *v.* To be inactive; having little motion.

slum *n.* A neighborhood marked by poverty.

slum-ber *v.* To sleep.

slump *v.* To decline or fall suddenly.

slur *v.* To insult; connected notes in music.

slurp *v.* To eat or drink with noisy sounds.

slush *n.* Melting snow. **-iness** *n.*

sly *adj.* Sneaky.

smack *v.* To slap; loud kiss.

small *adj.* Little in size.

small-pox *n.* A contagious disease.

smart *adj.* Intelligent.

smash v. To break into small pieces.

smear v. To smudge. **-er** n.

smell v. Notice of scent; odor.

smile v. To express amusement by movement of the mouth.

smock n. A loose-fitting outer garment.

smog n. A mixture of smoke and fog.

smoke n. A cloudy mass from something burning.

smold-er v. To burn slowly without a flame.

smooth adj. Flat.

smor-gas-bord n. A buffet meal with a variety of foods.

smother n. Suffocate.

smudge v. To smear with dirt.

smug adj. Self-satisfied. **-ness** n.

smug-gle v. To import goods illegally.

snag n. A pull in a piece of fabric.

snake n. A scaly, long-bodied reptile.

snap v. To break suddenly. **-per** n.

snare n. Anything that entangles.

snarl v. To speak in an angry way. **-er** n.

snatch v. To make a sudden move to grab something.

sneak v. To move in a quiet, sly way.

sneer v. To express scorn by the look on one's face. **-ingly** adv.

sneeze v. To expel air from the nose.

snick-er v. To laugh partially under the breath.

snor-kel n. A device for breathing under water.

snow n. The frozen crystals of rain.

snub v. To treat with neglect.

snug adj. Comfortable and safe. **-ly** adv.

snug-gle v. To lie closely for warmth or comfort.

soak v. To become saturated with water.

soar v. To rise higher than usual.

sob v. To weep deeply.

so-ber adj. Not intoxicated.

so-cia-ble adj. Enjoying the company of others. **-ness** n.

so-ci-e-ty n. Working together for a purpose.

so-ci-ol-o-gy n. The study of society.

sock n. A short knitted covering for the foot.

so-da n. A flavored, carbonated drink.

sod-om-y n. Anal sexual intercourse.

soft-ware n. The programs for computers.

sog-gy adj. Damp and wet.

so-journ *v.* To make a temporary stay.

sol-ace *n.* A comfort in time of grief.

so-lar *adj.* Relating to the sun.

soldier *n.* A person who serves in the military.

sole *n.* A single, the only one.

sol-emn *adj.* Very serious. **-ness** *n.*

so-lic-it *v.* Try to obtain.

sol-id *adj.* Definite form, shape and volume.

sol-id-ify *v.* To make solid; unite firmly.

sol-i-taire *n.* A single gemstone.

sol-i-tude *n.* Isolation.

so-lo *n.* A musical performed by one person.

sol-u-ble *adj.* Able to be solved. **-ness** *n.*

solve *v.* To find the answer.

som-ber *adj.* Dark; gloomy. **-ness** *n.*

some *adj.* Being an indefinite number.

song *n.* The music adapted for singing.

son *n.* A male offspring.

son-ic *adj.* Pertaining to sound.

son-net *n.* A poem of fourteen lines.

soot *n.* The black residue from fuel.

soothe *v.* To make comfortable.

so-phis-ti-cat-ed *adj.* Being worldly; subtle.

soph-o-more *n.* A second year high school student.

so-pran-o *n.* The highest female singing voice.

sor-cery *n.* Supernatural powers.

sor-did *adj.* Very dirty.

sore *adj.* Wound tender to the touch.

sor-row *n.* A mental suffering. **-fully** *adv.*

sor-ry *adj.* Feeling sympathy.

soul *n.* The spirit in man.

sound *n.* That which is heard. **-ness** *n.*

sour *adj.* Sharp to the taste. **-ness** *n.*

source *n.* Any point of origin.

south *n.* The direction opposite of north.

south-paw *n.* A left-handed person.

sou-ve-nir *n.* An item kept as a remembrance.

sov-er-eign *n.* A ruler with supreme power.

spa-cious *adj.* Large and roomy; vast.

space *n.* Unlimited area.

spa-ghet-ti *n.* Pasta made in long, thin pieces.

span *n.* The space between two objects.

spank *v.* To strike with the hand on the buttocks.

spar *v.* To fight; box.

spare *n.* An extra.

spar-kle *v.* To reflect light.

sparse *adj.* Scant; few. **-ness** *n.*

spasm *n.* A muscle contraction.

spat-ter *v.* To splash a liquid.

spat-u-la *n.* An instrument used in cooking.

spawn *n.* The eggs of water animals.

speak *v.* To utter words. **-able** *adj.*

spear *n.* A weapon with a pointed head.

spear-mint *n.* Mint plant.

spe-cial-ize *v.* To study a particular subject.

spec-i-men *n.* A sample.

spec-ta-tor *n.* One who watches or observes.

spec-trum *n.* The band of colors.

spec-u-late *v.* To think deeply. **-lation** *n.*

speed *n.* The rate of movement.

spell *v.* To form words with proper letters.

sphere *n.* A round object.

spice *n.* A pungently aromatic plant.

spic-y *adj.* Being highly seasoned.

spig-ot *n.* A faucet.

spi-der *n.* An eight-legged insect.

spike *n.* A large, thick nail.

spill *v.* To allow something to run out of something.

spin-ach *n.* A widely cultivated leafy plant.

spine *n.* The backbone.

spir-it *n.* A vital essence of man.

spir-it-ed *adj.* Lively; full of energy.

spite *n.* A malicious bitterness.

splash *v.* To spatter a liquid.

splash-down *n.* A landing of a missile in the ocean.

splen-did *adj.* To be magnificent; wonderful.

split *v.* To part or separate something.

spoil *v.* To destroy the value of something.

spokes-man *n.* The one who speaks on behalf of another.

sponge *n.* The skeleton of a sea animal used for absorbing liquid.

spon-ta-ne-ous *adj.* Done on an impulse.

spoof *n.* A deception; play a trick on.

spool *n.* A cylinder for holding tape.

spoon *n.* An eating and cooking utensil.

spo-rad-ic *adj.* Occurring occasionally.

sport *n.* A physical activity with set rules.

spouse *n.* One's husband or wife.

spout *v.* To cause to shoot forth.

sprain *n.* The twisting of a muscle.

spray *n.* A liquid dispersed in a fine mist.

spread *v.* To unfold or open fully.

spr ht-ly *adj.* Vivacious, lively. **-ness** *n.*

sprin-kle *v.* To scatter in small drops.

sprint *n.* A short, fast race.

spruce *n.* An evergreen tree.

spry *adj.* Quick; lively.

spur *n.* A sharp device worn on a rider's boot.

sput-nik *n.* Soviet earth satellite.

spy *n.* A secret agent who obtains information.

squab-ble *n.* Petty argument.

squad *n.* A small group of policemen.

squall *n.* A sudden violent gust of wind.

squan-der *v.* To spend wastefully.

square *n.* A parallelogram with four equal sides.

squash *n.* An edible vegetable; game played with rackets.

squat *v.* To sit back on the heels.

squaw *n.* American Indian woman.

squea-mish *adj.* Easily shocked. **-ness** *n.*

squeeze *v.* To press together.

squelch *v.* To suppress completely; silence.

squint *v.* To close eyes partially.

squir-rel *n.* A rodent with gray-brown fur.

squirt *v.* To eject in a thin stream. **-er** *n.*

stab *v.* To pierce with a pointed weapon.

sta-bi-lize *v.* To keep from changing.

sta-ble *n.* A place for lodging farm animals.

stack *n.* A large pile of something. **-er** *n.*

sta-di-um *n.* A large structure for holding sporting events.

staff *n.* The people employed to assist in business.

stag *n.* An adult male of animals.

stag-ger *v.* To walk unsteadily. **-ing** *adj.*

stag-nant *adj.* Standing still. **-cy** *n.*

stain *n.* A discoloration from dirt, etc.

stair *n.* A step or a series of steps.

stake *n.* A pointed rod; money put up as a wager.

stale *adj.* Having lost freshness. **-ness** *n.*

stalk *n.* A supporting

stem of a plant.

stall *n*. A place to confine animals.

stal-wart *adj*. Large in frame; muscular.

stamp *v*. To put foot down with force.

stand *v*. To be in an upright position.

stand-ard *n*. A model which stands for comparison.

stand-ing *n*. A reputation, or achievement.

sta-ple *n*. A piece of metal for holding papers, etc.

star *n*. The celestial bodies seen at night in the sky.

starch *n*. The nutrient carbohydrates.

stare *v*. To look with direct gaze. **-er** *n*.

stark *adj*. Utter; desolate.

star-let *n*. A young actress.

star-tle *v*. To suddenly surprise.

starve *v*. To suffer from not having food.

stash *v*. To hide or store for safekeeping.

state *n*. A nation; make known verbally.

stat-ic *adj*. Not moving.

sta-tion *n*. A scheduled stopping place.

sta-tis-tic *n*. A numerical data. **-tical** *adj*.

stat-ue *n*. Carved figure.

stay *v*. To remain.

stead *n*. A position of another.

stead-fast *adj*. Not changing. **-ly** *adv*.

stead-y *adj*. Firmly placed.

steal *v*. To take another person's property.

steam *n*. The water in the form of vapor. **-iness** *n*.

steel *n*. Various mixtures of iron, and carbon.

steer *v*. To guide the course of something.

stem *n*. The main stalk of a plant.

sten-cil *n*. A form cut into a sheet of material. **-ing** *n*.

ste-nog-ra-phy *n*. A writing in shorthand.

step *v*. To move one foot at a time.

ste-re-o-phon-ic *adj*. A three-dimensional effect of auditory perspective.

ster-e-o-type *n*. A conventional opinion or belief.

ster-ile *adj*. Sanitary; unable to reproduce.

stern *n*. The rear of a boat or ship.

steth-o-scope *n*. An instrument used to listen to the internal sounds.

stew-ard *n*. The one who manages another's property. **-ship** *n*.

stick *n*. A small branch of a tree; cause to ad-here.

stiff *adj.* Not flexible. **-ness** *n.*

sti-fle *v.* To suffocate; to smother.

stig-ma *n.* A mark of disgrace. **-tize** *v.*

still *adj.* Being silent; motionless.

still-birth *n.* The birth of a dead fetus.

stim-u-late *v.* To increase vital energy.

stim-u-lus *n.* Something that excites to action.

sting *v.* To cause sharp pain.

stin-gy *adj.* Not giving freely. **-giness** *n.*

stink *v.* To give off a foul odor.

stip-u-late *v.* To settle something by agreement.

stir *v.* To mix substance by moving round and round. **-ring** *adj.*

stir-rup *n.* A support for the foot on a saddle.

stitch *n.* The work done by sewing.

stock *n.* A supply of goods kept on hand.

stock-ade *n.* A barrier for protection.

stock-y *adj.* Short and plump. **-iness** *n.*

stole *n.* A long, narrow scarf.

stom-ach *n.* A digestive organ.

stone *n.* A small rock.

stool *n.* Three or four leg seat without a back.

stop *v.* To bring to a standstill.

stor-age *n.* An act of storing.

store *n.* A business offering merchandise for sale.

storm *n.* A violent wind with rain, snow, etc.

story *n.* Fictitious tale.

stout *adj.* Strong; sturdy. **-ness** *n.*

stove *n.* A device for cooking.

stow *v.* To pack or put away.

strad-dle *v.* To spread legs wide apart.

straight *adj.* Being without curves.

strain *v.* To stretch beyond a proper limit.

strait *n.* A passageway which connects two bodies of water.

strand *n.* A land that borders a body of water; run aground.

strange *adj.* Being odd; peculiar. **-ness** *n.*

stran-gle *v.* To kill by choking.

strat-e-gy *n.* A skillful planning.

stray *v.* To roam or wander.

streak *n.* A narrow line or stripe.

stream *n.* A small body of flowing water.

street *n.* A thoroughfare

in a city.

strength *n.* The power in general. **-ened** *adj.*

stren-u-ous *adj.* Vigorous effort. **-ly** *adv.*

stress *n.* A special significance.

stretch *v.* Extend fully.

strew *v.* To scatter about.

strick-en *adj.* Suffering, as from illness.

strict *adj.* To be holding to rules exactly. **-ly** *adv.*

strike *v.* To hit with the hand; means of protest.

strin-gent *adj.* Strict requirements.

stroke *n.* The movement of striking.

stroll *v.* To walk in an unhurried way.

stroll-er *n.* A baby carriage.

strong *adj.* Physical power.

struc-ture *n.* The manner of building.

strug-gle *v.* To put forth effort against opposition.

stub *n.* A short, projecting part.

stub-born *adj.* Difficult to control or handle. **-ness** *n.*

stud *n.* Upright post, as in a building frame.

stud-y *n.* Act of applying the mind to acquire knowledge.

stun *v.* To knock senseless. **-ningly** *adv.*

stunt *n.* Unusual performance of skill.

stu-pid *adj.* To be mentally slow.

stu-pen-dous *adj.* Be astonishing. **-ness** *n.*

stur-dy *adj.* Strongly built.

stut-ter *v.* To speak with repetitions of sound.

sty *n.* An inflammation of the edge of an eyelid; pen for swine.

style *n.* A manner, type.

suave *adj.* Being smoothly pleasant in manner.

sub-con-scious *adj.* Not fully conscious.

sub-di-vide *v.* To divide into parts.

sub-due *v.* To bring under control.

sub-ject *n.* A control over another.

sub-ma-rine *adj.* Underwater vessel.

sub-merge *v.* To go under water.

sub-mit *v.* To surrender to another's authority.

sub-or-di-nate *adj.* Being of lower class.

sub-se-quent *adj.* Following in order.

sub-side *v.* To become less intense.

sub-sid-i-ar-y *adj.* The one that helps.

sub-si-dy *n.* Financial aid.

sub-sist *v.* Continued existence.

sub-stance *n.* A matter of which anything consists.

sub-stan-tial *adj.* Of considerable size.

sub-sti-tute *n.* One who takes the place of another.

sub-ter-ra-ne-an *adj.* Located underground.

sub-tle *adj.* Cunning.

sub-tract *v.* To take away from.

sub-urb *n.* A community near a large city.

sub-way *n.* A railway beneath the surface of the street.

suc-ceed *v.* To accomplish.

suc-cess' *n.* An achievement of something.

suc-ces-sive *adj.* Following in order.

such *adj.* Of that kind or thing.

sud-den *adj.* Without notice; unexpected.

sue *v.* To seek justice by legal processes.

suede *n.* A soft leather.

suf-fer *v.* To feel pain or distress. **-ing** *n.*

suf-fi-cient *adj.* As much that is needed or desired.

suf-fix *n.* A form added to the end of a word.

suf-fo-cate *v.* To stop breathing due to lack of oxygen.

sug-gest *v.* To give an idea for action.

su-i-cide *n.* A taking one's own life.

suite *n.* A connected series of rooms.

sulk *v.* To be sullenly silent.

sul-len *adj.* Ill-humored; depressing. **-ness** *n.*

sul-try *adj.* Hot and humid; muggy.

sum *n.* A result obtained by adding.

sum-ma-ry *n.* Giving the sum; expressed in few words.

sum-mit *n.* The top and highest level.

sum-mons *n.* An order to appear.

sun *n.* A star around which other planets orbit.

su-per *adj.* Excellent.

su-per-fi-cial *adj.* Pertaining to a surface.

su-per-in-tend-ent *n.* A person who oversees.

su-pe-ri-or *adj.* Being of higher rank.

su-per-la-tive *adj.* Highest degree of excellence.

su-per-sede *v.* To take the place of. **-er** *n.*

su-per-son-ic *adj.* Speed greater than sound.

su-per-sti-tion *n.* A belief from faith in chance.

su-per-vise *v.* To direct and control.

sup-ple adj. Bending easily without breaking.

sup-ple-ment n. A part that compensates for what is lacking.

sup-ply v. To provide with what is needed.

sup-port v. To hold the weight of something.

sup-pose v. To assume as true. **-edly** adv.

sup-press v. To end something by force.

su-preme adj. Highest authority.

sure adj. Impossible to doubt. **-ly** adv.

sur-face n. An external layer of something.

surge v. To increase suddenly.

sur-geon n. A physician who practices surgery.

sur-mise v. To guess.

sur-mount v. To overcome. **-able** adj.

sur-name n. A family's last name.

sur-pass v. To be greater than.

sur-plus n. An amount beyond what is needed.

sur-prise v. To come upon unexpectedly.

sur-ren-der v. To cease resistance.

sur-ro-gate n. A person acting in place of another.

sur-round v. To extend around all edges.

sur-veil-lance n. A close observation.

sur-vey v. To examine in detail.

sur-vive v. To continue to exist.

sus-cep-ti-ble adj. Capable of emotional impression.

sus-pect v. To distrust.

sus-pend v. To cause to hang; temporary relief of a position.

sus-pense n. A feeling of being uncertain.

sus-tain v. To hold up and keep from falling.

su-ture n. Stitching together of an incision.

swab n. A mop for cleaning floors, decks, etc.

swal-low v. To cause food or liquid to pass from the mouth to the stomach. **-er** n.

swamp n. A low marshy ground saturated with water.

swap v. To trade something for something in return.

swarm n. A large number of insects.

swat v. To hit something with a violent blow.

swatch n. A strip of cloth cut off a larger piece.

swath n. An area of grass cut by a machine.

swathe v. To bind or wrap with a bandage.

swear v. To make an affirmation under oath.

sweat v. Secrete moisture from the pores of the skin. **-iness** n.

sweep v. To clean with a broom.

sweet adj. Sugary flavor. **-ness** n.

swell v. To increase in size or bulk.

swel-ter v. To suffer from extreme heat.

swerve v. To turn aside from the regular course.

swin-dle v. To practice fraud. **-dler** n.

swine n. A domesticated hog or pig.

swing v. To move freely back and forth.

swirl v. A whirling motion, as of water.

switch n. To exchange. **-er** n.

sword n. A weapon with a long blade.

syl-la-ble n. A pronouncing division of a word.

sym-bol n. Representation of something.

sym-pa-thy n. Affection during a time of sadness.

sym-pho-ny n. A concert by a large orchestra.

symp-tom n. Sign of change in body functions.

syn-chro-nize v. To take place at the same time.

syn-di-cate n. A unit of companies.

syn-drome n. The symptoms that indicate a disorder.

syn-o-nym n. A word that means the same.

syn-op-sis n. A shortened statement or narrative.

sy-ringe n. An instrument used to inject or draw fluids from the body.

sys-tem n. A method of doing something.

T

T, t The twentieth letter of the English alphabet.

tab n. A strip, flap, or small loop that projects from something.

ta-ble n. An article of furniture having a flat top, supported by legs.

tab-loid n. A small newspaper.

tac-it adj. Understood. **-ly** adv., **-ness** n.

tack n. A small, short nail with a flat head. **-er** n.

tacky adj. Slightly sticky; shabby; lacking style.

tad n. A small boy; an insignificant degree or amount.

tail n. The posterior extremity, extending from the end or back of·an for men.

tai-lor n. One whose profession is making, mending, and altering clothing.

taint *v.* To spoil, contaminate, or pollute.

take *v.* To seize or capture; to get possession of.

tale *n.* A story or recital.

tal-ent *n.* The aptitude, disposition, or characteristic ability of a person. **-ed, -less** *adj.*

talk *v.* To communicate by words or speech. **-er** *n.*, **-ative** *adj.*

tall *adj.* Of greater than average height; of a designated or specified height. **-ness** *n.*, **-ish** *adj.*

tal-on *n.* A long, curved claw found on birds or animals

tame *adj.* Not wild or ferocious. **-ly** *adv.*, **-er**

tam-per *v.* To change, meddle, or alter something. **-proof** *adj.*, **-er** *n.*

tan *v.* To cure a hide into leather by using chemicals.

tan-gle *v.* To mix, twist, or unite in a confused manner. **-ment** *n.*

tank *n.* A large container for holding or storing a gas or liquid. **-ful** *n.*

tan-ta-lize *v.* To tease or tempt by holding or keeping something just out of one's reach. **-er** *n.*

tap *v.* To strike repeatedly, usually while making a small noise.

tape *n.* A narrow strip of woven fabric.

ta-per *n.* A very slender candle. *v.* To become gradually smaller or thinner at one end.

tar-dy *adj.* Late; not on time. **-ily** *adv.*

tar-get *n.* An object marked to shoot at.

tar-iff *n.* Duty or tax on merchandise coming into or going out of a country.

tar-nish *v.* To become discolored. **-able** *adj.*

tar-ry *v.* To linger, delay, or hesitate.

tar-tar *n.* The reddish, acidic, crust-like deposit which forms as grape juice turns to wine.

task *n.* Work, usually assigned by another; a job.

taste *n.* The ability to sense or determine flavor in the mouth. **-ful, -less** *adj.*, **-er** *n.*

tat-tle *v.* To reveal the secrets of another by gossiping. **-er** *n.*

taught *v.* Past tense of teach.

Tau-rus *n.* The second sign of the zodiac; a person born between April 20 - May 20.

taut *adj.* Tight; emotionally strained. **-ly** *adv.*, **-ness** *n.*

tax *n.* A payment imposed and collected from individuals or businesses by the government. *v.* To strain. **-able** *adj.*, **-ation, -er, -payer** *n.*

tax-i *v.* To move along the ground or water surface on its own power before taking off.

tax-i-der-my *n.* The art or profession of preparing, stuffing, and mounting animal skins. **-ist** *n.*

teach *v.* To communicate skill or knowledge. **-ing** *n.*, **-able** *adj.*

teach-er *n.* A person who teaches.

team *n.* Two or more players on one side in a game.

tear *v.* To become divided into pieces.

tease *v.* To make fun of; to bother; to annoy; to tantalize.

tech-nique *n.* A technical procedure or method of doing something.

teem *v.* To abound; to be full of.

teeth *pl.*, *n.* The plural of tooth.

tel-e-gram *n.* A message sent or received by telegraph.

tel-e-graph *n.* A system for communicating.

tel-e-phone *n.* A system or device for transmitting conversations by wire.

tel-e-scope *n.* An instrument which contains a lens system which makes distant objects appear larger and nearer. **-ic** *adj.*

tel-e-vi-sion *n.* Reception and transmission of images on a screen with sound.

tel-ex *n.* Teletype communications by means of automatic exchanges.

tell *v.* To relate or describe; to command or order. **-able, -ing** *adj.*

tem-per *n.* The state of one's feelings.

tem-per-a-ment *n.* Personality; a characteristic way of thinking, reacting. **-al** *adj.*

tem-per-a-ture *n.* A measure of heat or cold in relation to the body or environment.

tem-po-rar-y *adj.* Lasting for a limited amount of time; not permanent.

tempt *n.* To encourage or draw into a foolish or wrong course of action; to lure. **-ation, -ter** *n.*

ten *n.* The cardinal number equal to 9 + 1; the number before eleven.

ten-ant *n.* A person who pays rent to occupy another's property.

tend *v.* To be inclined or disposed.

ten-den-cy *n.*, *pl.* **-ies** A disposition to act or behave in a particular way.

ten-der *adj.* Fragile; soft.

Ten-nes-see *n.* A state

located in the central southeastern part of the United States.

ten-nis *n.* A sport played with a ball and racket by 2 or 4 people.

ten-or *n.* An adult male singing voice, above a baritone.

tense *adj.* Taut or stretched tightly.

ten-sion *n.* The condition of stretching or the state of being stretched.

ten-ta-tive *adj.* Experimental; subject to change. **-ly** *adv.*

ten-ure *n.* The right, state, or period of holding something. **-ed, -rial** *adj.,* **-rially** *adv.*

term *n.* A phrase or word; a limited time or duration.

ter-mite *n.* The winged or wing-less insect which feeds on wood.

ter-race *n.* An open balcony or porch.

ter-rain *n.* The surface of an area, as land.

ter-ri-ble *adj.* Causing fear or terror; intense. **-ly** *adv.,* **-ness** *n.*

ter-ri-fy *v.* To fill with fear or terror; to frighten. **-fied, -fying** *adj.*

ter-ri-to-ry *n., pl.* **-ies** An area which is controlled by a particular government. **-ial** *adj.*

ter-ror *n.* Extreme fear; one who causes terror.

ter-ror-ism *n.* The state of being terrorized or the act of terrorizing.

test *n.* An examination or evaluation of something or someone.

Tes-ta-ment *n.* One of the two sections of the Bible.

tes-ti-fy *v.* To give evidence while under oath. **-fier** *n.*

tes-ti-mo-ny *n., pl.* **-ies** A solemn affirmation made under oath; an outward expression of a religious experience.

tes-tis *n., pl.* **testes** The sperm producing gland of the male.

Texas *n.* A state located in the southwestern part of the United States.

text *n.* The actual wording of an author's work. **-ual** *adj.,* **-ually** *adv.*

tex-tile *n.* A cloth made by weaving.

tex-ture *n.* The look, surface, or feel of something. **-al** *adj.,* **-ally** *adv.*

than *conj.* In comparison with or to something.

thank *v.* To express one's gratitude; to credit.

thank-ful *adj.* Feeling or showing gratitude. **-ly** *adv.,* **-ness** *n.,*

that *adj., pl.* **those** The person or thing present or being mentioned.

conj. Used to introduce a clause stating what is said.

thaw *v.* To change from a frozen state to a liquid or soft state.

the *definite adj. or article* Used before nouns and noun phrases as a determiner.

the-a-tre or the-a-ter *n.* A building adapted to present dramas or motion pictures.

the-at-ri-cal *adj.* Extravagant; designed for show, display, or effect.

theft *n.* The act or crime of stealing; larceny.

their *adj. & pron.* The possessive case of they.

the-ism *n.* The belief in the existence of God. **-ist** *n.,* **-istic** *adj.*

them *pron.* The objective case of they.

theme *n.* The topic or subject of something. **-atic** *adj.*

them-selves *pron.* Them or they; a form of the third person plural pronoun.

then *adv.* At that time; soon or immediately.

the-ol-o-gy *n., pl.* **-ies** The religious study of the nature of God, beliefs.

the-o-ry *n., pl.* **-ies** A general principle which covers the known facts.

ther-a-py *n., pl.* **-ies** The treatment of certain diseases. **-pist** *n.*

there *adv.* In, at, or about that place; toward, into, or to.

ther-mal *adj.* Having to do with or producing heat.

ther-mom-e-ter *n.* A glass tube containing mercury which rises and falls with temperature changes. **-tric** *adj.*

these *pron.* The plural of this.

the-sis *n., pl.* **-ses** A formal argument or idea.

they *pron.* The two or more beings just mentioned.

thick *adj.* Having a heavy or dense consistency.

thief *n., pl.* **thieves** A person who steals.

thieve *v.* To take by theft. **-ry** *n.*

thigh *n.* The part of the leg between the hip and the knee of man.

thin *adj.* Having very little depth or extent from one side or surface to the other; not fat; slender.

thing *n.* Something not recognized or named.

think *v.* To exercise thought; to use the mind; to reason. **-able** *adj.*

third *n.* Next to the second in time or place.

thir-teen *n.* The cardinal number equal to 12 + 1.

this *pron., pl.* **these** The person or thing that is near, present, or just mentioned.

tho-rax *n.* The section or part of the human body between the neck and abdomen. **-ic** *adj.*

thorn *n.* A sharp, pointed, woody projection on a plant stem.

thor-ough *adj.* Complete; intensive; accurate. **-ness** *n.*, **-ly** *adv.*

thor-ough-fare *n.* A public highway or road.

those *adj. & pron.* The plural of that.

though *adv.* Nevertheless; in spite of.

thought *n.* The process, act, or power of thinking; a possibility; an idea. **-ful**, **-less** *adj.*

thou-sand *n.* The cardinal number equal to 10 X 100.

thread *n.* A thin cord of cotton or other fiber.

threat *n.* An expression or warning of intent to do harm.

three *n.* The cardinal number equal to 2 + 1.

thresh *v.* To separate seed from a harvested plant mechanically.

thresh-old *n.* A horizontal piece of wood which forms a doorsill.

thrift *n.* The careful use of money and other resources.

thrill *n.* A feeling of sudden intense excitement, fear, or joy. **-ing** *adj.*, **-ingly** *adv.*

thrive *v.* To prosper; to be healthy; to do well in a position.

throat *n.* The front section or part of the neck containing passages for food and air.

throb *v.* To beat, move, or vibrate in a pulsating way.

throm-bo-sis *n., pl.* **-ses** The development of a blood clot.

throng *n.* A large group or crowd. *v.* To crowd around or into.

throt-tle *n.* The valve which controls the flow of fuel to an engine.

through *prep.* From the beginning to the end; in one side and out the opposite side.

through-out *prep., adv.* In every place; everywhere; at all times.

throw *v.* To toss or fling through the air with a motion of the arm.

thru *prep., adv. & adj.* Through.

thrush *n.* A small songbird having a brownish upper body and spotted breast.

thrust *v.* To push; to shove with sudden or

vigorous force.

thud *n.* A heavy, dull thumping sound.

thug *n.* A tough or violent gangster.

thumb *n.* The short first digit of the hand.

thump *n.* A blow with something blunt or heavy.

thun-der *n.* The loud explosive sound made as air is suddenly expanded by heat and then quickly contracted again.

thun-der-bolt *n.* A flash of lightning immediately followed by thunder.

thun-der-cloud *n.* A dark cloud carrying an electric charge and producing lightning and thunder.

thun-der-show-er *n.* A brief rainstorm with thunder and lightning.

Thurs. *or* **Thur.** *abbr.* Thursday.

Thurs-day *n.* The fifth day of the week.

thus *adv.* In this or that way; therefore.

thwart *v.* To prevent from happening.

thy-roid *adj. Anat.* Pertaining to the thyroid gland. *n.* The gland in the neck of man that produces hormones.

thy-rox-ine *n.* A hormone secreted by the thyroid gland.

tick-le *v.* To stroke lightly so as to cause laughter.

tide *n.* The rise and fall of the surface level of the ocean.

ti-dy *adj.* Well arranged; neat. **-ily** *adv.*

tie *v.* To secure or bind with a rope, line, cord or other similar material.

ti-ger *n.* A large carnivorous cat having tawny fur with black stripes.

tight *adj.* Set closely together *adv.* Firmly.

tight-en *v.* To become or make tighter. **-er** *n.*

tile *n.* A thin, hard, flat piece of plastic, asphalt, baked clay.

tilt *v.* To tip, as by raising one end.

tim-ber *n.* Wood prepared for building.

time *n.* A continuous period measured by clocks, and calendars.

tim-id *adj.* Lacking self-confidence; shy.

tin *n.* A white, soft, malleable metallic element, symbolized by Sn.

tinge *v.* To impart a faint trace of color; to tint.

tin-gle *v.* To feel a stinging or prickling sensation.

tin-kle *v.* To produce a slight, sharp series of metallic ringing sounds.

tin-sel *n.* Thin strips of glittering material used for decorations.

tint *n.* A slight amount or trace of color. *v.* To color.

ti-ny *adj.* Minute.

tip *v.* To slant from the horizontal or vertical.

tip-sy *adj.* Partially intoxi-cated. **-iness** *n.*

tire *v.* To become or make weary; to be fatigued.

tis-sue *n., Biol.* Similar cells developed by plants and animals.

tit-il-late *v.* To excite or stimulate in a pleasurable way. **-ting, -tive** *adj.*

ti-tle *n.* An identifying name of a book, poem, play, or other creative work.

TN *abbr.* Tennessee.

to *prep.* Toward, op-posite or near; in contact with; as far as.

toad *n.* A tailless am-phibian, resembling the frog but without teeth in the upper jaw.

toast *v.* To heat and brown over a fire or in a toaster. *n.* Sliced bread browned in a toaster.

toast-er *n.* A device for toasting bread.

to-bac-co *n.* A tropical American plant widely cultivated for its leaves.

to-bog-gan *n.* A long sled-like vehicle. **-ist** *n.*

to-day *adv.* On or during the present day. *n.* The present time, period, or day.

tod-dle *v.* To walk unsteadily with short steps.

tod-dl-er *n.* A small child learning to walk.

toe *n.* One of the exten-sions from the front part of a foot.

tof-fee *n.* A chewy candy made of butter and brown sugar.

to-geth-er *adv.* In or into one group, mass, or body; regarded jointly. **-ness** *n.*

toil *v.* To labor very hard and continuously.

to-ken *n.* A keepsake.

tol-er-ate *v.* To put up with; to endure; to suffer. **-ance, -ant** *adj.*

toll *n.* A fixed charge for travel across a bridge or along a road.

to-ma-to *n., pl.* **-toes** A garden plant cultivated for its edible fruit.

tomb *n.* A vault for bury-ing the dead; a grave.

tomb-stone *n.* A stone used to mark a grave.

to-mor-row *n.* The day after the present day.

ton *n.* A measurement equal to 2,000 pounds.

tone *n.* A vocal or musi-cal sound that has a dis-tinct pitch.

tongs *pl., n.* An imple-ment with two long arms

joined at one end.

tongue *n.* The muscular organ attached to the floor of the mouth.

to-night *n.* This night; the night of this day.

ton-sil *n.* One of a pair of tissue similar to lymph nodes, found on either side of the throat.

ton-sil-lec-to-my *n.* The surgical removal of tonsils.

too *adv.* Also; as well; more than is needed.

tool *n.* An implement used to perform a task.

tooth *n., pl.* **teeth** One of the hard, white structures rooted in the jaw and used for chewing and biting. **-ed, -less** *adj.*

top *n.* The highest part or surface of anything; a covering or lid.

top-ic *n.* The subject discussed in an essay.

top-ple *v.* To fall; to overturn.

torch *n.* A stick of resinous wood which is burned to give light.

tor-ment *n.* Extreme mental anguish or physical pain. **-ingly** *adv.*

tor-na-do *n., pl.* **-does** *or* **-dos** A whirling, violent windstorm accompanied by a funnel-shaped cloud that travels a narrow path over land.

tor-pe-do *n., pl.* **-oes** A large, self-propelled, underwater missile launched from a ship.

tor-pid *adj.* Having lost the power of motion or feeling. **-ity** *n.,* **-ly** *adv.*

tor-rent *n.* A swift, violent stream; a raging flood.

tor-sion *n.* The act or result of twisting. **-al** *adj.*

tor-so *n., pl.* **-sos** *or* **-si** The trunk of the human body.

tor-toise *n.* A turtle that lives on the land.

tor-tu-ous *adj.* Marked by repeated bends, turns, or twists; devious. **-ness** *n.*

tor-ture *n.* The infliction of intense pain as punishment. **-er** *n.*

toss *v.* To fling or throw about continuously.

tot *n.* A young child; a toddler.

to-tal *n.* The whole amount or sum; the entire quantity.

tou-can *n.* A brightly colored tropical bird.

touch *v.* To allow a part of the body, as the hands, to feel. **-able** *adj.*

tough *adj.* Resilient and strong. **-ly** *adv.,* **-ness** *n.*

tou-pee *n.* A wig worn to cover a bald spot on one's head.

tour *n.* A trip with visits to points of interest. **-ist** *n.*

tou-sle *v.* To mess up; to

disarrange.

tout *v.* To solicit customers. **-er** *n.*

tow *v.* To drag or pull, as by a chain or rope.

to·ward or towards *prep.* In the direction of; just before.

tow-el *n.* An absorbent piece of cloth used for drying or wiping.

tow-er *n.* A very tall building or structure. **-ing** *adj.*

tox-e-mi-a *n., Pathol.* Blood poisoning.

tox-ic *adj.* Relating to a toxin; destructive, deadly, or harmful.

tox-in *n.* A poisonous substance produced by chemical changes in plant and animal tissue.

toy *n.* An object designed for the enjoyment of children.

trace *n.* A visible mark or sign of a thing, person, or event. **-able** *adj.*, **-ably** *adv.*, **-er** *n.*

track *n.* A mark, as a footprint, left by the passage of anything. **-able** *adj.*, **-er** *n.*

tract *n.* An extended area, as a stretch of land.

trac-tor *n.* A diesel or gasoline-powered vehicle used in farming to pull another piece of machinery.

trade *n.* A business or occupation; skilled labor; a craft; a swap.

tra-di-tion *n.* The doctrines, knowledge, practices, and customs passed down from one generation to another. **-al** *adj.*, **-ally** *adv.*

traf-fic *n.* The passage or movement of vehicles.

trag-e-dy *n., pl.* **-ies** An extremely sad or fatal event or course of events.

trail *v.* To draw, drag, or stream along behind.

trail-er *n.* One who trails; a large vehicle that transports objects and is pulled by another vehicle.

train *n.* A long moving line of vehicles or persons. **-able** *adj.*, **-er**, **-ing**, **-ee** *n.*

trait *n.* A quality or distinguishing feature.

trai-tor *n.* A person who betrays his country, a cause, or another's confidence.

tra-jec-to-ry *n., pl.* **-ies** The curved line or path of a moving object.

tramp *v.* To plod or walk with a heavy step.

tram-ple *v.* To tread heavily; to stomp.

trance *n.* A stupor, daze, mental state.

tran-quil *adj.* Very calm, quiet, and free from disturbance. **-lity** *n.*, **-ly** *adv*, **-ize** *v.*

trans-act v. To perform, carry out, conduct, or manage business in some way. **-ion, -or** n.

tran-scend v. To pass beyond; to exceedass. **-ent** adj., **-ence** n.

tran-scribe v. To make copies of something.

tran-script n. A written copy.

trans-crip-tion n. The process or act of transcribing.

trans-fer v. To remove, shift, or carry from one position to another. **-able** adj., **-ence, -er** n.

trans-fig-ure v. To change the outward appearance or form.

trans-fix v. To pierce; to hold motionless, as with terror, awe or amazement. **-ion** n.

trans-form v. To change or alter completely in nature, form or function. **-able** adj., **-er** n.

trans-fuse v. To transfer liquid by pouring from one place to another. **-ion, -er** n.

trans-gress v. To go beyond the limit or boundaries. **-ion, -or** n.

tran-sient adj. Not staying or lasting very long.

tran-sit n. Passage or travel from one point to another.

trans-late v. To change from one language to another. **-tion, -tor** n.

trans-lu-cent adj. Diffusing and admitting light but not allowing a clear view of the object.

trans-par-ent adj. Admitting light so that images and objects can be clearly viewed; obvious. **-ency** n., **-ly** adv.

trans-port v. To carry or move from one place to another. **-able** adj.

trans-pose v. To reverse the place or order of.

trap n. A device for holding or catching animals.

trau-ma n. A severe wound caused by a sudden physical injury.

tra-vail n. Strenuous mental or physical exertion; labor in childbirth.

trav-el v. To journey or move from one place to another. **-er** n.

tra-verse v. To pass over, across, or through. **-able** adj., **-al, -er** n.

trawl n. A strong fishing net which is dragged through water.

tray n. A flat container used for carrying something.

treach-er-ous adj. Disloyal; deceptive; unreliable. **-ly** adv., **-ery** n.

tread v. To walk along, on, or over; to trample.

trea-son n. Violation of

one's allegiance to a sovereign or country. **-able, -ous** *adj.*

treas-ure *n.* Hidden riches.

treas-ury *n., pl.* **-ies** A place where public or private funds are kept.

treat *v.* To behave or act toward. **-able** *adj.,* **-er** *n.*

tree *n.* A tall woody plant, usually having a single trunk of considerable height.

trem-ble *v.* To shake involuntarily.

tre-men-dous *adj.* Extremely huge, large, or vast. *Slang* Wonderful.

trem-or *n.* A quick, shaking movement.

trench *n.* A ditch; a long, narrow excavation in the ground. **-er** *n.*

tri-al *n.* In law, the examination and hearing of a case before a court of law.

tri-an-gle *n., Geom.* A plane figure bounded by three sides and having three angles.

trib-ute *n.* An action of respect or gratitude to someone.

tri-ceps *n., Anat.* The large muscle at the back of the upper arm.

trick *n.* An action meant to fool, as a scheme.

trick-er-y *n.* Deception.

tri-cy-cle *n.* A small vehicle having three wheels, propelled by pedals.

tri-dent *n.* A long spear with three prongs, used as a weapon.

tried *adj.* Tested and proven reliable or useful.

tri-fle *n.* Something of little value or importance.

trig-ger *n.* A lever pulled to fire a gun; a device used to release or start an action. *v.* To start.

trill *n.* A tremulous utterance of successive tones.

tril-lion *n.* The cardinal number equal to one thousand billion.

trim *v.* To clip or cut off small amounts in order to make neater.

tri-o *n.* A set or group of three.

trip *n.* Travel from one place to another.

trip-le *adj.* Having three parts. *v.* To multiply by three.

tri-pod *n.* A three-legged stand.

trite *adj.* Used too often; common.

tri-umph *v.* To be victorious. **-ant** *adj.,* **-antly** *adv.*

triv-i-al *adj.* Insignificant; of little value.

troll *v.* To fish by pulling a baited line slowly behind a boat.

trol-ley *n.* A streetcar powered by electricity from overhead lines.

troop *n.* A group or assembly of people or animals. **-er** *n.*

tro-phy *n., pl.* **-ies** A prize or object awarded to someone for his success or victory.

troth *n.* Good faith; the act of pledging one's fidelity.

trou-ble *n.* Danger; affliction; need; distress. **-er** *n.,* **-lingly** *adv.*

trough *n.* A long, narrow, shallow container.

trou-sers *pl., n.* An outer garment that covers the body from the waist down.

trout *n.* A freshwater game or food fish.

trowel *n.* A flat-bladed garden tool. **-er** *n.*

tru-ant *n.* A person who is absent from school without permission.

truce *n.* An agreement to stop fighting.

truck *n.* An automotive vehicle used to carry heavy loads. **-er** *n.*

trudge *v.* To walk heavily; to plod.

true *adj.* In accordance with reality or fact. **-ly** *adv.*

trump *n.* In cards, a suit of any cards which outrank all other cards for a selected period of time.

trust *n.* Confidence or faith in a person or thing.

truth *n., pl.* **truths** The facts corresponding with actual events or happenings. **-ful** *adj.,* **-fully** *adv.*

try *v.* To make an attempt. **-ing** *adj.,* **-out** *n.*

tsp *abbr.* Teaspoon.

tub *n.* A round, low, vessel with handles on the side.

tube *n.* A hollow cylinder.

tuck *n.* A flattened fold of material.

Tues. *abbr.* Tuesday.

Tues-day *n.* The third day of the week.

tug *v.* To strain and pull vigorously.

tu-i-tion *n.* Payment for instruction.

tum-ble *v.* To fall or cause to fall.

tu-mor *n., Pathol.* A swelling on or in any part of the body.

tu-mult *n.* The confusion and noise of a crowd; a riot. **-uous** *adj.*

tu-na *n., pl.* **-na** *or* **-nas** Any of several large marine food fish.

tu-nic *n.* A loose garment extending to the knees.

tun-nel *n.* An underground or underwater passageway.

tur-bu-lent *adj.* Marked by a violent disturbance.

tu-reen *n.* A large dish, often having a cover.

turf *n.* A layer of earth with its dense growth of grass and matted roots.

tur-key *n.* A large game bird of North America.

tur-moil *n.* A state of confusion or commotion.

turn *v.* To move or cause to move around a center point.

tur-quoise *n.* A blue-green gemstone.

tur-tle *n.* A scaly-skinned animal having a soft body covered with a hard shell.

tusk *n.* A long, curved tooth, as of an elephant.

tux-e-do *n.* A semiformal dress suit worn by men.

tweed *n.* A coarse woolen fabric, woven in two or more colors.

twelve *n.* The cardinal number equal to 11 + 1.

twen-ty *n.* The cardinal number equal to 19 + 1 or 2 X 10.

twig *n.* A small branch which grows from a larger branch on a tree.

twi-light *n.* The soft light of the sky between sunset and darkness.

twill *n.* A weave that produces the parallel rib on the surface of a fabric.

twin *n.* One of two persons born at the same time to the same mother.

twine *v.* To weave or twist together.

twin-kle *v.* To gleam or shine with quick flashes.

twirl *v.* To rotate or cause to turn around.

twitch *v.* To move or cause to move with a jerky movement.

twit-ter *v.* To utter a series of chirping sounds. **-y** *adj.*

two *n.* The cardinal number of 1 + 1.

TX *abbr.* Texas.

ty-coon *n., Slang* A person of wealth and power.

type *n.* A class or group.

ty-phoon *n.* A tropical hurricane.

typ-i-cal *adj.* Exhibiting the characteristics of a certain class or group.

typ-ist *n.* The operator of a typewriter.

tyr-an-ny *n.* Harsh and unfair rule by a king.

U

U, u The twenty-first letter of the English alphabet.

ud-der *n.* A milk-producing organ.

ug-ly *adj.* Unpleasant to look at.

u-ku-le-le *n.* A musical instrument.

ul-cer *n.* The destruction of tissue.

ul-ti-mate *adj.* Final; ending.

ul-ti-ma-tum *n.* The final

demand.

ul-tra-son-ic *adj.* Faster than speed of sound.

um-bil-i-cal cord *n.* Connecting fetus to placenta.

um-pire *n.* A person who rules on plays in a game.

un-ac-cus-tomed *adj.* To be not ordinary.

u-nan-i-mous *adj.* To be agreed to.

un-can-ny *adj.* To be mysterious.

un-civ-i-lized *adj.* To be without culture.

un-con-scious *adj.* To be not mentally aware.

un-couth *adj.* Act or speak crudely.

un-der *prep.* In a place lower.

un-der-brush *n.* The weeds growing under trees.

un-der-grad-u-ate *n.* A student studying for a degree.

un-der-hand *adj.* To be done secretly.

un-der-mine *v.* To weaken someone or something.

un-der-stand *v.* To comprehend.

un-der-stud-y *n.* A substitute actor.

un-der-take *v.* To set about to do a task.

un-der-tak-er *n.* One who prepares the dead for burial.

un-der-tone *n.* A low, quiet voice.

un-der-tow *n.* A backward pull of current.

un-der-write *v.* To subscribe.

un-de-sir-a-ble *adj.* State of being offensive.

un-du-late *v.* To have a wavy shape.

un-dy-ing *adj.* Without end.

un-earth-ly *adj.* To be strange.

un-eas-y *adj.* Feeling discomfort.

un-em-ployed *adj.* To be without a job.

un-e-qual *adj.* To be not even; not fair.

un-e-vent-ful *adj.* To be lacking in significance.

un-faith-ful *adj.* Break a promise or agreement.

un-fore-seen *adj.* Not anticipated.

un-for-tu-nate *adj.* Having bad luck.

un-furl *v.* To unroll or unfold.

un-guent *n.* An ointment.

u-ni-corn *n.* A mythical one-horned horse.

u-ni-form *n.* An official clothing; identical.

u-ni-fy *v.* To come together as one.

un-ion *n.* The act of joining together of groups.

u-nique *adj.* To be unlike any other.

u-ni-son *n.* A harmony.

u-nit *n.* Several parts regarded as a whole.

u-nite *v.* To join together.

u-ni-ty *n.* A state of being one.

u-ni-ver-sal *adj.* Having to do with the world.

u-ni-verse *n.* The whole world.

u-ni-ver-si-ty *n.* Educational institution

un-just *adj.* State of being not fair.

un-kempt *adj.* To be poorly groomed.

un-lim-it-ed *adj.* Having no boundaries.

un-load *v.* To remove the load.

un-luck-y *adj.* To be unfortunate.

un-mis-tak-a-ble *adj.* To be obvious.

un-nerve *v.* To frighten.

un-oc-cu-pied *adj.* To be empty or void.

un-pleas-ant *adj.* Not agreeable.

un-pro-fes-sion-al *adj.* Having no professional status.

un-rav-el *v.* To separate threads.

un-re-li-a-ble *adj.* Not dependable.

un-re-served *adj.* To be unlimited.

un-ru-ly *adj.* State of being disorderly.

un-set-tle *v.* To cause to be upset.

un-sight-ly *adj.* State of being ugly.

un-think-a-ble *adj.* To be unimaginable.

un-til *prep.* Up to the time of.

un-u-su-al *adj.* To be uncommon or different.

un-veil *v.* To uncover.

un-whole-some *adj.* To be unhealthy.

up-grade *v.* To increase the grade of something.

up-hol-ster *v.* To cover furniture.

up-per *adj.* To be higher in status.

up-ris-ing *n.* A rebellion.

up-roar *n.* A commotion.

up--to--date *adj.* The most recent.

urge *v.* To encourage.

ur-gent *adj.* Immediate attention.

urine *n.* A secretion from kidneys.

ush-er *n.* One who directs people to the correct seats.

u-ter-us *n.* The female womb.

u-til-i-ty *n.* The state of being useful.

ut-ter *v.* To express something verbally.

V

V, v The twenty-second letter of the English alphabet.

va-cate *v.* To leave.

vac-ci-nate *v.* To inject

with a vaccine.

vac-cine *n.* A substance for inoculation against disease.

vac-u-um *n.* An empty space.

va-gar-y *n.* An eccentric action.

va-grant *n.* A person who wanders.

vague *adj.* Not clearly expressed.

vale *n.* A valley.

val-iant *adj.* Brave.

val-id *adj.* Sound on facts or truth.

val-ue *n.* Worth of something.

van-dal-ism *n.* A malicious destruction of property.

van-ish *v.* To disappear suddenly.

van-i-ty *n.* Conceit.

va-por *n.* The moisture in the air.

var-i-able *adj.* Changeable.

var-y *v.* Change.

vas-cu-lar *adj.* Having to do with vessels circulating fluids.

vast *adj.* To be very large in size.

vault *n.* A room for safekeeping.

ve-hi-cle *n.* A type of motorized device.

vein *n.* The vessel carrying blood to the heart.

ven-i-son *n.* A flesh of a deer.

ven-om *n.* A poisonous substance.

ven-ti-late *v.* To expose to air flow.

ven-ture *n.* A course of action.

verb *n.* A part of speech which.

ver-ba-tim *adv.* Word for word.

verge *n.* The extreme edge or rim.

ver-sa-tile *adj.* Having many functions or uses.

verse *n.* A writing that has a rhyme.

ver-sion *n.* A translation.

ver-sus *prep.* Against.

ver-te-bra *n.* The bones of a spine.

ver-ti-cal *adj.* Straight up-and-down direction.

ves-per *n.* An evening prayer.

ves-sel *n.* A container; ship.

ves-tige *n.* A trace or a sign.

ves-try *n.* A room in a church.

vet-er-an *n.* One who has served in the military.

vet-er-i-nar-i-an *n.* One trained to treat animals.

ve-to *n.* The power of rejection.

vi-a-duct *n.* A type of high bridge.

vi-car-i-ous *adj.* Substituted.

vice *n.* An evil conduct.

vi-cin-i-ty *n.* The surrounding area.

vi-cious *adj.* Meanness.

vic-tim *n.* A person who is harmed by another.

vic-to-ry *n.* A defeat of an enemy.

vid-e-o *adj.* Transmission of television.

vie *v.* To strive for superiority.

view *n.* An act of examining.

vig-il *n.* A period of surveillance.

vig-or *n.* A physical strength.

vil-lage *n.* A small town.

vin-di-cate *v.* To set free.

vi-nyl *n.* A type of plastic.

vi-o-late *v.* To break the law or a rule.

vi-o-lence *n.* A physical force to cause harm.

vi-o-lin *n.* A small stringed instrument.

vi-per *n.* A poisonous snake.

vir-gin *n.* A natural state.

vir-tue *n.* A uprightness.

vi-rus *n.* A disease causing agent.

vis-i-ble *adj.* Exposed to view.

vi-sion *n.* The power of sight.

vis-it *v.* To journey to see someone.

vi-su-al *adj.* Visible.

vi-tal *adj.* Very important.

vit-re-ous *adj.* Similar to glass.

vi-va-cious *adj.* Lively.

viv-id *adj.* Bright.

vo-cab-u-lar-y *n.* A group of words and phrases.

vo-cal *adj.* Related to the voice.

vo-ca-tion *n.* A devine call to a religious career.

vo-cif-er-ate *v.* To cry out loudly.

vogue *n.* A leading fashion.

voice *n.* A sounds of speaking.

void *adj.* Containing nothing.

volt-age *n.* An amount of electrical power.

vol-ume *n.* The loudness of a sound.

vol-un-tar-y *adj.* From one's own choice.

vo-lup-tu-ous *adj.* Pleasureful.

vo-ra-cious *adj.* Having a large appetite.

vote *n.* An expression of one's choice.

vouch *v.* To support as true.

vow *n.* A solemn pledge.

voy-age *n.* A long trip or journey.

vul-gar *adj.* Showing poor manners.

vul-ner-a-ble *adj.* Open to physical injury or attack.

W

W, w The twenty-third letter of the English alphabet.

wad *n.* A small crumbled mass.

waft *v.* To drift or move gently.

wage *n.* A payment of money for labor or services.

waif *n.* A homeless, or lost child.

wait *v.* To stay until a later time.

wait-er *n.* One who serves food.

waive *v.* To forfeit one's free will.

wan-der *v.* To travel aimlessly.

want *v.* To wish for or desire.

war *n.* An armed conflict among states.

ward *n.* A section in a hospital.

warm *adj.* Moderate heat.

warp *v.* Bend out of shape.

war-y *adj.* To be cautious; careful.

waste *v.* To be thrown away.

watch *v.* To view carefully.

wa-ter-shed *n.* An area drained by a river.

watt *n.* A unit of electrical power.

wa-ver *v.* To sway unsteadily.

way-lay *v.* To attack by ambush.

we *pl., pron.* Refer to one or more other people.

wealth *n.* An abundance of valuable possessions.

weap-on *n.* The device used to harm someone.

wea-ry *adj.* To be exhausted.

weath-er *n.* A condition of the atmosphere.

wed-ding *n.* A marriage ceremony.

wedge *n.* A tapered, triangular piece of wood.

week *n.* The period of seven days.

weigh *v.* To determine the heaviness of an object.

wel-come *v.* To accept gladly.

wel-fare *n.* A state of doing well.

well *n.* A hole in the ground which contains water.

welt *n.* A swelling on the body.

west *n.* The direction of the setting sun.

whale *n.* A very large mammal which lives in the ocean.

what *pron.* Which one; which things.

wheat *n.* The grain ground into flour.

wheel *n.* A circular disk

which turns on an axle.

wheeze *v.* To breathe with a hoarse whistling sound.

when *adv.* At what time.

where *adv.* In what direction.

whet *v.* To make sharp.

wheth-er *conj.* Indicating a choice.

which *pron.* What one or ones.

while *n.* Length or period of time.

whim *n.* A sudden desire or want.

whine *v.* To squeal or make a plaintive sound.

whip *v.* To hit or spank with a stick.

whirl *v.* To move in circles; to twirl.

whirl-pool *n.* A circular current of water.

whisk-er *n.* The hair that grows on a man's face.

whis-per *v.* To speak in a low tone.

whit-tle *v.* To carve shapes into wood.

who *pron.* Refer to certain person.

whole *adj.* Complete.

whole-sale *n.* A sale of goods to a retailer.

whole-some *adj.* Contributing to good health.

whol-ly *adv.* Totally.

whom *pron.* Objective case of who.

whose *pron.* Having to do with one's belongings.

why *adj.* For what reason.

wide *adj.* To be broad.

width *n.* From side to side.

wield *v.* To handle something skillfully.

wild *adj.* Being untamed.

wil-der-ness *n.* An unsettled area.

wilt *v.* To cause to become limp.

wind *n.* A natural movement of air.

wing *n.* The appendages that allow birds to fly.

win-ter *n.* The coldest season or the year.

wire *n.* A small rod used to conduct electricity.

wis-dom *n.* A good judgment.

wit *n.* A sense of humor.

with *prep.* In the company of.

wit-ness *n.* A legally sworn observer.

wiz-ard *n.* A very clever person.

won-der *n.* The feeling of awe.

word *n.* A meaningful sound which stands for an idea.

work *n.* Employment; a job.

world *n.* The planet Earth.

wor-ship *n.* Reverence for a sacred object.

worth *n.* The value of something.

wran-gle *v.* To quarrel noisily.

wreak *v.* To inflict punishment.

wreck *v.* To damage by accident.

wretch *n.* A miserable person.

wrist *n.* The joint between the hand and forearm.

write *v.* To form letters.

wrong *adj.* To be incorrect.

X

X, x The twenty-fourth letter of the English alphabet.

X chro-mo-some *n.* A sex female chromosome, associated with female characteristics. .

xe-non *n.* The colorless, odorless, gaseous element found in small quantities in the air.

xen-o-phobe *n.* A person who fears and mistrusts foreigners or anything strange. **-bia** *n.*

X-mas *abbr., n.* Christmas.

X--Ra-di-a-tion *n.* Treatment with X-rays.

X ray *n.* Energy that is radiated with a short wave length and high penetrating power; a black and white negative image or picture of the interior of the body.

xy-lo-phone *n.* A musical instrument consisting of mounted wooden bars which produce a ringing musical sound when struck with two wooden hammers. **-ist** *n.*

Y

Y, y The twenty-fifth letter of the English alphabet.

yacht *n.* A light sailing vessel.

yak *n.* A longhaired ox of Tibet.

yam *n.* A variety of the sweet potato.

yap *v.* To bark in a high pitched.

yard *n.* A unit of measure that equals 36 inches.

yard-stick *n.* A graduated measuring stick that equals 1 yard or 36 inches.

yarn *n.* Twisted fibers, as of wool, used in knitting or weaving.

yawn *v.* To inhale a deep breath with the mouth open wide.

Y-Chro-mo-some *n.* A sex chromosome associated with male characteristics.

ye *pron.* You, used especially in religious contexts, as hymns.

yea *adv.* Yes; indeed; truly.

year *n.* A period of time starting on January 1st and continuing through December 31st.

yearn *v.* To feel a strong craving.

yeast *n.* Fungi or plant cells used to make baked goods rise.

yell *v.* To cry out loudly *n.* A loud cry; a cheer to show support for an athletic team.

yel-low *n.* The bright color of a lemon; the yolk of an egg *v.* cowardly.

yel-low fe-ver *n.* An acute infectious disease.

yeo-man *n.* Owner of a small farm; a petty officer who acts as a clerk.

yes *adv.* To express agreement.

yes-ter-day *n.* The day before today; former or recent time.

yet *adv.* Up to now; at this time; even now; more so.

yew *n.* An evergreen tree.

Yid-dish *n.* A language spoken by Jews combining German and Hebrew.

yield *v.* To bear or bring forward; to give up the possession of something.

yo-del *v.* To sing in a way so that the voice changes from normal to a high shrill sound and then back again.

yo-ga *n.* A system of exercises for the relaxing of the mind.

yo-gurt *n.* A thick custard-like food made from curdled milk.

yoke *n.* A wooden bar used to join together two oxen or other animals working together.

yo-kel *n.* An unsophisticated country person; a bumpkin.

yolk *n.* The yellow nutritive part of an egg.

Yom Kip-pur *n.* Jewish holiday observed with fasting and prayer for the forgiveness of sins.

you *pron.* A person or persons addressed.

you all *pron., Slang* **y'all** A southern variation used for two or more people in direct address.

you'll *contr.* You will; you shall.

young *adj.* Relating to the early stage of life; not old.

your *adj.* Belonging to yourself.

your-self *pron.* A form of you for emphasis when the object of a verb and the subject is the same.

youth *n.* The appearance or state of being young.

yowl *v.* To make a loud, long cry or howl.

yo--yo *n.* A grooved spool toy with a string

wrapped around the spool so it can be spun or moved up and down.

yt-tri-um *n.* The metallic element, symbolized by Y.

yule *n.* Christmas.

yule-tide *n.* The Christmas season.

Z

Z, z The twenty-sixth letter of the English alphabet.

za-ny *n., pl* **-nies** A clown; a person who acts silly or foolish.

zap *v., Slang* To destroy.

zeal *n.* Great interest.

zeal-ot *n.* A fanatical person.

zeal-ous *adj.* Full of interest.

ze-bra *n.* An African mammal of the horse family having black or brown stripes on a white body.

zeph-yr *n.* A gentle breeze.

ze-ro *n., pl.* **-ros, -roes** The number or symbol "O"; nothing.

zest *n.* Enthusiasm.

zig-zag *n.* A pattern with sharp turns in alternating directions.

zilch *n., Slang* Nothing; zero.

zinc *n.* A bluish-white crystalline metallic ele-

ment, used as a protective coating for steel and iron.

zip *n.* To act or move with vigor or speed.

zip code *n.* The system to speed the delivery of mail by assigning a five digit number, plus four to each postal delivery location in the United States.

zip-per *n.* A fastener consisting of two rows of plastic or metal teeth that are interlocked by means of sliding a tab.

zit *n., Slang* A pimple.

zom-bie *n.* A person who resembles the walking dead; a person who has a strange appearance or behavior.

zone *n.* An area or region set apart from its surroundings by some characteristic.

zonk *v., Slang* To render senseless with alcohol or drugs; to stun.

zoo *n., pl.* **zoos** A public display or collection of living animals.

zo-ol-o-gy *n.* The science that deals with animals.

zoom *v.* To move with a continuous, loud, buzzing sound.

zuc-chi-ni *n., pl.* **-ni** A summer squash that is long and narrow and has a dark-green, smooth rind.

zwie-back *n.* A sweetened bread which is baked, sliced, and toasted to make it crisp.

zy-mur-gy *n.* The chemistry that deals with the fermentation processes.

NOTES

NOTES